תורה אור

מספריה

ANATOMY OF FAITH

ANATOMY OF FAITH

Milton Steinberg

Edited, with an Introduction, by Arthur A. Cohen

HARCOURT, BRACE AND COMPANY/NEW YORK

FIRST EDITION

Library of Congress Catalog Card Number: 60-5442

Design/Elaine Lustig   Printed in the United States of America

For M. S.
who made it possible

To E. S.
who recognizes it

To E. C.
who endures it

I undertook to select, edit, and introduce this volume at the request of Edith Steinberg and her sons, Jonathan and David. No invitation could have been more gratifying. Milton Steinberg has meant more to me than it is possible to express—less his intellect and teaching than the unbelievable humanity and warmth which informed both. It had been my wish for many years to present the unpublished theological essays of Milton Steinberg, to articulate their unity, and to underscore that unity by presenting a biographic essay which might suggest something of the richness of the man and the thinker.

The letters, documents, and writings used here for the first time were made available to me by Mrs. Steinberg. I am indebted as well for both chronology and a record of incidents unfamiliar to me to the preliminary biographic essay prepared by Rabbi Simon Noveck and lent to me by Mrs. Steinberg.

For permission to reprint essays in this volume, acknowledgment and appreciation are to be expressed to: *The Reconstructionist, The Journal of Religion, The Menorah Journal,* and *The Proceedings of the Rabbinical Assembly of America.* The concluding essay, "New Currents in Religious Thought," appears here for the first time.

CONTENTS

Introduction by Arthur A. Cohen

On March 20, 1950, Rabbi Milton Steinberg died. Eight years earlier he had suffered a near-fatal heart attack. Although repeatedly counseled to reduce his activities to a minimum, he continued to maintain a schedule which would have been exacting for a healthy man. Characteristically he dismissed cautionary advice with the assertion that "the load does not bother me."

During the closing years of his short life, although prevailed upon to engage an assistant, he taught, preached, and wrote, in addition to attending to the pastoral requirements of his community. But two months before his death he delivered four extended and demanding public lectures on trends in modern theology; a month before his death he brought his unpublished novel, *The Prophet's Wife*, to that crucial point at which Hosea discerns the meaning of Gomer's waywardness and God's persevering love; a week before his death he studied the rabbinic exegesis of Ecclesiastes with a young student; and, in the closing hours of his life, having recited the confession that anticipates the advent of death, he sought to encourage his family, to ask their pardon for his untimely departure, and to reassure them that he would die without regrets.

The Climate of the Times

The early twentieth century into which Milton Steinberg was born on November 24, 1903, in Rochester, New York, was relatively gentle and untroubled. It was marked by a tranquility, a precision of manners, an ordered unfolding of life which served well to mask the forming currents of unrest which twice in subsequent decades would burst the dams of social and political containment. Europe was smug and secure; the United States was bursting with energy. The generality of Americans prospered in an era of industrialization and expansion; the middle class became entrenched; the laboring man began to organize.

Ever since the abortive emancipation that attended the Revolution of 1848, the United States had been the haven of Western European Jewish intellectuals, political dissidents, and the economically dispossessed.

The immigration of German Jews which commenced in the late eighteenth century and continued during the first half of the nineteenth consisted in great measure of single young men of poorer families. They arrived—without benefit of preparation or indoctrination—to discover that the existing Jewish community, largely composed of already acculturated Spanish-Portuguese immigrants, was religiously lax, hostile, and unco-operative. By 1840, however, the quality of German-Jewish immigrants had begun to change from artisans and farmers to displaced intellectuals. Among the new arrivals were numerous leaders of German Reform Judaism, who, in addition to liberality of doctrine, were learned in German culture and thought. Most of the immigrants, to be sure, were not intellectuals, but rather young people from Orthodox homes in rural German communities, who sought, against insuperable odds, to maintain their observance of tradition while recognizing on every side the natural conspiracy of American life to undermine it.

•••

By the middle of the nineteenth century the American-Jewish community had commenced to exhibit the attributes of alienation, loneliness, and disenchantment. Abraham Kohn, for example, who arrived from Bavaria in 1842, observed that his life as a peddler made it difficult for him to observe even the least demanding commandment of Jewish law. Is not such a life, he asks, "slavery rather than liberty"? Kohn was not alone in finding that Arcadia was already populated—that freedom was not the condition of wilderness in which an ideal and pristine life could be pursued. America was no longer the "*Wunderland.*" It was, as every social community, formed by prejudices and snobbisms, pressures and requirements.

In such an environment little wonder that the emergent ideology of Americanization should have found ready support in the Jewish world. Under German-Jewish leadership an effort was commenced to disentangle Judaism from the Jew, to establish the distinction between the Jew as special believer and the Jew as American. The Reform Jewish movement, denying as it did the ethnic and national identity of the Jewish community, opposing the restoration of Zion and the personalization of the Messiah, disclaiming the separatist tendencies of Jewish law, substituting the vernacular for Hebrew in prayer, sought to divest the Jew of those visible and identifiable marks of Jewishness. The ideology which was intended primarily to Americanize late German-Jewish arrivals was extended and emboldened by the influx of Eastern European immigrants whose numbers began to increase at the end of the 1860's.

The Jewish community of Eastern Europe, unlike the historic Jewish communities of the West, was relatively stable and cohesive. Emancipation—moving eastward from Paris and Berlin—had succeeded in eroding the traditional loyalties of Western European Jewry by the time it commenced to gnaw at the foundations of Eastern Jewries. Eastern European Judaism was well founded in the community—in the self-governing, integrated, religiously homogeneous towns and ghettos that defined the Pale. The intensification of anti-Semitism in the East, the introduction of compulsory military service in Russia and Poland, the organized pogroms of 1881-1882 in Russia, the spread of secularism and revolutionary socialism, and the increasing pauperization of the *shtetl,* served to accentuate cleavages already present in the Jewish world since the late seventeenth century. The opposition of rich and poor, traditionalist and Hasid, educated and unlettered, prestigious and dispossessed, was hardened and exacerbated by the external pressures mobilized by Russo-Polish anti-Semitism. While the patrician Jew stayed at home and the pious complained suspiciously of the low level of American-Jewish religiosity, the poor, the illiterate, and the dissident came to the United States by the millions.

By the turn of the century a new generation of American Jews, but years removed from the settlements of Eastern Europe, had been born. Their parents were still Yiddish-speaking, oriented to the distant but evocative world of European *Yiddishkeit*—Yiddish art and journalism, theater and poetry; Ashkenazic orthodoxy—the exacting cadence of Talmudic study and the vitalizing enthusiasm of Hasidic spirituality; the *shtetl* community—small-town protectiveness and insularity; Russian politics—the dawning world of revolutionary socialism and autoemancipation; and Zionism—the movement of national liberation which, though it addressed itself to distant Palestine, saw its consummation in the self-fulfillment of the Jewish people and its deliverance from gentile anti-Semitism.

The Eastern European Jew, unlike his German-Jewish co-religionist, was a fantast and an unrealist. Where the German-American Jew was stolid, bourgeois, and unabashedly assimilationist, his Eastern European counterpart was stubbornly romantic. The romanticism of the Eastern Jew derived from the fact that, though he dreamed of the "golden land," he constantly confused it with "the promised land." The United States and the resurrected Zion were always commingled and, failing an immediate achievement of the security and acceptance which he deemed minimum requirements, he withdrew into self-imposed isolation and reproduced a small Vilna, a minia-ture Warsaw, a minor Odessa on the East Side of New York or the West Side of Chicago. Where German Jewry produced little lasting Jewish culture in the United States, Eastern Jewries produced a flourishing culture that had neither contact nor relevance to the American world that surrounded it.

This was the impasse in the early twentieth century. The American Jewish community had two aspects: an en-riched, slightly effete, and already contemptuous enclave of well-established Spanish-Portuguese Jews and their later (but still sufficiently early) German equals, and a vast sea of poor, struggling, uneducated Eastern European Jews. The former felt compromised in their assimilation by the presence of co-religionists so obviously ill-equipped to be their "equals." The latter, sustained in traditional Jew-ish learning and identity, yet envious of the security which the German Jew enjoyed, felt increasing self-con-tempt and alienation. Both settlements—that of German Jewry and that of Eastern European Jewry—could share in common but one resentment: a resentment against the re-ligion which defined their plight. Religion insured their separation, impeded their mobility, and catalyzed the hos-tility of their environment. Were they no longer Jews, the arcane world of English, the forbidding reaches of "up-town" urban society, the secret precincts of university and profession, might be penetrated. To be sure, the cure was infinitely more simple than the problem posed. Judaism might be tempered and modernized, "Christianized" and socialized, decorated and uplifted, without mitigating the inescapable destiny of being and remaining Jewish. It was easier to escape Judaism than the Jew.

In the early part of the twentieth century—although Orthodox Judaism proliferated synagogues, and Reform Judaism built monstrous structures in a neo-Gothic and rococo style, and Conservative Judaism struggled to establish a toe hold in between—Jewish life took on a complexity befitting a community which was the "House of Israel" long after it had forgotten that it was "a kingdom of priests." Aid societies, cultural associations, *landsmanschaften*, Zionist clubs, Jewish lyceums, and Chautauquas flourished. Essentially the Jewish community stuck together in order the better to prepare to fall apart—to stay together in the interest of self-defense and self-education in order the more easily to get better jobs, to move to better communities, to give their children better opportunities. Judaism—the religion of the Jewish people—became an ancilla of Jewish life, one more instrument of survival.

The Bare Bones   *Rochester: 1903-1917*

An aloof, witty, and eloquent maternal grandmother who smoked long Russian cigarettes, but went unpretentiously on errands of charity; a maternal grandfather who peddled trinkets for a livelihood, but wore his Prince Albert and top hat on Jewish festivals or when accompanying emissaries of European *yeshivot* on fund-raising tours; a slight, tight-lipped, and humorless mother who was born with a limp and never forgave the offense; a thoroughly impractical, but classic Jewish father, who had studied at the Talmudic Academy at Volozhin, but found socialism and Eugene Debs more engaging; and three children, two daughters and Milton Steinberg, inhabited the white frame house at 247 Baden Street in Rochester, New York. It was a complex, variegated, and diffuse household, held together by a single prevailing immigrant attitude—the

United States was a tentative, and slightly unbelievable, hypothesis which had to be explored. The task of testing the American hypothesis, not merely its theoretical foundations, but its capacity for diversion and worth-while entertainment, was left by and large to Samuel Steinberg and his son, Milton—Samuel to forage the land and plant it and Milton to reap its eventual harvest.

Samuel Steinberg was not unusual among the millions of immigrants who arrived from Eastern Europe in the last decades of the nineteenth century and the first decades of the twentieth. As most immigrants he was totally unprepared for the promised land. Raised in the small Lithuanian town of Seraye, he was accustomed to the compactness, consistency, and familiarity of that remarkable rural Jewish township, now immortalized by literature as the *shtetl*. The *shtetlach* of the Pale—that vast expanse of land which encompassed eastern Poland, Lithuania, White Russia, and the area north of the Carpathian mountains—bespoke indigenous Judaism. Traditionalism defined the order of life; society was, at best, integrated, and, at worst, circumscribed and limited by the ordinance of Jewish law. It was a predictable world—a world of piety and poverty, hard labor, famine, pogrom; but withal it possessed a sureness that life was watched carefully by God. The God of the *shtetl* loved the Jews even if he had bizarre and often dreadful ways of expressing it.

The *shtetl* of the late nineteenth century was already in decline. The inherited patterns of stability and order were slowly giving way before the relentless insistence of civil authority that Jews be either educated (which meant essentially, as Russian and Polish policy made clear, secularized or converted) or driven out. The coercion of civil authority could be combated—by subversion, by indifference, or by voluntary migration. But the inner Jewish world was susceptible to more dangerous influence—the village dissenter was a reality whether he appeared as *maskil* (an "enlightener" emancipated from Jewish observance but communicating the concepts of emancipation in the familiar language of Yiddish), Hebraist (one who rejected Yiddish in favor of the secular revival of the theretofore sacred language), or Zionist (one who saw in the national regeneration of the Jewish homeland a solution to the Jewish problem). The influences of *maskil*, Hebraist, Zionist, conjoined with the secular socialist and revolutionary movements which, in their Jewish extensions, used the folk culture and literature of the Jewish people, made significant inroads into the insulated world of the *shtetl*. The Jew was no longer cut off from the world. Though he had a pitifully unsophisticated and naïve conception of what the "world" meant, he was convinced that it was brighter, richer, and more promising than the world he knew.

The Talmudic student, Samuel Steinberg, was a prize of Seraye. Pious, clever, learned in Jewish law, he won the scholarship maintained by his town at the great and internationally known Talmudic Academy of Volozhin. But Volozhin in those days was already opened to the divisive influences of enlightenment. Samuel Steinberg, his son recalled years later, had told him of using his meager candle rations for purposes other than the review of the Talmudic portion. When his companions had fallen asleep, Steinberg would light his candle and conceal behind the enormous folio pages of the Talmud the fashionable works of the enlighteners: Tolstoy in Russian, the Hebrew novels of Abraham Mapu, or the daring, and slightly scandalous, questioning of Mordecai Zeev Feierberg's *Whither?*, the essays of Bin-Gorion, or the Yiddish and Hebrew stories of Mendele, Peretz, and Sholom Aleichem. Already before his immigration to the United States Samuel had relinquished the world of his youth.

The disillusionment which the impoverished and persecuted Jew confronted was now juxtaposed to the open world which an authentic secularism had defined. The secularism of the Pale, unlike the secularism that was to overcome American Judaism, had a different quality. It was a Jewish secularism. Although seemingly a contradiction, Jewish secularism was precisely that: it accepted the uniqueness of Israel and the providential destiny of the Jewish people, but it was no longer content with the passivity and resignation which characterized Jewish piety in Eastern Europe. By the time of the pogroms of the early 1880's and the rise of that distinctive movement, "The Lovers of Zion," the fate of the Pale was already determined. The rich stayed behind, the secure landowners and urban professionals remained, the Russified, the revolutionaries, the aged intellectuals, and the pious, who looked askance at reports of American irreligion, stayed home. Samuel Steinberg migrated. In the 1890's he arrived and in 1898 he settled and married in Rochester, New York.

Rochester in the early part of the twentieth century was a thriving center of the needle trades—innumerable small factories and piece-goods producers dotted the city. With the garment industry came both Jews and socialism—the former because, being largely unskilled labor and the factory owners being largely Jewish, Jews expected to be treated with the humanity and consideration due co-religionists. This was not to be the case. Jewish factory owners in the early century were no better and no worse, alas, than other factory owners. Working conditions were appalling, wages low, respect for interfering and time-consuming religious practices scant. The Jewish worker was pitted against the Jewish owner. The relation of Jew to Jew fell away and the antagonism of worker to boss remained. In this atmosphere the ideology and platform of American socialism and the organizing spirit of rising unionism found ready support. Perhaps the single most powerful influence in the assimilation and Americanization of the immigrant generally and the Jewish immigrant most particularly was the labor movement and the optimistic theorems of socialism—the former because it provided a rallying point and object of solidity in the disappearing world of old ties and securities; the latter because it held out hope that there was something more immediate than the Kingdom of God and the Days of the Messiah to be achieved.

Samuel Steinberg was evidently an undistinguished businessman and provider. Of his business career nothing is remembered. It is recalled only that his businesses were numerous and indifferently profitable. The distrait intellectuality of the European Talmudist could not be forgotten. Though the Talmud was stored away and the learning of the sages filed for later use, the curiosity which underlies the Talmudic mind was not wasted. Samuel was soon involved in the world of the reformers, the protesters, and the organizers. Lincoln Steffens, Meyer London, Morris Hilquit, Abe Cahan, became his new teachers and the Socialist Library on Chatham Street or the forums and lectures of the Labor Lyceum his new academy.

Into this complicated world of dissolution and discovery Milton Steinberg was born on Thanksgiving Day, 1903. Little is remembered of his boyhood—the few pictures that survive suggest a concentration and reflectiveness, qualified suggestively by a slightly grave but gentle irony. Even as a boy Milton was serious—his recreations were all entertainments of the mind. Though later, as his son Jonathan recalled, Milton urged upon all young men an elaborate education which included fencing, horsemanship, drawing, and the writing of sonnets, only the latter was to be included among his actual accomplishments. (He was to win, to his considerable delight, the first prize in poetry at De Witt Clinton High School when Countee Cullen, the distinguished Negro poet, was his primary competitor.) As a boy, however, Milton was either declaiming from memory the immortal triumphs and defeats of Jack London and inventing rousing tales of adventure and accomplishment to delight his playmates; or else was hidden away in the Rochester Public Library reading, characteristically, but to the dismay of the librarian, the Russian novels of which his family spoke endlessly. He was an accomplished student, a quick learner, an insatiable reader, and a passionate speaker. Curiosity was his motivation, argument his method, and answers his end. This tended to a kind of diffuseness, a form of intellectual wandering which he was to urge upon all but was ultimately to deny to himself.

His own program of the mind demanded concentration and thoroughness, virtues which he learned early and sustained. At sixteen years of age, however, Milton was an amateur everything—student of the novel, skilled debater, tyro astronomer, talented Latinist. It was actually an experience in Latin class at East High School in Rochester that marked the subtle turning of his mind from irresponsible learning to a sense of obligation toward the preciousness of learning. Dr. Mason D. Gray, the famous Latin teacher, caught Milton one day studying astronomy in Latin class. It was Gray's custom to call upon his students in alphabetic order to recite and translate. Breaking habit one morning he called on Milton, who was singularly unprepared. At the conclusion of the hour Dr. Gray read him a short riot act on the misuse of the mind. Steinberg was informed that the mind has its own priorities—priorities which do not issue from the vagaries of will or the meanderings of interest, but from the requirements of the task. Astronomy for the proper hour, Latin for the Latin class. Both are valuable in their place, but to exchange their places, to sacrifice knowledge of the one to passion for the other, is to distort both activities and compromise the mind. It was a gentle voice and a gentle manner that spoke an anything but gentle riot act to a student particularly sensitive to obligations and appeals to conscience. From that hour on undoubtedly Steinberg was to do nothing without thoroughness, without an almost compulsive attention to completeness.

The Emerging Man

The events of Milton Steinberg's adolescence and maturity are discrete and independent, so many occasions bound together by the articulate line of intellectual development. The problem of unfolding the life of an intellectual is particularly besetting. The intellectual rarely displays his *crises du coeur*, his pubescent outpourings, his dramatic shake-ups. Events are smaller, quicker, their consequences imperceptible, but no less profound.

The intellectual as a young man, you might think, is not all that self-conscious. This is a mistake. The pursuit of ideas is not leisurely. It is, as Steinberg was later to have the hero of his novel, *As a Driven Leaf*, Elisha ben Abuyah, observe: ". . . stark inner compulsion, dire necessity and he against whom it moves has no more choice than a leaf driven in a gale." What are the events that mark the life of the mind, that generate interest in facts which are essentially uninteresting? The intellectual is rarely chevalier, mover of history, ruler of nations, commandant of armies; if he is, the role which these careers of public action play in the internal action of the mind is tributary and submissive. If the mind works on the events of history and re-creates them, the life of action becomes secondary, and the life of the mind achieves ascendency.

The humanity of the intellect is always present; it is concealed behind the face of the mind, breaking through to expression in those ordinary crises of life—living, loving and dying. Ordinary, indeed, but absolute and final. We of the twentieth century tend to confuse importance with magnitude and scale. The small life—the life marked by interior accomplishments and joys, by creativity and seriousness, by loving and transforming—these lives we contemplate with awe and uncomprehension because they seem evidently to ignore the scale on which our modern conception of values is founded: power, wealth, success, public triumphs, renown, all of the finally trivial, but undeniably radiant accomplishments of our time. A great and transforming speech to a handful of people leaves us unimpressed, though it may be a lasting victory (if the handful are really transformed), while an enspiriting, but platitudinous, shaking of thousands is acclaimed. It is wrong and it misses the point. The life of the mind is dramatic, if one can enter the mind and see how the decisive moments are encountered and survived; how and why books are written; how vocations are adopted and pursued, and how, nevertheless, through all this, human beings love, relations are consummated, and the routine of life endured and ennobled.

In re-creating the life of Milton Steinberg all of these problems confront us—the skeleton is bare, only the bones appear.

A fortuity was the occasion of the movement of the Steinberg family to New York during the winter of 1919. Milton's older sister, Florence, a student at the Rochester Conservatory of Music, was introduced at a social gathering to the eminent cantor, Josef Rosenblatt. She so impressed Rosenblatt with her singing that he urged her to continue her studies in New York. Anxious to make available to her talented daughter every opportunity to mature her voice, Fanny Steinberg and Florence moved to New York during the winter of 1919. Shortly thereafter the family joined them.

The locus is shifted, but the same life unfolds. Steinberg leaves the Latin classes of East High School and enters De Witt Clinton High School, one of the city's most remarkable experimental secondary schools. The experience is repeated, but the achievements are compounded. The desultory curiosity of youth sharpens and concentrates. Latin is subdued; trigonometry, American history, English poetry are survived victoriously. It is recalled that Steinberg's English teacher was so overwhelmed by his skill and proficiency that he gave him at term's end the ridiculous grade of 105. Such implausible praise left Steinberg publicly unmoved, but secretly the dilemmas multiplied.

Lionel Trilling, recently interviewed in connection with research on Steinberg's youth, admits to feeling that "he was a respectable citizen and a prig." These are perhaps the reminiscences of youthful competitiveness, for, on examination, Trilling's own contributions to the literary journal of De Witt Clinton, *The Magpie,* were relatively undistinguished and enthusiastically American—baseball stories and rather mannered criticism of J. M. Barrie's plays come to mind. But then Trilling had a point, for, coupled with his plausible demurral (to be a "respectable citizen" is also in many circles to be a "prig"—and rightly so), is his comment that "my impression is that he (Steinberg) was not on easy terms with the generality of the students. . . . My image is of a person conscious of his powers, and separated from the boys by reason of this, in effect, already no longer boyish."

We need not give undue importance to Trilling's observations if we choose to bury Steinberg—as was common in medieval cities—under the fortress of sanctity. But ours is not the task of apotheosis or of augmenting legend. Legend is built out of imagination and forgetfulness. It fabricates as it destroys. The more immediate challenge is taking the facts as they are recorded and to discover what they yield. When we look at the early maturity of Milton we are confronted with an incredibly brilliant, preoccupied, and busy human being. The world was viewed as so many obligations and tasks, whether studying or reading, whether organizing and even instructing the Greek class at De Witt Clinton, whether debating, whether earning money by tutoring in French or English, Steinberg had little time for the diverting boyishness of which Trilling speaks. And yet where others mature into solemnities, having exhausted the frivolousness of youth, Steinberg was to reverse the procedure. Life into his early thirties was to be all seriousness and work; life, after his marriage to Edith Alpert—a marvelously volatile and complicated mechanism—was to shift, moving from seriousness to simple pleasures, simple companionship, and, in his last years, the incongruity of which he spoke so often, to raising flowers, and growing vegetables, and making furniture in his country workroom.

The determining experience, the experience which precedes and ratifies Steinberg's life decision, was his entrance in 1921 into the College of the City of New York and his meeting with Morris Raphael Cohen.

City College, founded in New York at the end of the Mexican War, had been for nearly a century under steady fire from the conservative press. It was thought of as an ill-disguised device of using the wealth of the rich to finance the education of the poor. The fact that higher education had once been the privilege of the rich and an ornament and source of power is undeniable, but that City College was a challenge to such a view is equally undeniable. Its student body in the twenties was largely composed of children of immigrant parents, the majority of whom were Jewish. The program offered was rich and diversified, the tastes of its students broad and unconfined.

It is to the credit of City College to have decided, as a corollary to its own liberal educational doctrine, to break camp with those who considered the teaching of philosophy to be but a device of shoring up Christian doctrine—indeed at that moment in American education most professors of philosophy were divines in secular pulpits. To have appointed Morris Raphael Cohen, an immigrant, a reforming socialist, and a logician, as assistant professor of philosophy in 1912 was daring. City College inadvertently made a great contribution to the education of a whole generation of thinkers. Not the least of these was Milton Steinberg.

Writing to Morris Cohen's son Felix after Cohen's death in 1947, Milton expressed his indebtedness: "He was a very great man, and a very gifted teacher, perhaps the most gifted and inspiring teacher it has ever been my fortune to encounter." Morris Cohen was undoubtedly a great teacher, but he was equally a formidable and shattering experience. If Cohen conceived the role of the teacher to be the cleaning of the Augean stables of the mind, he often scoured much more than the mind when he set to work. He was, as he admits in his autobiography, *A Dreamer's Journey*, relentless, persistent, and dogged in his pursuit of an incomplete idea, a pretentious argument, or an unexamined dogma. Since he considered teaching to be the impossible situation of having to implant enduring ideas in such a short space of time as to have little or no opportunity to examine them, he chose to be, not a former of character, but a cleaner of minds. It was not for him to impose upon others his own questionable and untested views; rather it was more valuable to disabuse minds of cherished illusions, to break ideas on the rack of close reasoning. This he did. Many fought back and survived—coming to richer and more profoundly held convictions. Others broke. Cohen admits that he was correctly charged with being "merely critical, negative, or destructive." [1]

Milton Steinberg, who had at least four courses with Cohen during his years as an undergraduate at City College (in every one of which he received an A), responded differently. He neither entrusted his mind to philosophy, adopting the course which Cohen was to describe as "naturalistic metaphysics"—open both to the questions which positivism denied and to the methods which classic metaphysics considered irrelevant—nor did he flee from philosophy, beaten in the fight against his teacher. Milton did something else, which is perhaps more crucial. He came to the conviction that both the mind and the spirit had to be sustained together, that logic could be restored to the service of religion, that reason and faith were not only compatible, but indispensable one to the other.

What Milton came to believe, and it is the belief that underlies the whole of his mature life, is that mind and soul are indeed one. As the Bible was to use the Hebrew word *nephesh* to stand interchangeably for intellect and soul, so Milton came to believe that to separate them was not only a distortion but a disaster. One suspects from his writing that this intuition came first—that the rediscovery of God, of Judaism, and of the Jewish people grew from it as necessary corollaries of a primary judgment. Milton was always an admirer and opponent of Henri Bergson. Indeed it was to a study of Bergson and Schopenhauer that his master's dissertation in 1928 was devoted. He often quoted Bergson's observation in *Creative Evolution* about the role of the guiding intuition, that central, jarring, self-contained insight which marks out, not only a train of thought, but a way of life. The guiding intuition of Milton Steinberg was that the soul of man—that which sustained

•••

[1] Morris Raphael Cohen, *A Dreamer's Journey* (Glencoe, Ill.: The Free Press, 1949), p. 145 f.

his humanity and affections—cannot be separated from his mind. It is but a consequential movement to come to believe that this union is founded upon a more complete wisdom, a more comprehensive vision of the universe which not only metaphysics defines, but religious belief illuminates.

The Vocation

There is little in the youth of Milton Steinberg which suggests his later vocation. The religious environment of his home was sympathetic to Judaism and conversant with its habits of mind and action. It was not, however, a meticulously observant home; words of Torah, though spoken often, were a casual expression of the atmosphere rather than a religious exercise. Opportunities for intensive Jewish education were lacking in Rochester and the roll records of those religious schools which did exist do not disclose that Milton was availed of them. He was prepared for his Bar Mitzvah by a local *melammed;* the ceremony took place at the Leopold Street Synagogue not far from the Steinberg home, and those who attended are reported to have been impressed by his chanting of the prophetic portion and his *derashah.*

Thus far all is quite predictable and in order. The first sixteen years are religiously uneventful. But is even this quite accurate? The record may be undemonstrative, but the inner life may well have been intense and secretly exploding. The conditions for the rabbinic vocation were there, even though they were neither sufficient nor determining. Milton's parents, first and foremost, liked Judaism. Even though they were no longer pious in the accepted traditions of Eastern European Orthodoxy, they had profound and articulate affection for their faith, its culture, its history, and its God. In spite of his being a mild-tempered socialist caught up in the spirit of American reform, Milton's father undoubtedly recalled that the rabbis were often on his side, or on the side of the poor, the oppressed, and the toiling. Where others might draw their secular wisdom from Goethe or Shakespeare, Samuel Steinberg drew his from *mamrei hazal,* the sayings of the sages. Sabbath was observed, synagogue was attended (often the Orthodox *shul* founded on Hanover Street by immigrant Polish Jews), festivals were respected, and, above all, Jews and Jewish destiny were a source of abiding concern.

It is not unusual that newly arrived in the burgeoning Jewish community of New York's West Harlem—the area that ran westward from Central Park to Riverside Drive and upward from roughly 116th Street to 125th Street— the Steinberg family should have first sought to sink Jewish roots. They were strangers and alone, and a warm and comfortable community, centering about several distinguished synagogues, afforded companionship. Whether at the instance of his mother, who first tried a Reform synagogue and found it cold and formal, or of Milton, who entered one day and introduced himself to the youth director, the family joined Congregation Ansche Chesed on February 22, 1920, but a short time after their arrival in New York.

Ansche Chesed, one of the oldest and most distinguished synagogues of the Conservative movement, was led by Rabbi Jacob Kohn, an energetic thinker, a persuasive believer, and an animated preacher. Milton enrolled himself in the after-school and week-end educational program of the synagogue. In addition to the formidable requirements of his academic life at De Witt Clinton, he undertook a time-consuming course of general religious instruction; founded a secret society, SOHI (whose initials stood for a marvelously characteristic aspiration, "Society of Higher Ideals"), and became captain of the school's debating team. He shaped the program of SOHI, lecturing on an immense variety of subjects—Hannibal, Job, Hellenic culture (the minutes of the April 30, 1921, meeting of SOHI record that "Mr. Steinberg gave a very interesting talk on John Milton and his achievements").

At the time that Milton entered City College, however, his knowledge of Judaism was still slight. His experience with Ansche Chesed and its rabbi had defined an ambiance of engagement and intimacy, but not of knowledge. The periphery of Judaism had been circled, its outer garments handled and worn, but its inner texture was still closed to the one medium of contact which he required of himself and others: knowledge.

It may be presumed that the years of high adolescence, the years that immediately preceded his entrance into City College, were filled with the ambiguity and uncertainty that the intellectually demanding habitually manifest—the play of inquiry, the passionate digestion of learning, the reading widely, the feeling deeply, the projection of those dreams which, of necessity, are grand and glorious—and without whose growth the maturity that follows would be unavoidably pedestrian and uneventful. Among these dreams one is given substance—a recognition of the genius and misery of the Jewish people, a profound awareness of kinship and intimacy with the historical destiny of the Jew. In his youth and early maturity, the terrestrial image of Jewish history predominates—Milton's identification with the secular fortunes of the Jew, his omnivorous reading of Jewish history and literature. And yet secular history is precisely that: sacred history secularized. The sensitized mind pushes further: How does a people survive? Beyond all tenacity, all vigor, all stubbornness, there is an ideal order toward which the people struggles and which sustains it. The secular history of the Jews presses to the affirmation of divinity.

The decision to learn, which Milton made in 1921, was an inescapably Jewish decision. Once the Jew chooses to learn, he rarely turns back. He may abandon learning, he may become surfeited of its subtlety, exhausted by its detail, tried by its exaction, but the decision to learn is final and irreversible. Undoubtedly Rabbi Jacob Kohn, to whom Milton turned in his early years at City College, exposed precisely the same network of argument which later Milton was to use upon others. One suspects that the reading list was the same and the arguments—good arguments they were—have not lost their power. Essentially Rabbi Kohn sought to take the first principles of the metaphysicians and logicians and turn them to the service of theism. Every philosophic argument is pressed to that point at which an axiomatic principle is affirmed, a first and final premise is articulated. Such first principles are principles to which logic assents without proof. If, indeed, logic and science must bow to principles which reason cannot demonstrate, where then is the unreasonableness of theism? Theism insists only that there is a more ultimate cause for the unfolding and display of life: a supreme intelligence who is God. Beyond this, what greater sanction for the order and beauty of life than to hold that this intelligence is also moral, that it obeys the law it makes? And lastly, what greater tradition can there be than that which worships that moral intelligence, which seeks to bring man into closeness and rapport with such a God?

The argument undoubtedly took this form in the early 1920's. It is preserved and extended by Steinberg throughout his writings; it is the groundwork upon which his religion rested. It was, above all things, a rational faith. Of necessity it had to be, for it could not otherwise have survived the assaults of Morris Cohen. Morris Cohen was not as dispassionately objective as he might have wished—it is idle to pretend that he was. The intellect, even in the act of cleansing and purifying, has already determined the errors to be expunged and the illusions to be debased. Among these, Cohen numbered the assumptions of religion. He was willing, as Milton was not, to settle for a purer, even if less comprehensive, truth. Milton, on the other hand, was bent upon achieving an embracing view, a *Weltanschauung*—one of Milton's precious and revealing words—which would "invest his days with meaning and dignity."

The legitimacy of theism, the intelligibility and reasonableness of its origins and conclusions, were appealing and won the young Steinberg. The argument, however, was not over: belief victorious never meant to Milton that the inquiry had ended. Rather it had just begun. The process of winnowing belief was to continue for a lifetime.

Milton Steinberg—for all his Jewish background—came to Judaism out of the secular culture of America. He did not return to the ancestral faith; he had not strayed only to come home. In his youth Judaism was a companion of the atmosphere, appealing and endearing, but not compelling. The argument that compelled him to Judaism was the same argument that might have compelled him, as Morris Cohen dearly wished, to become a philosopher. Milton argued his way into Judaism. Judaism succeeded, but philosophy did not lose. The philosopher always lurked in the doorway of the synagogue, throwing up challenges and rebukes, warning and proposing, indicating pitfalls and suggesting new possibilities. Although Morris Cohen thought he had lost (indeed Cohen, who saw himself locked in combat with his students, believed that Milton's decision would cost philosophy more than religion gained), he had, in fact, more profoundly won. Milton was never to become a simple fideist, a believer without complication. His mind remained to the end of his life infinitely involved with the complexities of faith and reason, the demands of the affections, and the exactions of the mind. But, then, though Judaism did not win a thorough and unconditional submission, it won something more significant and symptomatic, the mind of a Jew who, possessing power of thought, could yet—in the face of modern rationalism and scientism—accept Judaism.

Shortly before his twentieth birthday, on September 18, 1923, Milton Steinberg applied for admission to the Jewish Theological Seminary. He possessed adequate familiarity with Hebrew, a knowledge of Jewish history and current events, an affection for the Hebrew prayer book, a love for the Bible, and an unreserved passion for the discovery of an authentic, comprehensive, and adequate view of the universe. But he was singularly ill-equipped to enter the Jewish Theological Seminary.

The Jewish Theological Seminary, whose president in those years was the dour, austere, and somewhat unimaginative Cyrus Adler, had been founded in the late years of the nineteenth century as a device for offsetting the influence of the Reformer's Hebrew Union College. The seminary did not flourish until it was reorganized in 1901 and secured the services of the great and creative European scholar, Solomon Schechter, who served as its president from 1902 to 1915. The function of the Seminary as defined in those years was to transmit that body of Jewish knowledge necessary to an informed rabbinate, to instill in its students appropriate theological attitudes, and to adjust the student to the role which he was to perform in the community. This was the expressed intention of the Seminary, but intention is not always, or necessarily, father to the deed.

The Seminary thrived under the vivid and dramatic leadership of Schechter—Schechter succeeded, as others have not, in establishing an intimacy between the official role he performed and the intellectual convictions he held in private. Schechter would have been dismayed to know that the Seminary which Milton Steinberg entered would be characterized by an atmosphere of indecisiveness, defensive orthodoxy, and a vagueness regarding the ideology which it was ostensibly dedicated to clarify and articulate.

The Seminary, Steinberg was later to observe, was an intellectual academy with a professional school attached—the latter paid for and justified the former, but it was the former that held the allegiance of its faculty and administration. To be sure there was genius available to the students of the Seminary in those years—the renowned Talmudist, Louis Ginzberg; the distinguished but fatiguing Biblical scholar, Jacob Hoschander; the encyclopedic but abstracted historian, Alexander Marx; the beloved Hebraist, Morris Levine; the dry-as-dust pedant, and the Seminary's professor of codes, Moses Hyamson; the inventive and enthusiastic teacher of medieval Hebrew literature, Professor Israel Davidson; the Seminary's professor of homiletics, Mordecai Kaplan—but it concerned itself, not with teaching and training, but with its own professional specialty and preoccupation. These teachers, most of them educated and trained abroad, considered teaching an unfortunate, but unavoidable, interference with their own education. Moreover, they were singularly uneasy and awkward in the presence of their American-Jewish charges: young men of undoubted Jewish commitment, but undoubted spiritual anxiety, religious confusion, theological backwardness. They taught and they taught brilliantly, but their words poured forth in formal lectures where discussion was minimal, and feedback and controversy was a needless impertinence. They were by and large uninterested in the background against which they taught; it might yet have been the *Hochschule für Wissenschaft des Judentums* or the *yeshivot* of Eastern Europe, so little did they concern themselves with the predicament of American Judaism.

In those early years at the Jewish Theological Seminary Milton Steinberg was, in his own words, "miserable." A friend of his has recalled at least a dozen occasions on which Milton was convinced that he had to leave the

Seminary. He had more than twenty hours of classroom work each week; innumerable hours with a Yiddish-speaking *rebbe* whom he was compelled, at the insistence of the Seminary, to engage to fill out his inadequate knowledge of the Talmud; an additional fifteen to twenty hours of weekly homework and review; a teaching position at a neighborhood synagogue to earn a portion of his keep; and the continuance of his private reading in the classics in preparation for a doctorate he hoped to undertake upon graduation from the Seminary.

The incredible burden of study was in no wise lightened by any compensating solidity of conviction or spiritual certainty. This was, as he later admitted, not unusual. To the contrary he held that "every man of soul in the Seminary must traverse this particular bit of wilderness"— the torment of conscience, the vacillation of conviction, the tempting allure of other professions and pursuits. Those, he continued, "who didn't have this experience were Rabbinical oxen. While mental disturbances are no guarantee of effectiveness in the Rabbinate, I certainly think that the absence of them is a serious reflection in the student." The torment and uncertainties through which Milton passed were, however, of a different order from those which dislocated more traditional students. Unlike them, Milton was not distressed to learn of the Higher Criticism of the Bible, the mythologies of the Near East which possessed epic creations and floods paralleling those of Genesis, or the evolutionary unfolding of Jewish law and liturgy. He had never been monolithic. It was not disturbing therefore to discover that beliefs which he had never held were no longer scientifically admissible. His torments were different and to these torments there was none, except one, to give answer.

The problems in which Milton found his métier and to which he later gave his passion were issues of metaphysical stature: the nature of God, his relation to man and history, the problem of evil, the tension of theology and science, the balance of reason and belief, the destiny of human life. These problems, dissolved in the alembic of Jewish study and observance, would tend to vanish if one allowed them to; the labored study of Holy Writ and its commentators, the precise mastery of the Talmud and the Codes (these primary areas of emphasis in Seminary training) could adequately consume and exhaust a life. Only one who stood out before, over, and against tradition, who mastered it, accepted it, but went on, in spite of all obstacles, to continue to ask leading questions of the universe, might endure. Milton Steinberg was not satisfied to be a rabbi, if to be a rabbi meant other than to speak only what he believed and to be discontented with anything on which he could not speak with conviction and belief. The tension between tentative and fulfilled conviction led to the intellectual drama which his later works illustrate. But in the days of the early 1920's, as a young man of precocious brilliance, all that sustained him was sheer energy and will. He had no answers, but he knew where to look. The Seminary, then as now, made little provision for the study of Jewish philosophy. If one wished to know what practicing Jews thought about their Judaism, one had either to study for oneself or go elsewhere. Between courses on Hellenism and Greek philosophy at Columbia and his program at the Seminary, Milton undertook to study with a fellow seminarian, Alex Bernstein, the texts of medieval Jewish philosophy. They agreed to study *The Book of Beliefs and Opinions* of the ninth-century Jewish philosopher, Saadya Gaon. It is not unusual that from this side study his prize-winning essay, "Reason and Faith in Saadya," should have resulted.

Institutions possess a marvelous faculty of self-deception. They build their own walls and man the battlements, but invariably contrive to leave an escape door in an ob-

scure portion of the fortress. They forget that as easily
as it might serve them to escape, it will as readily give
entrance to the invader. Mordecai Kaplan has been, for
more than forty years, the escape door of the Jewish Theological Seminary. Had it not been for the inventive and
imaginative techniques which he devised to rationalize the
Judaism into which the Seminary was inducting its students, it might have lost—in those years of religious at-
trition, the late twenties, thirties, and early forties—literally scores of future rabbis.

Mordecai Kaplan, unlike those who were to be his colleagues and very much like those who were to be his students, survived the same fires of uncertainty and skepticism through which he was literally to force his students
to pass. Kaplan was a hybrid—his youth was passed in a
small Russian community; at the age of nine he came to
the United States, where his Jewish education continued,
while his knowledge of English was left to be garnered
from street playmates. By his twelfth year he was permitted simultaneously to enter public school and the preparatory adjunct of the Seminary. At the age of twenty-one
he graduated from the Seminary and, after continuing post-
graduate studies, both Jewish and secular, he accepted a
call to an Orthodox pulpit. Troubled by the challenges of
Higher Criticism of the Bible, dissatisfied by the apolo-
getic rationalism of the medieval philosophers, skeptical
of the essential truth and necessity of much rabbinical
ordinance and exegesis, he was, and has remained, nevertheless, a thoroughly observant Jew. Although strenuous in
his exactions upon himself, he has been lenient, temporizing, and tolerant in his program for others.

It is not unusual that Kaplan's own intellectual uncertainty should have been communicated to his orthodox
congregants. His position became untenable, his own ambivalence of attitude too exhausting and dishonest to be
maintained for long. Within weeks of his decision to

abandon the rabbinate, he was asked by Solomon Schechter to succeed the recently deceased Joseph Asher as professor of homiletics, while continuing in his capacity as dean of the newly organized Teachers Institute of the Seminary.

In the years from 1909 to 1923, Mordecai Kaplan undertook to appraise the foundations, unfolding, and future of Judaism. In a generation in which Jewish scholarship was devoted to conservation and self-perpetuation, he had the daring to reopen pressing questions of doctrine and theology.[2] In a generation where no one rose to think, when rabbis were founts of torrential platitudes and Jewish thinkers were little more than homileticians, Kaplan transformed homiletics into an instrument and technique of articulating a new and significant preachment. The breach left open by the Seminary—that minor and somewhat insubstantial position of professor of homiletics—was converted by Kaplan into a pulpit of his own, a pulpit which, though many tried, was never toppled, and which, moreover, was extended in later years to include what the Seminary, with disarming ambiguity, now calls "philosophies of religion."

As Mordecai Kaplan was later to acknowledge, Milton Steinberg was one of his most brilliant students, perhaps the only student of philosophic genius it had been his good fortune to teach. Whatever Steinberg had been to Kaplan, Kaplan was undoubtedly much more to Steinberg. The early twentieth century witnessed the collapse and intel-

• • •

[2] For further information regarding the life of Mordecai Kaplan one may consult his essay, "The Way I Have Come," in his *An Evaluation* (New York: Jewish Reconstructionist Foundation, 1952), pp. 283-321; also his recent address, "Rabbis and Teachers as Guides for the Perplexed," *The Reconstructionist*, XXV, 11 (Oct. 2, 1959), pp. 8-14. For a critical discussion of Kaplan's thought, see the present writer's forthcoming book, *The Jewish Mind* (New York: Pantheon, 1961).

lectual disarmament of classic theisms. Although Protestantism had already succumbed to modernism and Roman Catholicism had artificially withstood its assault, Judaism, the last to be reached, received the backwash of modernist doctrine. The findings of comparative anthropology, cultural Darwinism, sociology of religion, archaeology, and Biblical criticism reached Judaism in the twentieth century. Where Reform theology was still characterized by a Judaized neo-Hegelianism and Orthodoxy was intransigent, Conservative Judaism stood resolutely noncommittal and astride all positions. This uncomfortable stance had, however, marginal benefits. It attracted students who were sufficiently concerned with the survival of a traditional Judaism to be antipathetic to Reform and sufficiently acculturated to be unsusceptible of Orthodoxy. A student body existed for whom there were no teachers but Mordecai Kaplan. In a very real sense Kaplan—opinionated, passionate, and unrelenting—gave both his students and his institution a hard time. He renovated Judaism while he taught it; he exploded convictions while he formulated his own; he disabused Judaism of cherished theological illusions while substituting equally debatable doctrines.

What Mordecai Kaplan had to teach, however, Milton Steinberg never forgot: Judaism had to be worth the struggle to preserve it. Supernaturalism was passé; revelation was irrational; the chosen particularity of classic Judaism was deemed antiuniversal. Kaplan was, as Steinberg came later to believe, often wrong and unconvincing. He was always thinking, however—a virtue which could not be imputed with ease to any other Jewish thinker in his generation. Kaplan was a Morris Cohen of the religious order —a disabuser and a cleanser of inherited prejudices and unexamined assumptions. During his Seminary years Milton's devotion was unreserved; he owed much of his survival power in the Seminary to strength derived from Mordecai Kaplan.

...

On May 24, 1928, Rabbi Milton Steinberg graduated with distinction from the Jewish Theological Seminary. He had passed through four complex and demanding years—years of exemplary academic achievement, but years of impatient searching; years of dissatisfaction with the Seminary, combat with its administration, and criticism of its curriculum; years of patient learning with Louis Ginzberg and devotion to Morris Levine and fascination with Israel Davidson; years of unraveling his conception of Judaism in dialogue with Mordecai Kaplan. He had completed an M.A. dissertation in philosophy at Columbia; he had enjoyed the wild confusion of being a counselor at Camp Modin; he had occupied High Holy Day training pulpits in Austin, Illinois; Ithaca, New York, and Indianapolis, Indiana.

The Milton Steinberg who left the Jewish Theological Seminary in 1928 was resolute and serious. He carried himself with a prepossession and sureness which betrayed his age—for he was, notwithstanding, a shy, tentative, and somewhat awkward twenty-five. Milton had already defined, however, the major lines of his intellectual position; he had successfully refined his position of the marginalia of petty doubts and uncertainties. He had, as he wrote to his close friend Ira Eisenstein, arrived "at a satisfactory intellectual attitude toward Judaism both actively and passively—actively in that one reads, one wrestles with the problems, passively, in that one's attitude and position gradually clarify themselves, almost of themselves, like a precipitate dissolving in the presence of some unknown, unseen reagent." The marks of this self-assured clarity he went on to describe:

"1. When one knows what one's own position is very definitely—and one has definite arguments that are convincing (to oneself at least) for holding that position.

"2. When one ceases to be afraid of people who disagree and to dread the reading of hostile books.

"3. When the restlessness departs—and peace sets in.

"4. When everything one reads seems either false or else confirmatory of one's attitude."

The irony of Steinberg's position was that it expressed real and honest conviction which he was never to change, although it left unexplored that desert of the spirit which the experiences of involvement and love, discovery and intense passion, were to humanize. Milton Steinberg was graduated from the Jewish Theological Seminary full of knowledge, but not yet wise. The wisdom was to come, for it was the wisdom which only the heart could teach.

The Mature Years Before the Middle Years

Most men live without discretion, pushing their dreams before them, keeping risk from view, changing little, and dying in their threescore ten, unfulfilled, tired, and not a little bored. Other men live as if every moment were their last—struggling always to know themselves better, to discover their concealments and deceptions, to reveal more of themselves, to give the most they can. Such men become human beings early; they are mature before their middle years; and if they chance to die before the time convention adjudges decent, they often die fulfilled.

Milton Steinberg died young and he matured early and deception was no part of his life. The world was too enormous and his passion for living too intense to be wasted. Unlike others his youth was not passed in the small games of discovery and the traditional pleasures of childhood. It is no wonder that he should have written to his future wife, Edith Alpert—and to her alone—but a year after his graduation of the single fear that animated his life: "What I cannot attempt to approach is human beings." The occasion of this self-accusation—an outburst of petty jealousy and a touching apology—possessed, however, its core of truth. Milton was uncommonly sensitive to the alienating power of the intellect. To take refuge in the mind, in its capacity for clear and strict logic, and in its righteous intolerance for uninformed argument and prejudice may be sound training for a human being, particularly for a human being whose vocation was to be the teaching and instruction of the uninformed, the narrow, and the otherwise prejudiced. Milton understood this, but was unsuccessful in his early years in combating it. He had for so long pressed an inward argument, an internal struggle for clarity and conviction, that the necessity of moving outward—from the tight enclave of the Seminary to the broad and uncongested world of public affairs and public activity—was undoubtedly frightening.

His first pulpit, Beth El Zedeck in Indianapolis, had been so impressed by his conduct and preaching during a visit to their congregation for the High Holy Days in 1926 that they had importuned him to become their rabbi upon his graduation from the Seminary. The years in Indianapolis, which began in 1928, were training years. Into those years Milton compressed a lifetime of vigor and involvement, engagement and intensity. He did everything but consider himself and his proper task; he strained his marriage to the breaking point; he placed his young and vivacious wife under extraordinary pressures; but, withal, the shock of nearly losing her recalled him to himself.

The Jewish community of Indianapolis, like small communities the world over, was ingrown and possessive. It unfailingly confused affection with power; it saw its public servants as recipients of favor and attention for which they were expected to reciprocate with submission. The community defined the standards and the rabbi and his wife were expected to fulfill them. For several years Milton did not consider this unreasonable—for that matter he was not particularly aware of the subtle slights and indignities which he was asked to suffer. His finances were a matter of public discussion; his wife's friends and amusements were scrutinized; her piety or impiety an issue of communal assessment. While he tried unsuccessfully to justify his privacy to the congregation and the ways of his congregation to his wife, he found himself—quite willingly —in constant demand. In addition to revitalizing his own congregation and embarking upon an elaborate program of Jewish education, he took on innumerable speaking engagements—at interracial meetings, at Zionist rallies, at civic luncheons, at Butler University. No lecture was too trifling to be passed. Through this press of activity and public success an undercurrent of unrest moved. Not only had his wife left him briefly to reconsider the future of their marriage and to give him time to rethink what it was he really wanted, but he had, in the years at Indianapolis, so committed himself to public affairs as to leave unattended his long-standing obligations to work privately, to think, and to write.

There is a real sense in which Steinberg's acceptance of the offer of the Park Avenue Synagogue in New York to become its rabbi in early 1933 represented the end of his apprenticeship as both a rabbi and a human being. He and his wife were splendidly reconciled—he, committed to a more sympathetic and attentive concern for the requirements of privacy, and she, increasingly tolerant of the unavoidable inconveniences of being a rabbi's wife. Moreover, they were delighted at the prospect of returning to a metropolitan wilderness where personal anonymity became possible once more, where private work could be pursued, where intellectual companionship could be found, where one's society was not limited to the membership of one's congregation.

The return to New York was accompanied by yet another decisive commitment. Milton had always wanted to write, to set down the argument of his own inner pilgrimage, to be a call and a trumpet blast to American Jewry. He had long since proved his capacity as a rhetorician and polemicist—his ringing speech at an Emancipation Day rally in Indianapolis before the Negro community, his tercentenary address on Spinoza at Butler College, his on-the-spot, quick, and pointed lectures and sermons had confirmed his verbal power. But there was something more that catalyzed his intellectual ambition—his conviction that since he had thought his way into Judaism, Judaism was truly a thinking man's faith, a religion of enormous moral power, reasonableness, and beauty, to which others could be induced to return if Jewish history and thought could be effectively dramatized.

It is the sense of drama, perhaps more than all else, which should be underscored in Steinberg's recounting of the history and fortunes of the Jewish people. Steinberg, in spite of being a rationalist and an intellectual, lost all pomposity and sternness when he entered the active rabbinate. Although he was to complain often of the low level of intellectual companionship in the rabbinate, of the meager intellectual resources of his audiences, of the "stale sachet, composite perfumes, and the savor of unappetizing fish courses" of the unchanging and endless women's luncheon—he was by no means a snob. His real passion was to break through the formal barriers erected by modern religion to keep the parishioner from the truth—the sermon, the luncheon, the banquet, the social—and to teach, to engage his congregation in common discussion and exploration.

The center of Milton's sense of Jewish history was its magnificent drama. Its drama bespoke the mystery of Jewish existence and survival—the wondrous techniques of conservation and exploration which Jewry had matured through centuries, the devices of study, memory, and teaching which it had fashioned as instruments of self-perpetuation, the dignity and courage which it maintained before a hostile world. These were the elements not of intellectual history, but of drama. It is this drama which underlay "How the Jew Did It," the first of a two-part article which he wrote for the *Atlantic Monthly* in 1933, and his first book, *The Making of the Modern Jew,* which Bobbs-Merrill had commissioned in the closing months of his stay in Indianapolis.

The first months of his return to New York were chaotic beyond belief. The Steinberg household became, as Edith described it, "a smaller version of Grand Central Station, except for the arrival and departure of trains." The Park Avenue Synagogue demanded immediate attention—its membership had declined, its services were a hodgepodge of the worst elements of Reform and the least impressive emendations of Conservative Judaism, its executives were demoralized; the Jewish community at large immediately put Milton on call; Edith was expecting the birth of their first child, Jonathan; and Milton was under contract to deliver the manuscript of *The Making of the Modern Jew* by fall. The Steinberg house was a somewhat frantic display, midway between the antics of an Arthur Kober story and an early George S. Kaufmann comedy. In spite of the pressure, Milton maintained an unrelenting schedule and *The Making of the Modern Jew,* perhaps his most daring and exciting book, was completed in slightly more than six weeks.

In a footnote to *The Making of the Modern Jew* the emergence of Milton's religious platform was signaled. He refers in passing to a movement in Conservative Judaism "concerned with the evolution of a more adequate ideology." The leader of this movement, Mordecai Kaplan, was at the same time readying for publication his own *Judaism as a Civilization.* As Steinberg glosses, "With its appearance, a new page may be turned in the effort to adjust tradition to its times." [3]

It is not unusual therefore that Milton was asked during

• • •

[3] *The Making of the Modern Jew* (New York: Bobbs-Merrill Co., 1933; New York: Behrman House, Inc., 1943), p. 288 *passim.*

the spring of 1934 to join with his former teacher, Mordecai Kaplan, and others in the expansion of The Society
for the Advancement of Judaism, Kaplan's own organization, and the inauguration of a magazine, *The Reconstructionist*. Milton had been a Reconstructionist for more than
a decade; he had given articulate expression to his sympa-
thies with Kaplan's program, both explicitly and by in-
direction throughout *The Making of the Modern Jew;* he
was commencing to mold the service and attitudes of the
Park Avenue Synagogue accordingly. Although Milton was
a programmatic Reconstructionist, an ideological supporter
of the movement, he never became a supporter of its
theology.

The distinction between ideology and theology is one
which nontheologians will not grasp and antireligionists
will consider wildly funny, but it is a real one. An ideology,
conventionally understood, is a program of practical principles held together in loose confederation by a mixture
of sound truths and rhetorical slogans. The dubiety of its
ultimate grounding in no wise compromises the consequences and viability of its practical recommendations.
Mordecai Kaplan was convinced—he has not changed in
this—that Judaism has an ill-starred future if it does not
regain relevancy to the times, if it does not modify or
scrap portions of its doctrine and practice which depend,
in his view, upon outmoded and antiquated procedures.
At the same time Kaplan believes that Judaism is unusual,
although not unique; that it is a true, valuable, and significant civilization which the world requires and which
Jews desert only at the peril of inauthenticity. Kaplan's
program directed itself to the building of Jewish civilization in the United States, in other lands of the dispersion,
and in the rejuvenated Zion. Since civilizations mature
and change, unfold and evolve, and Judaism is a civilization, it loses nothing—indeed, it gains and survives only
if it changes and moves with history.

The ideology of Reconstructionism is a *praxis*, not a *theoria*. It is a program, not a doctrine; a *Weltanschauung*, not a metaphysic. The former is useful and constructive if it works, if it brings Jews home, if it reinvests the synagogue with meaning, if it revitalizes prayer and worship, if it justifies ritual. Steinberg saw it as this—not with such conscious clarity in the early years, but surely in his last years. He joined, therefore, in editing and writing for *The Reconstructionist*, assisting in the formulation of the movement's ritual program, co-operating actively in the publication of its Sabbath Prayer Book, which he introduced, albeit with admitted reservations, into his own congregation. But the reservations which he held (which he expressed on the occasion of the fifteenth anniversary of *The Reconstructionist* but a month before his death [4]) were significant, for they underscore the later development of his thought. Reconstructionism was founded upon a useful rhetoric, but a dull and uninspired sense of poetry; Reconstructionism expressed a viable ideology, but it lacked not only a metaphysic, but a metaphysical concern. Essentially what Reconstructionism lacked—poetry and philosophy—was precisely what Milton demanded. It was one thing to instruct the Jew, bring him to prayer, confirm him in his faith. Undoubtedly, one needs active Jews if one is to have Judaism. But Milton insisted that not every Judaism was true and trustworthy simply because Jews believed it. There were indispensable questions which had to be asked not because they had practical significance—but because they lay at the heart of man's wondering about the universe. These questions, the questions which inform all his writing and particularly the essays in the present volume, have no practical consequence, but they are essential, for on them depends truth. They are the philosophic ques-

• • •

[4] *A Believing Jew* (New York: Harcourt, Brace & Co., 1951), pp. 166-78; cf. particularly p. 174 f.

48

tions. But even then, philosophy is not sufficient, for what is philosophy without the sense of mystery and awe? And the latter is the poetry of religion, the judgment that ultimate truth—truth about God and His kingdom—cannot be spoken in platitudes, but that the poet's touch must inform the shaping of theology.[5]

The poet's touch and the theologian's anxiety were combined most magnificently in the next project which Milton was to undertake, the fictional narration of the life of Elisha ben Abuyah, a rabbinic sage of the first century A.D., who, though a member of the Sanhedrin and a colleague of the sainted Rabbi Meir, deserted to Rome in the waning hours of the Jewish nation. The struggle of Elisha, the *passio* of Elisha, and the death of Elisha all received his warmth and compassion. Elisha shared not a little with Milton, and the world of Elisha shared not a little with the world of the twentieth century. Unquestionably he saw the life of Elisha as a modern homily, an example and a warning to the modern world. Elisha was, more than personal companion and homily, a further explication of Milton's own religious life. Where *The Making of the Modern Jew*

• • •

[5] There is a magnificent letter from Steinberg to Mordecai Kaplan, November 17, 1947, declining the latter's invitation to join with him and his associates in the preparation of a High Holy Day *Mahzor*. Aside from technical and personal reasons for his refusal, Steinberg cannot accept Kaplan's aesthetic. Kaplan appeared willing to excise exquisite prayers, because he demurred from some formulation or attitude which they expressed. Steinberg argued: "I have always maintained that departures from traditional forms are justified only when clearly and demonstrably indicated by intellectual or ethical necessity." He goes on to list cases where proposed deletions are justified by neither canon. In sum, though he sympathized with Kaplan's exposed ideology, he was more and more incapable of accepting a position which had already hardened sufficient slogans and clichés so as to make it unyielding to theological speculation and closed to the requirements of poetry.

articulated his public stand—his pride in his vocation, his love for the Jewish people, his intense desire to bring alive in others what was aflame within himself—*As a Driven Leaf* was something else. It was most superficially an intellectual penance: Milton had long intended to write a doctorate for Columbia University on the influence of classic culture on rabbinic Judaism. The research was done fitfully, his notes were enormous, his library fitting testimony to this enduring concern—an assessment of the bridge between his own two worlds, that of Greece and Rome and that of Israel. The thesis was never written. As he wrote to Rabbi Joshua Loth Liebman in 1946: "I'm not at all perturbed at the fact that the book [*As a Driven Leaf*] is nontechnical. While all of us who have been extensively exposed to academic procedures tend to value scientific work more highly than popular, I for one have increasingly freed myself of late from that obsession. That is why my thesis is still unwritten, whereas other things have been finished and are in process."

As a Driven Leaf was, however, something more than a penance; it was a making use of learning which would otherwise have remained untested and unapplied. It was an explanation of himself to himself, an articulation of why a Jew stays a Jew and why a Jew deserts Judaism. And the problem—the beautiful problem of *As a Driven Leaf*— is that Elisha was unsatisfied with the Biblical rendering of the mystery of the universe, the antiphilosophic scruples of the rabbis, the hostility which they displayed to Greek learning; moreover, he was tempted—as all religious men are tempted—to go over to the regnant paganism which exists always and at every moment. The passion and immolation of Elisha, which Steinberg beautifully re-creates, centers around Elisha's dissatisfaction with the simple faith and regimen which piety enjoined. It wanted more; it wanted to bring God down from heaven to confirm his existence; it wanted proofs—not signs and wonders. Although superficially the battle of Elisha and the rabbis is narrated in terms of the age-old contest of faith and reason, that is but the intellectual shell in which the argument of life is enclosed. What comes alive in *As a Driven Leaf* is Milton's own sense of the vindication of *struggle* itself, without contempt for those for whom the struggle has already ended in acceptance of a traditional way. Rabbi Meir is beautiful and so is Elisha ben Abuyah. Rabbinic tradition accounts the former a saint and the latter a rebellious and accursed deserter. Steinberg accounts them both blessed, for both teach us the thorny way of the religious life—the one resigns himself to personal tragedy and continues to believe, the latter affirms an enduring and uncompromised Promethean *hubris*. Both are man's way—the way of trust and the way of philosophic question and scrutiny. There is nothing less than the grandness and misery of man in *As a Driven Leaf*.

The Making of the Modern Jew had been written easily and had enjoyed a vast success. It had sold well and it brought Steinberg national prominence. *As a Driven Leaf* was wrought, however, with considerably greater pain. Since it was so profoundly personal, since it involved the treatment of so much with which Milton was unfamiliar and of which he was not a little afraid, it became a work of agonizing collaboration—Milton's writing and his wife's unfailingly subtle and precise sense for its ring of truth. Edith Steinberg was fatefully honest; she lived so successfully at the edge that she spared none, least of all herself.

In a brilliant unpublished essay, "Midwife to a Novel," Edith has described most amusingly, but with undisguised recognition of the traumatic undertaking which such a collaboration involved, the writing of *As a Driven Leaf*. The early part of the essay sketches the inception of the novel, the three agonized years of researching, the tentative blocking of the novel, the preparation of the first draft. It is with the completion of the first draft that her narrative becomes most revealing—revealing of the profound tension and profound love in which they pursued their common lives:

> One evening he handed me a sheaf of untidy pages, saying briskly, "Here—it's finished. . . ." And I read it, eagerly as I started, with a sinking heart as I continued, sick with dismay long before I reached the end.
>
> It was bad, and I would have to tell him so. The hero acted alternately like an imbecile and a cad. The dialogue was consistently stilted and unnatural. And the women were what might have been expected of a clergyman—creatures not to be found in heaven, on earth, nor in the waters under the earth.

Although Milton insisted that the manuscript was finished and sent it to his publisher, Bobbs-Merrill, Edith's judgment was confirmed. The publisher responded that the manuscript's appeal was "almost entirely intellectual," and recommended a complete recasting of the novel. It is in the description of the process of revision that "Midwife to a Novel" is so diverting and well worth recall:

> I became a habit with him, a prop to lean on, a butt for abuse when the words would not march. I never wrote a line, yet every passage had to pass muster with me. To encourage naturalness in the dialogue I developed the practice of testing the lines by declaiming them out loud. . . . It turned out to be an enlistment for the duration. Even when he wrote I had to be on the scene, unheard but seen. For woe betide me, should I be out of the room when he needed me as actor or audience. . . . Those tempestuous hours when I would be bellowed at for exhibiting curiosity as to which child had murdered the other. Or the tirade that would beat upon me when I would have to hand back a passage. . . . There were occasions when he took disapproval in good grace. But sometimes he was physically

exhausted or disagreed with me—or was just furious for allowing himself to get so dependent upon me. Then he would let loose and the fur would fly. At least once a week our raised voices stopped the piano-player next door. The temptation to throw was at times very strong. . . . It was jolly fun.

But if the cooperative writing of a novel cannot be recommended as a pedagogic device, it had the most salutary effect on me. Instead of being merely an important member of a firm, I had been raised to partnership status. . . . And our marriage too reached a new high. . . . Day after day, we cut, redid, stripped, polished, all but planned the manuscript. We filled two drawers in the desk, our morgue, with material we had discarded, irrelevant chapters, infelicitous bits of dialogue, unfortunate descriptions. Out of it all, there emerged at last two freshly typed volumes of novel. To the publishers they went—this time not to return.

Although delayed slightly by the publication in the fall of a dubiously competitive novel by Sholem Asch, *As a Driven Leaf* was published in January, 1940. It received vast praise and compliment. His first teacher, Rabbi Jacob Kohn, his professor of Talmud, Louis Ginzberg, his colleagues in the rabbinate, received it with unparalleled pleasure, indeed, gratitude. Alfred Kazin, writing in the *New York Herald Tribune*, considered it "a rare and moving book, creative in its thought, sensitive, scholarly without being a document. . . . It has a warmth of conception and intellectual intensity that are exciting." Only one slightly acid, and as yet unexplained, dissent was voiced, that of Maurice Samuel. Writing in the *Newsletter* of Hadassah, the woman's Zionist confederation, Samuel succeeding in missing the whole point of the novel, in accusing it of defects which were in fact its virtues. If Steinberg was to be chastized for taking Elisha at his word and interpreting his ruin as the price paid for a "sheer hunger for truth," Samuel had failed to grasp the elemental concern of the novel. Other weaknesses *As a Driven Leaf* possessed—weaknesses which Milton willingly admitted—but to charge it with a defect of purpose was neither just nor accurate. A close friend ceased to be quite as close as he had once been. It was obviously dangerous for a rabbi to attempt the craft of a rival, but not notably successful, novelist.

Life proceeded with unceasing complication. Steinberg had been active in the reformulation of the religious program of the Y.M.H.A., had served as chairman of the Social Justice Committee of the Rabbinical Assembly, the professional body of Conservative Judaism, had begun lecturing—with an undoubted sense of urgency and danger—on the disaster then threatening European Jewry and the necessity of pressing for the upbuilding of Palestine, and maintained his active participation in and contribution to the work of *The Reconstructionist*.

The lines of his life were marked and defined by 1940. The timidity and unsureness had passed; the combustible Steinberg ménage—now increased by the presence of Jonathan and David, two growing and wonderfully inventive children—had settled into a slow, steady, but considerably gentler pace; his success and tenure at the Park Avenue Synagogue had already been assured by a splendid outpouring of affection at a celebration held in his honor two years earlier on the fifth anniversary of his return to New York; his public image was formed and firm.

The Years of Prescience

Milton Steinberg was not permitted to enter the active chaplaincy when the United States declared war in 1941. The Jewish Welfare Board, which supervised the placement and call of Jewish chaplains, had diagnosed a slight heart impairment which made it impossible to call him for full service. At his importuning Milton was appointed, however, to a theoretically less exacting position. He was invited to act as trouble shooter and traveling inspector of Jewish chaplains, moving from base to base inquiring after the handling of Jewish religious needs and problems. This assignment was not calculated to relieve strain. While not altering in the least his usual program of activity, he undertook to make a national tour of Army bases in the late fall of 1942. On December 7, 1942, while en route from Brownwood, Texas, he suffered a severe coronary attack. After several months in a local hospital he returned to New York, to his home on East 92nd Street, to his bed, from which he was but infrequently—and only with unacknowledged effort and stress—to arise.

The seven years that were to remain to Milton Steinberg were undoubtedly years of prescience—his wife, with growing awareness and terror, was undoubtedly cognizant of the seriousness of his condition. Numerous doctors had already made clear that unless his schedule was radically curtailed, unless the Park Avenue Synagogue availed him of adequate assistance, unless sufficient funds were given to him to reduce the necessity of public lecturing, they could not assume responsibility for his life. While his wife suffered and his children grew, Milton maintained a face of magnificent imperturbability. If anything, the leisure to which he was compelled to submit allowed him to redouble his activity. His attention to the formal obligations of his congregation was considerably reduced by the engagement of Rabbi Morris Kertzer and later Rabbi Simon Noveck as assistant rabbis; he preached less, reserving his strength for particularly significant occasions—festivals and holy days, or for consideration of issues he deemed of paramount importance, his critique of *Commentary Magazine* being one of note.[6] His attention shifted reluctantly from the public arena to the fulfillment of more immediate

• • •

[6] *A Believing Jew*, pp. 136-65.

and apparently less arduous tasks, the cultivation of younger friends to whom he gave inordinate attention, the Zionist movement for which he continued to agitate, the United Jewish Appeal for whom he wrote his memorable appeal, "When I Think of Seraye," [7] and the writing of books.

The Making of the Modern Jew implied a sequel. It ended with the arrival of Judaism in the twentieth century, with the adumbration of the future of the Jew. But the question to which answer had still to be given was: Having arrived in the modern world, having reached American shores, what was the Jew to be? *A Partisan Guide to the Jewish Problem* (1945),[8] whatever its simplifications, contained gallery portraits of possible answers. In this atypically polemical work, Steinberg sought to create categories, formulate alternative stances, define the various postures of the Jew. The one which he advocated in the elegiac conclusion to *A Partisan Guide* was a composite, for it enfolded the best of all alternatives and the best of all alternatives are available to no man. It had the undeniable merit, absent from most popular Jewish books, of being enormously literate, felicitous in style, abundant in the richness of its historical sense and allusion. The Jewish man to which he sought to give life was the ideal man, the man reverential, but open; uncompromisingly Jewish, yet unambiguously American; capable of multiple literacies —English and Hebrew; traditional, yet flexible; God-fearing, yet reasonable and amenable to the findings of science. What he advocated, he had in large measure achieved: a balance and blending, an integrated being all of whose parts were yet discriminable and clear-cut. But what he asked of himself, he characteristically asked of

• • •

[7] *Ibid.*, pp. 181-95.

[8] *A Partisan Guide to the Jewish Problem* (New York: Bobbs-Merrill Co., 1945).

others. The weakness of *A Partisan Guide* is that he over-simplified the prospects of achieving the ideal—this was the pure and untempered idealist in him, the undimmed optimist and enthusiast.

The years which spanned the publication of *As a Driven Leaf,* the onset of his illness, and the writing of *A Partisan Guide* were fitful years, years in which his personal life had reached a profound level of contentment and satisfaction, but years as well in which the prescience of disability and premature death accompanied every waking hour. Many were the restless nights, for night is the time when death becomes most familiar to the living. He consumed the night hours reading endless mystery stories and cheering Edith, who knew what fear shadowed both his thoughts and hers. But as well he realized that, as his heart did not mend and his energy waned, time was playing against him. It was inescapable that he should, at some point, have grown to a conscious decision that the life of an unproductive semi-invalid, confined to an enforced rest, limited in hours available to others, was infinitely worse than to take the risk of blasting forth in the time that remained and accomplishing something of importance.

It was in these years that he plotted a book, *The Anatomy of Faith. The Anatomy of Faith* was to have been a descriptive phenomenology of belief—its nature, aspects, character, and end. It was never written, although many of the preliminary essays included in this volume were prepared for it. One project, however, which was completed was *Basic Judaism,*[9] the most successful of all his works. *Basic Judaism* was an explicit effort to move from history and descriptive sociology to Jewish religion. Even here, however, Milton's preoccupations as educator overrode his conscious and oft-expressed recognition of the danger of summary condensation and simplification. *Basic*

• • •

[9] *Basic Judaism* (New York: Harcourt, Brace & Co., 1947).

Judaism is a lucid, precise, and admirable book, but it was not—nor was it intended to be—a work of theology. The praise which it received was lavish; the criticism which it received hurt, because Milton knew the deficiencies of his approach, but felt the Jewish masses deserved the attention which more sophisticated and subtle Jewish intellectuals would rarely give them. *Basic Judaism* was frankly a popular work, but it hurt to have respected intellectuals misunderstand the fact that its author knew it to be popular.

It was in these years, the last years, from 1947 to his death, that he returned in full to speculative thought. These were the years of study and renewal—years in which he read Royce, Peirce, Bradley, Whitehead, Hartshorne; the continental theologians Kierkegaard, Barth, Brunner; the American neo-Orthodox, the two Niebuhrs, and Tillich; and the European social philosophers, Simmel, Dilthey, and Weber. These were the fructifying years with Will Herberg and Albert Salomon—years when both thinkers bore down hard on his, by then, habitual requirement of making the theologian pass for review and approval before the bar of science. There were even plans in late 1948 for the establishment of a small circle for Jewish theological discussion and the launching of a theological journal. Nothing came of the latter proposals, although Will Herberg, then in the process of writing his own *Judaism and Modern Man*, came weekly to Milton's home to review his own theological position, and to argue with indefatigable tenacity each point on which Milton took issue.

There can be little question, however, but that Milton's own intellectual life had reached a turning point. The existentialists, toward whom Herberg leaned and for whom Salomon had considerable sympathy, had their impact on Steinberg's thought. Though he continued to hold to his conviction that man's condition was neither as irretrievably sinful nor as unabashedly idolatrous as Herberg insisted, he did come to share with the Bible, with Pascal (whom he quoted for the first time in his late writings), with Kierkegaard, with Buber and Rosenzweig, the conviction that the religious life begins, not with a judgment of rational assent, but with an unconditional act of faith.

This position he maintained in a long and brilliant lecture before the Rabbinical Assembly Convention in 1949. It was expanded and refined once more in a series of public lectures which he delivered at his own Park Avenue Synagogue in January, 1950. These lectures marked the last public appearance of his life.

The pressured work and tension which accompanied the delivery of the Convention lectures six months earlier, the abortive and unco-ordinated invitation of the Jewish Theological Seminary to become visiting professor of Systematic Theology in late 1949, and his four public lectures which were enormously oversubscribed, proved both an emotional and a physical strain. He was confined to his bed in February, 1950, and on March 20, but a week before the *bar mitzvah* of his second son, David, he died.

In every generation there are those who do more than move with the tide of culture, who succeed in transcending its conditions and thereby altering them. Such individuals may anticipate the culture, breaking with it, in order to chart new directions for its unfolding. They may also summarize in themselves so much that was best in their environment that they anticipate and instruct the future without consciously shaping it. They become leaders because they articulate so generously the standards that ennoble culture that they revive those standards and re-establish their contemporaneity. They may not create tradition or break new ground, but they till the fallow soil with such industry and devotion as to make the work of later planters easier. Such leaders stand between the past and the future. They take their stand upon the mixed truth, the unfulfilled vision, the imperfect present, and yet their stance is in a real sense more dangerous than even the creators of the future, for they take the profounder risks. Theirs is not yet to know the truth, but to know the incompletion of what is; not to know the future, but to know the limitations of holding with the past; to be possessors, as Bergson observed, not of the creating intuition, but of the denying intuition—an awareness of what cannot be, but an uncertainty of what is. Theirs is the dangerous role, for they take all the risks and history profits by their judgments of wisdom and their oversights. They reap none of the rewards, for they rarely live to see their own consciousness of what is false and wrong transformed into what is true and right.

Milton Steinberg was born into a transitional half century of Jewish life and died before he had completed its full measure. He succeeded, however, as perhaps no other American-Jewish thinker has, in having been the accurate echo of his time. Unlike other echoes, who hear but do not understand, Milton not only heard but comprehended. He knew what history was trying to say about the Jew, he anticipated its hollow ring, its call to death by violence or by slow erosion, and he sought to return the echo to its source and silence it.

The last adventure on which Milton embarked—an adventure that was never completed—was a novel treating of the love of Hosea and Gomer. For years, ever since Milton had moved from fascination with the unsatisfied questionings of Job to wonder at Hosea's fullness of love, he had been tormented by the meaning of divine love. The novel was never finished, but the closing years had lived what Hosea understood; for, over and above all genius, Milton Steinberg was inexpressibly gentle and warm, understanding and compassionate. His books will survive the memory of his person, but those who live and remember his presence will recall not the book and the writings. They will recall rather that this was a rare creature who so loved his creator that he could withhold love from no man.

PART ONE

I

Toward the Rehabilitation of the Word "Faith"

Underlying much of Steinberg's thought and work in the last decade of his life was the conviction that American Judaism ran the risk of capitulating to the prevailing secularity of modern life. Although he strongly supported those movements on the American scene, notably the Jewish Reconstructionist Foundation, which sought to strengthen the preservative homeostats of Jewish life— Jewish culture and letters, the Zionist movement, the Kehillah—Steinberg sensed the temptation in Jewish leadership to forgo thought and intellection in favor of program and action. This is not to suggest that he played off thought against action, speculation against the daily task. Quite the contrary. He did feel, however, that Judaism could ill afford not to speculate, to refine a new metaphysic, to renovate and refurbish the classic intellectual armature of Jewish religion. This concern becomes particularly clear in the closing essays of his life and the closing essays of this volume. As early, however, as 1942 he conceived the idea of writing a book which would deal primarily with the nature of belief—the modes of belief and the varieties of cognition. The present essay, which first appeared in THE RECONSTRUCTIONIST *in 1942 and is reprinted with its permission, was a preliminary study in what was to have been a volume to be called* THE ANATOMY OF FAITH.

EDITOR

Words have a destiny of their own. They too can be the victims of circumstances. Consider, for example, the rise and fall in prestige of the terminology employed in philanthropy. No one who was not constrained to it would nowadays use the adjective "eleemosynary." The accents of the noun "charity," to which the bosoms of our forefathers thrilled, are vaguely discordant to us. And it is questionable whether the phrase "social work" will ever recover from the devastating picture of the social worker in Elmer Rice's *Street Scene.* In each case, connotations once altogether pleasurable have turned more or less sour. Old idioms then constantly pass from favor, and new ones are forever being invented or adapted to serve in their stead. All of which would be of little consequence were it not for the fact that, in some areas of human interest, specific values are inextricably associated with specific words. In such instances, the scraping of verbiage may be of large moment. The baby is likely to go out with the bath.

No other item in the vocabulary of the Western world has fallen so spectacularly as the word "faith," that monosyllable which denotes the readiness to believe that which cannot be completely proved. Once, and that not so long ago, it was the most exalted and honorable concept in the realm of the intellect. It has become one of the lowliest and most despised. Many, perhaps most modern men, simply disregard it as an instrument for the solution of the deeper problems which confront them. Urge on them its availability as a tool of the mind and they will brush it aside as a broken reed, fit only for those who lack the power to think. Even its name has become suspect. Let the protagonist of a philosophical position admit that he rests it on an act of faith, and his case is damned before he has made it.

To the evil fate which has beset both this word and the mental process which it represents, the advocates of faith have themselves made no slight contribution. Medieval men seem to have had a limitless capacity for belief. There was apparently no theological caprice, no scientific vagary, no historical conceit which could not win some acceptance for itself by an appeal to credulity.

Faith then was called on to sanction not only plausible propositions which had, at the least, the virtue of being moderately sensible; it was exploited to justify also the wildest figments of the imagination. And since, at the time, there was nothing in experience or reason to challenge such notions, men got along with them quite comfortably. But with the Renaissance and the scientific revolution, the incompatabilities between hunches and logic became too numerous and too conspicuous to be ignored. Then the custodians of the various traditional systems of doctrine blundered miserably. They stood by their ancestral outlook resolutely, refusing to surrender even its most untenable jots and tittles. In the name of faith, they rejected the most unexceptionable results of scientific research. Indeed, they opposed the entire program of free inquiry, unless it would guarantee in advance the acceptability to them of its conclusions. So it came to pass that the word came to be tainted with connotations of blind loyalty to the irrational, and stubborn resistance to intellectual light; that many modern men cannot hear *"credo"* ("I believe") without responding instinctively, *"quia absurdum est"* ("because it is absurd").

The degradation of faith was, however, only in part the result of the sins of its spokesmen. In equal, perhaps in greater, measure it was an oblique consequence of the triumphs of science. By the dawn of the seventeenth century, men began to suspect the existence of a hitherto unused instrument for the discovery and the determination of the truth. This *novum organum* consisted, first of all, in open-mindedness. Thence it might proceed either according to the empirical methods of Bacon, or the rationalism of Euclid. But whichever the course, its point of departure was a general skepticism; its goal, a demonstration.

The more enthusiastic proponents of this new technique, particularly during the earlier stages of its application, expressed unlimited optimism as to its efficacy. Flushed by its first successes, they foresaw the time when it would solve the last riddles of man and the world he inhabits. So much it has not achieved, and we know now that it never will. But its accomplishments have nonetheless been breathtakingly impressive. It has caused men to understand much in themselves and the universe which was, for untold generations, pure mystery. It has given them vastly larger control over their world than was ever at their disposal before. Naturally enough then, the prestige of faith sank as that of science ascended. For four centuries, a law of inverse proportion has regulated the position of these two enterprises in the scale of esteem. And since one has come to stand very high, the other has been brought almost as low as it can go.

To make matters worse, faith is today condemned not only for the intellectual mistakes of its custodians, but, somewhat unfairly, for their social offenses as well. Churches are institutions, and hence, by nature, corruptible. The human beings who administer or support them are, for all their association with ideal values, subject to the frailties of all mortals. They can be misled, frightened, and tempted. They are capable of blinding themselves and perverting their doctrine in self-interest. They may, for the sake of a variety of advantages, enter into unholy alliances with the state or the economic order. In the long course of history, every communion has, at some time or other, taken a stand on the wrong side of some social fence. In this regard, the over-all record of all religions collectively is far from being as good as it might be.

In rigid logic, faith as a tool of the intellect and an ad-

venture of the spirit ought be dissociated from the mis-
demeanors of those who claim to be the faithful. But men
are not impressed with an innocence that lies only a hair's
breadth from guilt. They know only that the church has
condoned or encouraged immoralities against which, in the
light of its commitments, it should have protested vigorously. To him who judges as he runs, it is all of a piece—
the belief itself, the process of believing, and the behavior
of the believer. The brush which tars one tars all.

The fact that for one reason or another the word "faith"
has acquired an unpleasant taste is of larger import than
would at first appear. It is, among other things, perhaps
the largest single influence now operating adversely to the
religious life. At this juncture in human affairs, a reawak-
ened interest in the churches has manifested itself. Men
who had once believed themselves permanently done with
them are asking whether science is adequate to satisfy their
curiosity concerning the universe, let alone to provide clear
guidance for their behavior. They wonder whether the evil
which has come upon them may not be at least in part
the consequence of a neglect of religious values. They are
haunted by a suspicion, which until most recently they
would have laughed to scorn, that about the old altars
there may be something of light and goodness essential to
their salvation. And yet there is no stampede on the part
of the unchurched into the historic communions.

For this paradox of men refusing to go whither they
are drawn, there is no single and simple explanation. One
person who is attracted to religion discovers that he cannot stomach rituals, another may gag over items of doctrine, a third over the institutionalizing of ideas and ideals.
Very many, however, are repelled for another reason altogether. Faith is still a requirement for entrance into religion, whether organized or personal. And with faith they
refuse to have traffic. The very sound of its name frightens

them off. And so they oscillate, swinging alternately to the churches and away from them, at rest neither within them nor without.

That it is the word rather than the intellectual process represented by it which is the stone of offense is apparent on even the most casual reflection. For the very people who protest that they cannot tolerate any undemonstrated doctrine of religion proceed blithely and without serious discomfort of conscience to believe all sorts of things in other areas of interest.

No one has ever "proved" the objective reality of the physical world, or, if it exist, that it conforms to our impressions of it. For all we know, the vast panoramas of earth and sky may be no more than the projection of our creative imaginations, or they may in "actuality" be quite different from our "ideas" of them. Not that men have not tried to attain demonstration in one direction or another. They have fretted over this issue for over two millennia. The upshot of all their effort has been this: that the only unarguable position is that of the solipsist who is virtually convinced that *he* exists, but cocks a skeptical eye at his fellows and the universe, because *their* reality has not been established in ruthless logic.

And yet, men continue to behave as though the world were there and their senses altogether trustworthy. And this applies not only to naïve souls who have never heard of that vexation of the spirit which goes under the name of "epistemology," but the epistemologist himself, though he is quite aware of the many unsolved riddles involved in the simplest acts of sight, taste, and touch. For, underneath all the doubtings of reason, men consciously or unconsciously act on the faith that the universe is, and that, within limits, their eyes and ears are reliable witnesses as to its character.

This pattern of believing that which is not altogether

demonstrated appears not only in the domain of sense, the most elemental stratum of the intellect; it manifests itself in higher realms as well. Among the enterprises of modern man none is more honorably regarded than science. The skeptic, in particular, is likely to invoke its awesome name to justify his rejection of theology and all its works. And yet the sciences are shot through with acts of faith, with assumptions and affirmations which admittedly are not and cannot be completely established in logic. These, to be sure, are carefully designated as postulates and hypotheses. But calling them by other names does not alter their character. They remain propositions which have not been proved.

Nor is their role in the realm of science trivial and secondary. In the deductive sciences, they sanction the validity of the syllogistic process and supply the basic premises from which everything else is derived. And the empirical sciences would be altogether impossible unless men were prepared to make elemental assumptions as to the rationality of nature and its uniformity in time and space, not to mention more specific and limited hypotheses in special fields of research. In other words, no scientific assertion is ever demonstrated absolutely. It is either posited in its entirety or derived from and shot through with hypothesis.

An interesting question now arises. If the readiness to believe the unproved is admittedly legitimate in one realm, why shall it be regarded as improper elsewhere? The answer would seem to be that in science hypothesis and postulate are employed carefully, under fixed and rigid restraints; whereas in theology the use of acts of faith has been free and easy. But suppose the same conditions were imposed on the latter as on the former? What would happen then? Either the religious outlook might prove unequal to the test, in which case it ought properly to be relegated to the limbo to which so many moderns have already consigned it; or, on the other hand, it might pass muster. Given the latter eventuality, it ought to be conceded a legitimacy akin to that which is allowed to scientific theory.

The question we have just put must be couched more exactly in this form: Can theological belief survive the same disciplines to which scientific beliefs are subjected? To resolve this issue we must examine briefly the standards which the scientist prescribes for his hypothesis.

In the first instance, he insists that it shall be *congruous,* more congruous than any other which he can form concerning the phenomena in which he is interested. For as scientist he is trying to catch multitudinous and diverse facts in a "law," that is to say, a general description of their behavior. The realities with which he deals may not be particularly co-operative. Confronted by a choice among them, he will select that one which seems to him best to "fit" the facts, to "cover" them. And if neither of the alternatives does quite that, then he will fasten on the theory which matches more of the facts, and the more salient among them.

Now judgments of congruity are by necessity largely subjective. They arise from a sense of harmony between theory and experience. They constitute, as it were, an aesthetic of reason and hence, like opinions of the beautiful and ugly, are eternally debatable. There is need then for a second criterion by which the scientist may be led to favor one hypothesis amid the welter of possibilities. He concerns himself therefore with another consideration: the comparative *practicality* of diverse theories. That is to say, he will prefer to posit that proposition which is most conducive to experiment, most exact in its predictions, and hence most susceptible to confirmation.

Simplicity is his third standard of judgment. He follows the counsel of William of Occam, who said long ago, *Entia non sunt multiplicanda praeter necessitatem,* which, freely translated, means that we should not assume the existence of unexperienced realities unless we absolutely have to. If driven to such a course, he will be sparing and niggardly, getting along with as few of them as is feasible. And even as he likes his concepts uncluttered, so he desires them as little involved as possible. Not that he fears complexity. He will, however, as a matter of policy, adopt the aesthetically neat formula rather than the untidy, the logically orderly rather than the tangled.

Let a theory meet these three requirements of higher congruity, superior practicality, and greater simplicity, and the scientist is ready to grant its validity. And well he may, for if he insisted on complete demonstration of his first principles he would never get beyond them; or if, by some marvel, he contrived that, he would never arrive at a conclusion. As matters stand, there is never an unchallengeable Q.E.D. after any assertion. It is all hypothesis in one fashion or another, controlled, tamed, disciplined— but hypothesis nonetheless.

Every religion is four elements fused into an organic unity: It is an interpretation of reality as a whole, the ethical implications which flow from it, a system of ritual acts, and a complex of emotional drives and associations. Only the first of these concerns us at the moment, for it is here that faith, as an act of the intellect, is operative. Now, observe the word "interpretation"; it is employed deliberately to designate that special function of religion which differentiates it from science.

When the physicist, chemist, astronomer, or, for that matter, the sociologist, economist, or psychologist presents a formula, what is its essential purport? It is, to put it succinctly, a description of the general behavior of that aspect of the world in which he is interested. It informs us that bodies, whether meteors, apples, or the bird that has been shot on the wing, will fall with such and such a velocity; that gases, whether of this type or that, will contract in particular proportion to the pressures exerted upon them; that money of one sort will tend to drive money of another sort out of circulation, that emotional impulses which are suppressed will find a devious, symbolic release for themselves. In each case then the "law" constitutes a widely inclusive description of the recurrent conduct exhibited by some phase of reality.

Now the knowledge of laws of nature is of incalculable value to man. Not only does it satisfy a deep and legitimate curiosity as to the universe; it supplies the tools of mastery over it. And yet science neither gratifies the whole of man's desire to understand, nor does it, of and by itself, give him adequate guidance for action. For it leaves unresolved a number of issues of the largest import: What in the reality which has been described is to be regarded as good and what as evil? What as beautiful and what as ugly? Why, last of all, should the universe behave as it does? What construction as to its essential constitution is best justified by its conduct? There is, then, room and need for another activity beyond science. After the *descriptions* come the *interpretations*, judgments of moral value, of aesthetic quality, and of ultimate character. It is here that both religion and philosophy function, seeking an interpretation of reality at its core and in its entirety.

Nor is the role of theology and metaphysics a temporary one as has so often been supposed. It is no interim operation to be maintained until scientific research completes itself. For even when the end of days comes for the scientist, when all the permutations and combinations of matter and energy in all time and space have been caught in one all-embracing law, that formula will be a description, vastly more comprehensive than any now at our disposal, but still a description. Even then, therefore, the task of interpretation will still confront the inquiring mind and eager heart. Or to put it otherwise, the better the camera, the better the picture. But no camera, not even a perfect camera should one ever be invented, decides whether the person who has been photographed is good or bad, beautiful or ugly, sane or insane. This is a matter for the observer to judge. It is an evaluation, an interpretation.

It should be noted that there is a two-edged implication in this division of labor. On the one hand, it legitimatizes speculation, metaphysical and theological, by assigning to it a realm in which it may properly operate. On the other hand, it delimits the scope of religious and philosophical propositions. These may be interpretative to their hearts' content. They may not be descriptive. They must not attempt to determine the phenomenal facts of the world or the laws of their behavior.

Now, of making interpretations of the universe-as-a-whole there is no end. Every person alive does some reflecting on the nature of things and arrives at some conclusions concerning it. But for all the number and variety of their theories, men on this issue divide themselves into two groupings. There are those who look reality in the face and decide it is self-existent and self-explanatory, devoid of unity and unifying motivation, empty of design, that it all adds up to "a tale told by an idiot, full of sound and fury, signifying nothing." Contrariwise, there are those who insist that the world declares the glory of a God, that it reveals the operations, behind its mask, of a cosmic Mind-energy, a Reason-Will, a Spirit. In the latter fashion all the historic religions of the Western world have construed the universe. This is their common essential interpretation of it. It is in this that they ask us to have faith. By our ability to accede to their request, they stand or fall ultimately.

One of the gravest tactical blunders of theologians in the past has been their quest after an absolute demonstration of the reality of God. For this error they ought not to be condemned too harshly. After all, they lived at a time when some of the postulates of mathematics and the physical sciences were regarded as indisputably true, because supposedly their opposites were inconceivable; when the propositions of Euclidian geometry, for example, were held to be established beyond the shadow of a doubt; when in brief, reason was conceived as capable of achieving final proofs. In such atmosphere, they sought naturally enough to win similar certainty for their central and most essential doctrine.

And so they set out to prove the existence of God, to find some argument, ontological, cosmological, epistemological, which would make the fact of Deity as sure as the relation of the hypotenuse to the legs of a right triangle. It was foreordained that they fail, operating as they did on an exaggerated estimate of the powers of pure logic. The case they made was at times ingenious, impressive, even persuasive. In the nature of things, it could not be conclusive. No one, not even the systematic theologian, has ever been compelled to the God-concept by sheer logic alone. The agnostic was never reduced to total silence. He could always, as Kant indicated so brilliantly in his antinomies, set up some kind of case against theirs. "One can always reason with reason," was the way Bergson put it. For like all other propositions, that of the existence of God is not completely provable. It remains the conclusion of an act of faith.

We return then to the crucial question: What is the character of the particular act of faith? Is it wanton and unjustified in reason? Or is it in essence a sober, disciplined position akin to its analogues in science and warranted by the same sanctions? To put it more pointedly—is the religious interpretation of reality more plausible, more practicable, and of greater simplicity than its alternative?

The universe itself has all the imperturbability of a sphinx. It can be variously construed. And yet, underneath all the self-contradiction of its demeanor, certain traits of its character manifest themselves constantly. It is, in the first place, a dynamic universe, in which all things move and nothing abides. It is furthermore a creative universe. Out of old materials, it is forever evolving novelties, whether new solar systems, new botanical species or human geniuses. And it is—at least, it seems more reasonable to believe that it is—a rational universe in the sense that everything within it conforms steadfastly to the principles of its special being. In all nature, from the vast suns that flame in space to the least infinitesimal of matter, nothing is outlaw. Given such a universe, which interpretation is the more congruous: that it is an idiot's tale in character, or that it is the progressive manifestation of Spirit? The plausibilities are heavily in favor of the latter. Only the postulation of God explains the world with any measure of adequacy, only it makes its salient characteristics intelligible. Only it renders comprehensible the soul of man, invested with sanity, moral yearning, and sensitivity—a phenomenon which otherwise must remain an anomaly. Only it offers an accounting for the law-abiding quality of the cosmos, for the fact that it is cosmos and not chaos.

The truth is never determined by a show of hands. That most men, even that all men, think something to be so does not make it so. But what they believe does testify to what they believe, that is to say, to what opinions they find most acceptable. Now on the God-concept there has always been a large consensus. Were it only the formally religious who shared in it, their assent might be dismissed as the product of childhood indoctrination, social pressure, fear, or superstition. Even so, it would be difficult to conceive that any position could have maintained itself so long and so widely by these alone—without the support of at least an air of rationality. But it is not only the churched who have affirmed God. In the course of philosophical speculation there have been those who were open rebels against the communions of their time, who had, thanks to persecution, abundant reason to reject everything which the priest or rabbi represented and who, nonetheless, found themselves compelled to the God-idea by its essential reasonableness. It is then no accident that man has historically been so partial to religion. For, over and beyond all other considerations, the God-interpretation of reality has appeared to him more nearly congruous than any conceivable alternative.

Superior practicality, the second criterion by which any theory is to be judged, also argues for the religious outlook. This assertion, to be sure, cannot be established with the definiteness which the sciences achieve on behalf of their propositions. The scientist treats with limited aspects of reality and such as are susceptible to mathematical determination. Our concern, on the other hand, is with the comparative pragmatic utility of two world outlooks. To that end we must deal with the whole universe and the reactions to it of the whole man, body, heart, and mind. But if there are no exact measuring rods at our disposal for our enterprise, we are not left without standards of judgment. Human morale—that is to say, man's respect for mankind, his feeling of the worth-whileness of his existence and that of his fellows, his confidence that his career and that of humanity are invested with significance—and human morality—these, if not precise, are canons nevertheless of the broadest scope and highest order.

Once again then we set theism and atheism against each other, this time to contrast their effects on the temper and conduct of man. In the light of which are morale and morality likely to run stronger? Will the sense of human dignity be the more vivid should man regard himself as a colloidal solution accidentally compounded, rather than as an objectification of an infinite Spirit? Will he tend to feel the game of living more nearly worth the candle, if it is in his eyes the sport of blind elements rather than the manifestation of creative Will? Will he view the pilgrimage of mankind as the more meaningful, if it appears to him a purposeless blundering from one oblivion to another rather than the progressive revelation of a creative Reason? And in the realm of the ethical, which position will be the more encouraging to earnest efforts toward self-realization on the part of the individual, to reverence for his fellows, to the readiness to live with them co-operatively, to treat them with compassion and justice? The questions answer themselves decisively as soon as they are put. It is not willful caprice which drives men to seek out religion and to cling to whatever faiths they succeed in finding with a passion close to desperation. Men need God with an urgency that is almost physical. Only through Him can they look at the universe and consequently at themselves and pronounce with Scripture "and behold it is very good."

And as for the relative simplicity of the two interpretations of reality, here too the scales incline heavily toward the religious. Given the one concept, God, and the whole of reality bursts into lucidity. The rationality of the universe, its uniformity, the emergence of life, of consciousness and conscience all become intelligible. Not that no elements of turgidity remain. No one solvent is so potent as to dissolve all things and their relations into total clarity. But even such precipitates as persist—the existence of evil, for example—can be forced toward solution. On the other hand, let this one premise be denied and the whole turns to deep obscurity into which sight is denied. Or else, for want of a single principle of explanation, many partial principles must be posited, so that Occam's rule shall be violated. Within and about the God idea reside large, solemn difficulties. But it remains the simplest theory for the mysterious world in which we find ourselves.

This then is the intellectual structure of religious faith: it is a hypothesis interpreting the universe as a whole as scientific hypotheses describe aspects of it. It is posited on the same grounds on which all hypotheses rest, namely, superior congruity, practical cogency, simplicity.

This is not to say that the God-faith is as certain of truth as scientific theory, that it is as well established as, let us say, the doctrine of heliocentrism. For that matter, the Copernican hypothesis itself is far less sure than our elemental perceptions of the sun, stars, and planets with which it deals. The folk rule, "the higher one goes, the harder he can fall," applies to concepts as well as bodies. The intellectual enterprise is, as it were, a structure in three stories: the lowest, sense impression; resting on that, scientific description; and superimposed on the whole, interpretation moral, aesthetic and metaphysical. At each level, faith, the readiness to believe the unproved, serves as cornerstone. In each stratum, therefore, the possibility of error inheres. And this peril is cumulative as one moves upward. The third floor of a building is quite obviously a more dangerous abode than those below it. It may collapse not only because of its own architectural defects but also because of those of any of the strata underneath. But then, up high, the view is better, and those who wish to see must take their chances. All of which is to assert what has long been known, that every opinion is a gamble, that the element of adventure increases progressively as one moves from judgments concerning sense to scientific formulas, and thence to interpretations of the cosmos. In the God idea, the risks are admittedly highest, but so too are the stakes.

Nor do we mean to imply that religious men are necessarily aware that their affirmation is of the nature of interpretative hypothesis, or that they arrive at it by following, in orderly sequence, the steps of our argumentation. Except for an occasional metaphysician, no one ever puts himself into the position of Rodin's *Thinker* and thinks unswervingly to a God by weighing the two alternative

Weltanschauungen in the scales of plausibility, practicality, and simplicity. It is no secret that men rarely, if ever, reason on any matter according to the rules of textbooks in logic. The syllogisms of education, the canons of inductive inference, do not represent the thought process as it is in actuality. They are graphs of how, ideally and in the abstract, it ought to move, and a system of controls to tame its waywardness and correct its errors. Of those who, at any given time, profess a religious position, some have been born to it, in the sense that it was communicated to them early in life through the home or church, others achieve it for themselves, and still others have it thrust upon them by social pressures. But though few of them are articulately aware of the logic of their case, most of them sense, even if somewhat inchoately, its fundamental reasonableness, utility, and simplicity. Under normal circumstances these considerations operate underground. But when, as now, the God faith is challenged, the awareness of its fittingness, practicality, and economy becomes acute. Then it stands forth clearly as a dignified response to the requirements of man's mind and heart alike.

Perhaps the authoritative spokesmen of the historic churches ought to assemble in some solemn convocation and by official resolution substitute for the word "faith," with all its association of opprobrium, the word "hypothesis," so rich in honorific connotations. But then, who knows what unpleasant destiny awaits the word "hypothesis"? The custodians of the religious traditions might, by such a decision, make of their nomenclature a weathervane swinging to each new wind of fashion.

For the abuses of faith which are responsible for its ill repute, no defense is offered here. But the word, in essence, represents an honorable and necessary enterprise; it is charged with precious memories of prophets, sages, and saints. Perhaps then it would be wiser and simpler to get along with it after all.

II

The Common Sense of Religious Faith

It is interesting to note that, but a generation apart, two distinguished Jewish thinkers sought to ground authentic faith upon the empirical foundations of common sense.

Both Milton Steinberg and the German-Jewish theologian Franz Rosenzweig (1886-1929) turned to common sense with renewed respect. Common sense was no longer the abused and slightly vulgar intellectual weapon of the uneducated. Common sense reported the quality of uncertainty which suffuses the sciences, disclosed the connections which link the thinking man, the objective world, and the creative God into unity, indicated the reasonableness which attends the view of provident design.

This is not the occasion to explore the comparison of Steinberg and Rosenzweig further; but it is worth remarking that at a moment in Jewish history when philosophic attention to religious questions was profoundly needed within Judaism, two thinkers—vastly different in temperament and presupposition—were employing the twin arms of philosophy and theology to define them anew. "The Common Sense of Religious Faith" has the characteristic marks of apologetics—the dismissal of obviously inadequate and corrosive views, the dispatch of trivializing considerations, the formation of a careful, lucid, and essentially simple argument. It was characteristic of Steinberg that— whether attempting to clarify metaphysical questions, as in "The Theological Issues of the Hour" (pp. 155-213),

or exposing the essential lineaments of Judaism in BASIC
JUDAISM—*his strenuous intellection was cut short by the
demands of communication. Steinberg was always more
sensitive to the audience and his usual superiority to it
than he was preoccupied with carrying through a devastating piece of argument to its really drastic conclusions.
For this reason his theology is always to be hunted on the
moors of homily—the passion and the concern to communicate exceeded his submission to the demands of argument.
This is evident in the essay "The Common Sense of Religious Faith," where the conclusions were such that even*
THE RECONSTRUCTIONIST, *by whose permission a slightly
shortened version is published here, noted in a prefatory
remark to the appearance of Part 1 on February 21, 1947,
that "Reconstructionism, though committed to belief in
God, is not committed to any particular conception of God
or to any particular argument for that belief." Steinberg
had touched—as he was to many times more—an exposed
flank in the fortifications of his own position. Reconstructionism lacked a theology—and a position favoring any
and all theology was not a sufficient answer. (Cf. Steinberg's comments on Reconstructionism in "The Test of
Time,"* A BELIEVING JEW, *op. cit., pp. 174-176; "Theological Issues of the Hour," pp. 155-213, and "New Currents
in Religious Thought," pp. 214-300.)*

EDITOR

•

I • *The Importance of Religious Faith*

1

Does believing in God make sense? Or is religious faith
something for the ignorant, the muddleheaded, those too
wishful, lazy, or cowardly to think the matter through?

This essay answers these questions in favor of religion.
It argues that not only is intelligence no enemy to the
affirmation of God, but that if a man will but think long

enough, hard enough, broadly and freely enough, he will almost inevitably come to such an affirmation.

The case to be made will be all the way an appeal to reason and experience. At no time will the reader be asked to accept any proposition on any other ground. He is, of course, free to take recourse to authority or revelation if he feels the desire or need to do so. Neither figures in any fashion in the discussion that follows. . . .

Being in fact greater than creed alone, a religion is experienced and acquired in more ways than through reason. To one man, it will be primarily a matter of intuition and feeling, to another of tradition, to a third of morality or of esthetics, or of group solidarity, and to still another of some combination of all these. Indeed, a person may be intensely devout and yet be but little occupied with theology.

On the other hand, the religion of some people is basically intellectual. Philosophical reflection is, in many instances, the beginning of piety. . . .

The thesis of this essay, that common sense supports faith, must not be misunderstood. It does not mean that religion is intellectually a matter of common sense only. Religion among other things is an awareness of mystery and poetry, of that which is too deep or too subtle or too vast or too grand for human comprehension. Religion is furthermore a sensitivity to the realms beyond realms of possibility, in which, as Ibn Gabirol put it, "our thoughts weary themselves to find a stopping place." The "sense" of religion, in other words, is *uncommon* as well as *common*. But—and this is the crux of the matter—it is always *sense*. It may and should transcend reason, it must never run contrary to it.

One more preliminary observation. Every communion, as has already been indicated, propounds a *Weltanschauung*, a view of things. In some religions, Confucianism, for example, or early Buddhism, that view is nontheistic, being indifferent to the idea of God. Conceivably a church might be organized which would be actively atheistic, propagating a theory of reality which explicitly denied God. Jewish religion, on the other hand, and the faiths which derive from it are committed to theism, that is to say, they construe the universe in terms of a God, such a construction being essential to them. If the words "religious outlook" do not invariably connote theism, that is their usual meaning for us, and it is so that we shall understand them in the ensuing discussion.

2

Religion sets a philosophy of reality and life before men. But are they in need of it? Or is it something without which they can get along quite well?

Undeniably, some people can. These are the persons whom William James once characterized as "tough-minded." To them all abstract and nonpractical issues seem remote and artificial. They require no metaphysics, whether theistic, nontheistic, or atheistic.

Most men, however, would seem to belong to the "tender-minded," James's other class. The riddle of the universe haunts them. They are forever restless, aching to search out why things are as they are, what meaning they may have, what may be the good for which mankind exists, and why it is the good.

Whence comes this preoccupation, this disquiet of the spirit? Part of it is straight curiosity, a yearning to understand the awesome pageant which is the cosmos and the baffling experience which is life. That part is of one piece psychologically with the impulse that moves science. Another part expresses a deep and unquenchable hope of the human heart, that there may be an intelligible scheme to things, one sympathetic to man's ideals, so that his career may possess significance and his aspirations validity beyond himself and his brief span. The last motivation is practical. Men are ever being called on to decide between alternative courses of action. But what is right or wise as to conduct depends, at least partially, on the nature of reality and life. Given a cosmos of one character, one code of conduct may be indicated. In another sort of world another ethic may be appropriate. Willy-nilly then, the riddle of the universe keeps forcing itself on men.

That is why so much of mankind, including many of its keenest minds and noblest spirits, has always been so mightily exercised over theology. In it they have seen their classic opportunity, perhaps the sole one, to understand reality, find it congenial, and know how to deal with it and themselves.

Now too we can perceive why agnosticism, a permanent suspension of judgment, is inadequate, and all but impossible, for most men. It leaves the curiosity of the intellect unanswered, the hungers of the heart unsatisfied, the soul aquest after goodness unilluminated and uninspired. Worst of all, it leaves the hand undirected. Whatever else may be true about agnosticism, this much is certain: no one can practice it. Life forbids. Life is forever putting men into situations in which they *must* turn one way or the other, in which they *must* make up their minds, for the purpose of action if for nothing else, as to what is true and what false, what good and what evil. They may talk indecision to their heart's content, they must live decisively. To cap the climax, it is not true, as the agnostic claims, that only *his* position is consistent with intellectual integrity. For, as we shall soon discover, the evidences for the religious outlook are more than adequate to justify a decision in its favor. Mental honesty is no monopoly of anyone, let alone of those who refuse to make up their minds.

3

This discussion of the motivations behind faith should help to dispel the widespread misconception that religion has its origins in, and panders to, disreputable human interests. It was the fashion among eighteenth-century rationalists to account for it as the handiwork of witch doctors and priests eager to make a "good thing for themselves" of human credulity. Marxists habitually deprecate religion as the "opiate of the masses." Some of the advocates of the new dynamic psychology maintain that the beginnings of religion are to be sought in fear, or in the quest of a father substitute or in what not else.

Were all this completely true, it would be of only academic relevance, since the value of an idea or practice depends not on its origins but on the validity it eventually attains for thought and action. It would be as silly to condemn present day religion because of its supposed beginnings, as to reject chemistry because of its involvement, in ages gone by, with alchemy.

The truth is, however, that this argument against religion is only fractionally true in sober fact. No doubt fear, superstition, social manipulation, and class interest have had and continue to have a share in the rise and course of religion. Certainly religion, like all other human pursuits and institutions, has at times been perverted to the service of obscurantist or wicked causes. But that is neither the whole story nor even its larger part. Most fundamentally, religion is the expression of a thirst for understanding, a hope of meaning, a quest for goodness, and a sanction for it. These motivate religion on its deepest level. They make the cultivation of it a fascinating, unavoidable, and thoroughly legitimate enterprise.

But why religion for the fashioning of world outlooks? Why not science? Given its precise methods and careful disciplines, is it not a more reliable guide?

Science can help us in framing a philosophy of the universe. Indeed, we must look to it for most of the materials we use to that purpose. But it cannot itself do the job for us—and that for three reasons:

First, every science deals with some single and limited aspect of reality. This is the nature of a science, this the goal of its techniques and skills: to explore a particular category of things. Yet men are vitally interested not only in limited classes of things but in the nature of "things as a whole," and for "things as a whole" there is and can be no science. Here metaphysics, whether religious or not, must step in.

Second, science deals with phenomena, with that which can be weighed, measured, counted—in sum, with those objects and forces which can be grasped through sense perception or inferred from it. Beyond these, however, are vast areas of human concern with which science does not deal: the nature of the beautiful, of the good, of the ultimate reality, if there be one, of which phenomena are an outward manifestation. These are respectively the domain of aesthetics, ethics, philosophy, and theology.

Third, the function of a science is *description*, that of a world outlook *interpretation*. Every science describes some aspect of reality, rendering an account of *what* composes it and *how* it behaves. Even when science asks *why*, thus giving the appearance of engaging in interpretation, its question is always intended to evoke an answer in terms of cause and effect. Its very *why*, in other words, is really a *how*, a demand for a *description* of the fashion in which things come to be as they are. On the other hand, a world outlook, whether religious or not, has for its subject matter not the *what* and *how*, but *of what worth* and *to what end*, that is to say, issues of value and purpose. And when *it* inquires *why*, it is not with reference to cause and effect but to some possible ultimate reality in the light of which all else is illumined.

Religion and science operate then in different spheres. Not, as some have suggested, because science deals with the known and religion with the unknown. Both deal with the known, and from it leap to the unknown. The materials are the same; it is the purposes which are different. One confines itself to parts, the other to the whole. One busies itself with the quantitative and the phenomenal, the other with whatever may be outside and beyond these categories. One is devoted to description even when it seems to interpret and evaluate, the other entirely to interpretation and evaluation even when it appears to describe.

In sum, science is, as it were, a camera which furnishes schematic photographs of reality, whereas religion uses these photographs—and those supplied by other forms of human experience—to arrive at a judgment of the character of reality, whether it be sane or insane, purposeful or blind, good or evil. Whence it follows that religion has every reason to hail scientific progress, since the better the camera, the clearer and more trustworthy the pictures available for interpretative and evaluative purposes.

But if so, why the protracted and bitter conflict between religion and science?

Most of the fault for this unhappy condition rests with religion, but some with science also.

Religion has been guilty of invading areas where it has no business, of trying to tell the scientist what the facts of the world are: how old it is, for example, or how man came into being, or whether natural laws are suspendible. Even graver, it has at times advocated authoritarianism, seeking to limit freedom of inquiry or to dictate its results in advance.

In other words, religion is not necessarily or invariably a good thing. The popular saying that it doesn't matter what a man's religion may be so long as he has one is sheer poppycock. It makes as much sense as would the assertion that it makes no difference what a man's character may be so long as he has one. Insofar as a religion supports exploitation, resists social and moral progress, and engenders more of hostility than of good will among men, it is evil, not good. And it is no less a curse when, in the fashion we have just indicated, it infringes on scientific inquiry or seeks to limit its freedom.

But if much of the blame for the conflict between religion and science is assignable to the former, no slight part must be charged against the latter. Whether in reaction to the tyranny of churchmen or in expression of an intolerance of their own, many scientists have displayed disinterest or impatience with the quest after a religious interpretation of reality, and indeed, in some extreme instances, with all interpretative and evaluative efforts. On either side, the attitude has too frequently been, to paraphrase Job: "We are the people, and all wisdom will die with us."

Fortunately, conflict between the two sides has rarely been total; at no time has it been really necessary; it can be avoided with especial ease these days when so much of religion is liberal and science has been so sobered. All that is required is that either camp recognizes the limitations of its own pursuit and the legitimacy of the other. Let religionists leave to science the enterprise of photographing reality. Let scientists admit that even when their job is finished, another task awaits doing, that of construing and evaluating.

●

II. *The Reasons for Religious Faith*

Religion's world outlook centers about God.

Before attempting to indicate what we mean by that word, let us first make clear what we do not mean.

"God" does not denote an old man on a throne somewhere up in the sky. That notion is in part a survival of the infancy of the human race, in part a hangover from our personal childhood, from those days when, having first heard about God and possessing only limited intellectual resources, we pictorialized Him according to our naïveté. However the conception is come by, it is far less innocent than is generally supposed. It impels many a person to regard himself as an atheist, simply because he does not believe that there really is an old man in the heavens. On the other hand, it condemns individuals capable of ripe spirituality to the stuntedness, perhaps life-long, of puerile, unsatisfying, and undignified convictions.

To believe in God, maturely, intelligently, is to believe that reality did not just "happen," that it is no accident, no pointless interplay of matter and energy. It is to insist rather that things, including man's life, make sense, that they add up to something. It is to hold that the universe, physical and moral, is a cosmos, not an anarchy—made a cosmos instead of an anarchy, meaningful rather than mad, because it is the manifestation of a creating, sustaining, animating, design-lending Spirit, a Mind-will, or to use the oldest, most familiar and best word, a God.

Here at last we come to the crux of our investigation. Are there any reasons for maintaining that the world is of this character rather than that, that Deity rather than Nullity moves behind and through it?

There are such reasons, not one but a number, all good, indeed compelling.

1

God is the only tenable explanation for the universe.

Here we are, creatures of a day, in the midst of a vast, awesome world. Sometimes it strikes us as a big, blooming tumult. But through the seeming confusion some traits persist, constant and all-pervading.

Thus, the universe is *one*, an organic unity, subject everywhere to the same law, knitted together with inter-dependence.

Again, it is *dynamic*, pulsating with energy, movement, life.

It is *creative*, forever calling new things into being, from stars and solar systems to new breeds of animals, new ideas in the minds of men, new pictures on the artist's canvas.

It is *rational* in the sense that everything in it behaves according to law! Electrons and protons according to the rules of their being, plants in harmony with their nature, animals after the patterns of their respective kinds, and man in consonance with the mandates not only of chemistry, physics, and biology but of psychology and the moral order as well. Everywhere: form, design, predictable recurrence, law.

The universe, furthermore, is *purposive;* at least it is in some of its phases. An insect laying its eggs in a place where the larvae yet to be born will be assured of food as they will require it; a spider weaving its web, a bird building a nest, an engineer designing a bridge, a young man charting his career, a government drawing up a policy, a prophet blueprinting a perfected mankind—all these are instances, rudimentary or advanced, conscious or instinctual, of planning ahead. Purposiveness is indisputably an aspect of reality, and no theory can be said to explain the latter if it does not account for the former as well.

The universe further contains *consciousness.* It has produced man. At least in him it discloses intelligence, a thirst for truth, sensitivity to beauty, a desire for goodness. And man is a component of reality. Whence it follows that no explanation of the entirety can be acceptable if it does not illumine the existence and nature of this most complex, challenging and mysterious of its components.

This then is the world in which we live: one, dynamic, creative, rational, and inclusive of elements of purpose, consciousness, and goodness. For such a universe the religious theory is by far the best "fit." Only *it* accounts at all adequately for the striking features just enumerated. That is why men of all eras, cultures, and capacities, including most of the world's great philosophers, have tended so generally to arrive, no matter what their point of departure, at some kind of God-faith. For, once one begins to reflect on the nature of things, this is the only plausible explanation for them.

But what about the evil of the world? Can the God-idea account for *that?* Not entirely, and not to anyone's complete satisfaction. This fact unquestionably counts against faith. On the other hand, there are many interpretations of evil from the religious viewpoint whereby its existence can be reconciled, partially if not thoroughly, with the existence of God.

But even if evil were a total mystery on which theology could not make so much as a dent, the God-faith would still be indicated. For, at the worst, it leaves less unexplained than does its alternative. If the believer has his troubles with evil, the atheist has more and graver difficulties to contend with. Reality stumps him altogether, leaving him baffled not by one consideration but by many, from the existence of natural law through the instinctual cunning of the insect to the brain of the genius and heart of the prophet.[1]

This then is the intellectual reason for believing in God: that, though this belief is not free from difficulties, it stands out, head and shoulders, as the best answer to the riddle of the universe.

2

The second reason for belief in God is that man cannot live joyously, hopefully, healthily, perhaps not at all, without it.

•••

[1] For a fuller discussion of the problem of evil in the light of the general position of this essay, the reader is referred to the author's "God and the World's Evil" in *The Reconstructionist,* IX, 6 (April 30, 1943); reprinted as "God and the World's End," in *A Believing Jew* (New York: Harcourt, Brace & Co., 1951), pp. 13-31.—EDITOR.

Consider what the universe and man look like under the assumption of atheism.

Reality appears totally devoid of point or purpose. Like everything else, man is seen as a by-product of a blind machine, his history a goalless eddy in an equally directionless whirlpool, his ideals random sparks thrown off by physiochemical reaction in the colloidal solution, compounded by chance, which is his brain. Everything adds up in the end to exactly nothing.

What is the consequence of such a view for man and society? Can it be other than discouragement, demoralization, despair? What else shall one say of it except that "that way madness lies."

Now consider what face the universe takes on once God is assumed.

Because there is Intelligence behind it, its countenance is now intelligible, not vacant. The things that exist both within and without ourselves cease to be capricious, irrational, and isolated episodes. To the contrary, they are bound together into unity, reasonableness, and pattern by the Mind and Being before which, by virtue of which, they exist.

The spectacle unfolding before our eyes, this awesome pageant which has for its actors stars and atoms, plants, animals, and men, our private worlds of thought and feeling—this is a pageant after all, executing a design, spelling out a message.

What is more, it is a friendly visage which, given God, the universe turns upon us. The suns flaming in space are not altogether alien to us; trees, blades of grass, and beasts are all our kin, near or remote; and we humans, for all our differences and contentions, are brothers one to another by virtue of the Father we share.

As the God-faith transforms the cosmic countenance, so it illumines the darkness within ourselves. It dispels the misgiving lest our strivings serve no purpose, lest our ideals be mere idiosyncrasies, without validity beyond ourselves and hence doomed to extinction with us. Instead, our aspirations come to be seen as refractions of God's purpose, our struggles as elements in the working out of the divine scheme. Before us opens an exit from our human impasse. Frail and short-lived though we be, we can still transcend our limitations by serving God's will, advancing His design and so partaking, by identification, of His infinity and eternity. Finally, the God-faith sends us into the battle for the good in ourselves and society with heightened morale. We know, as we join issue with the forces of evil, that we do not fight alone. In the face of seemingly insuperable odds we can reassure ourselves with the words of the prophet: "Fear not; for they that are with us are more than they that are with them" (II Kings 6:16).

Such are the emotional states distilled respectively by denial of God and by the affirmation of Him. Between them, who can hesitate?

3

Man's moral life requires belief in God.

Under atheism, as we have just seen, all ideals depreciate in value. Regarded as the creations of cosmic chance, if not indeed as the expression of mere human preference, they lose in validity and authority, until, in the end, the reasonableness of their continued observance comes under question. Men begin to ask themselves what logic there may be to devotion and self-sacrifice on behalf of ethical principles and human welfare, if these principles are as rootless and man's career as pointless as the atheist position implies.

That this is the upshot can be seen from Bertrand Russell's *The Free Man's Worship,* one of the noblest and most thoughtful statements of irreligion ever penned. Mr. Russell is a rare atheist; he is a thorough enough logician to follow his premise to its consequences, and is too earnest to prettify them once he has discovered their true character. He grants point blank that from his point of view there is neither basis nor sanction for moral ideals.

These, he concedes, are altogether alien and inappropriate in a blind world machine. Nevertheless, Mr. Russell concludes, he will cling to them. Not that he has any foundation or logic to justify them. He accepts them, as he is frank to admit, arbitrarily, capriciously, in part because, thanks to indoctrination and habit, he has come to love them; in part, *zu l'hachis*, as it were, to defy and spite an uncomprehending and soulless universe. All of which is noble, if a bit theatrical, of Mr. Russell. But it is far from constituting an adequate basis for ethics. And it leaves unanswered the question of what Mr. Russell would have to say to persons who insist on logic to their morality and who wait for arguments more convincing than a dramatic gesture before they will be persuaded to dedicate their lives to the classic ethical code.

The very origin of our higher moral aspirations supports the thesis immediately before us, that a close connection exists between them and religion. Ethical conceptions such as the worth of the individual, human brotherhood, the future regeneration of mankind are not self-evident. None of the great, ancient civilizations, not even the Greek or Roman, attained to them. Even in our time acceptance of them is far from universal.

These principles were first formulated by the prophets of Israel, in association with their God-faith and, in part at least, as inferences from it. Not that the prophets first framed their theology and then proceeded systematically to deduce a morality from it. History is never that precisely logical. As a matter of fact, the faith of the prophets and their ideals evolved pretty much side by side, with now one element, now the second, ahead of the other and stimulating it, now both being prodded by social circumstances. But the special theology of the prophets, their doctrine of a God, who is a universal Spirit, just, merciful, holy, was an ever-active agent in the development of the Jewish conception of the good life.

From the theology the morality flows directly, unswervingly, irresistibly. If every person incarnates God, then every person is sacred, too precious to be oppressed or degraded. Because every man embodies the Divine uniquely, he is entitled to an opportunity for the expression of his individuality. Since all men manifest God, they are brothers, owing each other the duties of brotherhood. Since God is good and rational, the present world order, marred by evil and irrationality, cannot be His final work. Some day it must yield to another, more truly reflective of His nature, a perfected society of perfected men, the Kingdom of God.

In other words, the ideals we take for granted are not self-generating. In historical actuality, they came into being in relation to a particular God-faith, in which to find their theoretical justification to this day. Whether they can long endure without it is, as the instance of Bertrand Russell has suggested, profoundly questionable.

Ideals, be it remembered, demand self-sacrifice, and self-sacrifice has to appear justified or it will not be undertaken. A man may give up his comfort or lay down his life for something that seems to him to be worth the cost. But who will do either for what is regarded as of superficial value or of none at all? Yet, in the light of atheism, ideals can be no more than the phosphorescence emitted by physiochemical process within the organic compound which is man. And as for mankind, in the eyes of an irreligionist, it must appear as only a bigger accident than he is. And it is for such as these that a man may reasonably call on himself to suffer and perhaps to die?

But is this fair to atheists? Have not some of them been

among the most unselfish and self-forgetting of mortals? And on the other hand, are not many of the most bestial and least idealistic of human beings religionists?

No, what we have just said, had it been said of atheists, would have been grossly unfair. But it does no injustice whatsoever to atheism, the inescapable effects of which are to trivialize ideals, to present the human enterprise as a futility, and so to undermine the classic ethic of justice, mercy, and self-negation on behalf of moral principle and human welfare.

But, if so, how is one to account for the goodness of so many irreligionists? Very simply. Men often behave better than their philosophy. Only they cannot be expected to persist in doing so. In the end, how a man thinks must affect how he acts; atheism must finally, if not in one generation then in several, remake the conduct of atheists in the light of its own logic.

The fact of the matter is that most irreligionists, Bertrand Russell included, are living by the Judeo-Christian morality which follows from Judeo-Christian theism. At the same time, they profess a world outlook which in all its implications denies the code to which they conform. Eventually the contradiction between theory and practice must reveal itself. Then one or the other will give way. Either disbelievers will yield to the pressure of their doctrine and begin to act on its implications, or, refusing to accept the implications, will have to work back to a philosophy which sanctions the morality by which they desire to live, by which alone society can endure.

It is just such a crisis in choice on a mass scale through which mankind seems to be passing right now.

For several centuries irreligion has advanced steadily, all, it seemed, without appreciable effect on human behavior. The bulk of men continued, it appeared, to be about as good or as bad as they had ever been. And then suddenly new moral cults emerged. In ever-increasing numbers, men began openly to deny the worth of the human personality. (They had always acted in denial of this principle, but this was the first time in two thousand years that they repudiated it publicly.) They preached the glorification of violence and conquest. They deprecated justice and mercy. They rejected overtly the notion of the brotherhood of man.

What had been happening, all unobserved, within the human spirit? What, except that having adopted irreligion, men were beginning to be in earnest about its thoroughly unmistakable directives for conduct?

When the props beneath an edifice rot away, it does not fall immediately. The decay is likely to be gradual, and slower in some areas than in others. Again, the building may hold together by inertia and the interweaving of its parts. But ultimately a collapse must come. This, there is reason to believe, is what we are now undergoing: a moral breakdown consequent on the disintegration in modern man of religious faith.

The belief in God then is necessary to morality. For, without it, moral values turn arbitrary, even trivial; self-sacrifice for an ideal becomes irrational; the life of the individual loses all direction except, of course, that of self-interest; society suffers and may in the end be ruined. Only on the faith which gave them birth do ethical values retain their vitality.

Two objections may remain in the reader's mind to the thesis just propounded, that the classic moral code is ultimately dependent on the classic religious outlook.

The first of these is: What of the religious immoralist? What of the man who professes all the correct doctrines and performs all the prescribed rituals, and then behaves like a beast of prey? What of pious tyrants like Francisco Franco, and devout exploiters like Judge Elbert Gary, and religious racialists whose number is too great for telling?

Yes, they exist, men of this ugly stripe. If people are

often better than their philosophy, they are, alas, often worse. They may refuse to draw the inferences of their doctrine, or, having drawn them and found them unwelcome, may suppress, pervert, and corrupt them.

The point, however, is that the religious immoralist is acting contrary to his convictions, is either consciously or unconsciously a hypocrite, whereas the irreligious immoralist is thoroughly consistent with his creed.

In other words, a man's world outlook exerts a steady pressure on his conduct. That pressure may be diverted or resisted for a time, perhaps for a long time, but in the end it must make itself felt.

The second question which may be present in the reader's mind is this: Cannot self-interest and fear be relied on to keep men in line, regardless of their philosophies? Suppose it be true that the religious position leads to one pattern of behavior and the irreligious to another, what difference does that fact make when men know that no one can be secure unless everyone behaves himself, when they are aware in addition that society has weapons with which to punish deviations from its codes?

Unquestionably, some respect for law derives from considerations of this sort. Some, but never enough. First, the policeman is not always at hand. Indeed, just when he is most needed, in the hour of social crisis, he is likely not to be on the job at all.

Besides, it would be a sorry morality which is no more nor better than the law requires and the policeman can enforce.

As to the argument from self-interest, let us not be naïve. True, the classic morality is essential to the health and survival of society. But the convinced immoralist knows perfectly well that he can rely on the good citizenship of his fellows. No matter then what his own sins, society will keep on running, dispensing its benefits and securities not only on the righteous, who have earned them, but (so long as he continues to avoid detection) also on a sinner like himself.

To be sure, once enough people begin to play fast and loose with ethical principles, society will suffer. It may even fall apart in the end. But not at once. *"Après moi,"* the immoralist admits, *"le déluge."* But it will be long after, and by the time it breaks he will long since have shuffled off this mortal coil. Finally, there are some situations in which both fear and self-interest work against morality, when a man will be safe if he violates ethical principle and most certainly in peril if he stands by it, and when the policeman, the state, indeed all organized society are aligned not for but against the right. What becomes then of honesty in the hands of those who urge on its behalf only that it is the best policy?

No, there is no trustworthy basis for the ethical life in either advantage or fright. These factors may co-operate with the angels; they cannot be counted to do so always, or at all adequately. Human virtue admittedly does not rest on one foundation only; it has many props and shorings. Among these, however, the strongest and ultimately the most indispensable is the knowledge that reality is of such a nature as first to commend the good and then to support and sanction it.

4

Man learns of God from history, from the directions in which it persists in moving.

Look back over the weary way mankind has traveled down the ages. Consider how, though with frequent and heartbreaking retreats and deviations, a line of progress can be drawn from points of departure toward goals—from insensibility toward consciousness and knowledge, from servitude toward freedom, from brutality and ruthlessness toward compassion and conscience.

Is such a movement, so insistent and cumulative, likely to be no more than a chance eddy in a reasonless flow? Or is it more probably the consequence of a great propulsion working through man and driving him?

Or consider the pattern of human affairs: how falsehood, having no legs, cannot stand; how evil tends to destroy itself; how every tyranny has eventually invoked its own doom. Now set against this the staying power of truth and righteousness. Could the contrast be so sharp unless something in the scheme of things discouraged evil and favored the good?

If all history bespeaks God, that of Israel testifies to Him with especial eloquence and clarity. For this is the people which first discerned His true nature, earliest identified itself with Him, and has longest sought to do His will.

And Israel is alive this day.

The nations it knew in its youth and first maturity are memories. Not so this people. Consigned to an iron destiny, armed against it only with faith, it has survived the ages and their rigors. What is more, its influence has with extraordinary consistency been exerted on behalf of justice, compassion, freedom, and truth. And it has been creative far beyond its size and opportunities.

Jewish history demonstrates that the God-faith is life-giving, humanizing.

But is it likely that a belief will evoke such echoes from reality unless it is in tune with it?

5

Among all peoples and in all times some men have made the claim of contact with God, insisting that in an intuition transcending sensation or thought they have had firsthand experience of Him. The Prophets of Scripture brought such testimony, as did a variety of others; among Jews, numerous rabbis of the Talmudic era, Kabbalists, and Hasidim; in the classical pagan world, Plato, Aristotle, and Plotinus; among Christians, Augustine, the two Theresas, and Jacob Boehme; and in the East a great company of Brahmans, Taoists, and Moslems.

Now, these men and women, who are the world's mystics, have been of the most widely diverse backgrounds and temperaments. Yet, despite the many differences among them, they all report having undergone substantially the same spiritual episodes: an awareness, derived not from the senses or the mind but from some faculty beyond them, of the immediate presence of Ultimate Reality, a conviction of its goodness, so potent as to fill the soul with a feeling of illumination, purity, and redemption. It is on such spiritual events, personally undergone, that mystics rest their doctrines concerning God, His nature, and the good.

In the development of Judaism specifically, the role of mystics, though far from decisive, has been larger than is generally perceived. They had a hand in the making of the prophetic faith and morality. From time to time, they have rekindled the Jewish religion with their own fervor into incandescence. They are responsible for no slight part of its dynamism to this day.

Most of us, however, have never met with mystical adventures. What the mystic relates comes to us at second hand, on the word of someone else. We would be well advised therefore to credit it, if at all, with reservations.

Yet, even for incorrigible nonmystics, mystical evidences should carry some weight—about that which one would allow to some stubborn, widely diffused, and self-consistent rumor. Being hearsay and hence inadmissible as formal testimony, no case may be built on it. Yet a reasonable person will reckon with it in his calculations. And if the judgment arrived at on other grounds happens to account for this also—so much the better, both for the judgment and it.

•

III · *The Nature of Religious Faith*

1

In the foregoing discussion the logic of the theistic position has been presented. The nature of the world, the course of history and, for the mystic at least, the evidences of mysticism argue for God. The needs of human morale and morality make the God-faith desirable, even pragmatically necessary. But "argue for," "desirable," "pragmatically necessary" are not *proof*. And is it not proof which men want?

If the reader is asking for an indisputable case for God's existence, he will not find it here. Neither theism nor atheism is susceptible to final and unquestionable demonstration.

But then, nothing is. There is not a single proposition of any sort which can be established beyond challenge. The intellect never leads to absolute certainty.

From modern philosophy we have learned that the reality of the physical world cannot be verified, nor, if it exists, that it conforms to our notions of it. The deductive sciences —logic and mathematics, for instance—begin with axioms and postulates, so that any conclusions they reach are contingent ultimately on assumptions. That is why Euclid's geometry is no "truer" than any of the non-Euclidian systems, since all alike begin with intellectual "acts of faith."

And as for the physical sciences, from physics to sociology, these are of hypothesis all compact. They posit the knowability of nature, its uniformity, and innumerable more limited postulates. They take for granted concepts such as causality, matter, energy, time and space, ideas which are shot through with unresolved enigmas. And then, after all these assumptions, the empirical sciences achieve at best, as the scientist will be the first to admit, not certainty, but probability, more or less high.

In a word, intellectual finality exists nowhere, not even in the most exact of sciences. Nothing can be so proved as to be beyond dispute.

What then remains for men? They must do as best they can with what they have. Whether they be ordinary folk trying to make up their minds about some simple issue, or scientists weighing alternative theories, or all of us hesitating between religion and irreligion, they cannot do other than look at the various possibilities, select the best, and take that for the truth.

Such is the procedure of the scientist. Knowing that no absolute demonstration is attainable, he does not waste himself trying to achieve one. Instead he frames a *hypothesis*. That is to say, he studies his facts, considers the theories which apply, and posits as true the one which covers the facts best, works out best, and is the simplest.

Which, in a different field, is exactly what we have done. Confronted by a choice between the theistic and atheistic views, we have adopted the former.

It fits better.

It works better, both for morale and morality.

It is simplest; with one concept it unifies reality and makes it intelligible.

Or, to restate the point in formal, philosophical language: Religious faith is a hypothesis interpreting reality and posited on the same grounds as any valid hypothesis, viz., superior congruity with the facts, greater practicality, and maximal conceptual economy.

Does this sound awesome and far removed from religion

as we know it? Let us not be dismayed. All we are doing is to put into technical terms what all religionists have always said: that religion is in the end a matter of faith, and that that faith, far from being blind, arbitrary, or merely wishful, is indicated by compelling reasons, intellectual, practical, emotional.

This is not to say that theology is intellectually as exact or certain as is science, even if both are arrived at by the same general common sense. (For that matter a scientific theory in turn is less sure than the sense data it is devised to account for.) The hazards increase as one mounts upward in the edifice of the intellect, for at any level there will be present the risks of error implicit in that level plus all those in the levels below. The higher one climbs, the further he may fall. But then the view is almost certain to be better, the climate more healthful, and directions more clearly discernible.

The possibility remains however—and every religious person must face up to it—that, despite the preponderance of evidence in its favor, the theistic conclusion may be mistaken. One takes a chance with God. But, if so, it is a chance that has to be taken for the sake of head, heart, life itself.

Besides, who ever said that religion was something tame or safe? To the contrary, it is the greatest adventure of the human spirit, the boldest leap the soul can make; it is a man betting his life, with the evidences in his favor to be sure, but still betting his life, that things—the universe, ideals, the very life he is wagering—make sense and good sense to boot.

2

But if there is an admitted risk to faith, what about solidity of conviction? Is the religious person condemned to an everlasting tentativeness about what he believes?

Not at all. Firmness of opinion is attainable. Not on the basis of logic unaided, since, as we have already seen, argument is never definitive. But confidence fortunately comes from the heart rather than the head; it is an emotion rather than a proposition. It can be induced.

First, a man must purify his belief of logical and factual impossibilities, making it the most plausible belief available to him. For, if constancy in conviction is not to be fashioned in the intellect alone, it most certainly cannot be won, at least not by thinking moderns, without it, let alone in opposition to it.

Next, he must make up his mind. He commits himself, saying: "In view of the evidences and my needs, this is the position I adopt."

Then he lives by his decision. Only as he lives by it is sureness distilled within him. The view he has accepted becomes habitual with him; it is imprinted ever deeper on his consciousness by familiarity and, more effectively, by the cumulative evidences of its adequacy and value—until, in the end, though he can envisage other possibilities and though, as is inevitable, his moods go up and down, this emerges as the only position possible for him.

Acquiring faith, in other words, is only in part like proving a proposition in geometry. Equally, perhaps more, it is like falling in love. First the mind must assent; the fervor, however, wells from the heart, and the certainty, whether in marriage or religion, is the final upshot of the mind's assent, the heart's fervor, all confirmed and deepened to immovability by the testimony of the years.

3

The Jewish tradition makes no attempt to enforce a particular conception of God. Within Judaism, God has been envisaged as a Mind apart from and contemplating the world; or as a Spirit within it, as both, or in any number of other guises. In this respect, each Jew is left to his own needs and preferences.

And yet the reader who has followed our argument to this point may, especially if he be a stranger to religious speculation, lack the materials and skill to fashion a God-conception for himself. Conceivably, it would be helpful to him were some typical God-idea to be put before him, if only as an object of study. To this purpose, let me submit the particular envisagement I know best and most intimately, my own.

To me, whatever *is* is the outer shell of a Spirit. That spirit is the essence and ground of all things, sustaining and animating them, yet not exhausted by their totality.

Very often, I think of the world in relation to God in a parable. I imagine a mighty river with currents, waves, ripples, bubbles. Each current, wave, ripple, bubble, I recognize, has an independent existence. Yet each is but part of the stream and carried along by it in its course. What is more, there is more to the river, depths below depths, than is visible to my eyes.

As are the waves, ripples, bubbles to the river, so all things stand vis-à-vis God. Each has its individual identity. Yet each is but a manifestation of Him, pervaded by Him, existing only by virtue of Him, moving with His purposes. Touch anything and you may say: He is here. Yet add all things together and you will not have Him, for He is more than the world.

When I describe God as Spirit, I mean that He is not only a Power but a "Mind." His nature, in other words, is akin to our own. He is rational, which is why the universe is law-abiding. He is conscious with a consciousness like, though infinitely greater than, ours. Indeed He is the source of human consciousness, our private minds being individualizations of Him, sparks as it were of His fire.

When I speak of God as Spirit, I mean further that He is purposive. Whatever the case elsewhere in space, on our planet He has worked through inorganic nature to the plant, thence to the animal, thence to man, through whom He is now driving toward every increasing freedom, justice, and mercy, or, to use a good old theological phrase, toward the Kingdom of Heaven.

And man, how do I picture his role in this design? Man, I believe with the ancient rabbis, is a "partner with the Holy One, blessed be He," laboring with the God he incarnates toward ever increasing truth and goodness, toward, in sum, the realization of the cosmic design.

Of my specimen God-idea it should be observed that, without violating in the least the scientific description of the world, it yet satisfies all the needs for which a God-faith is posited to begin with. It accounts for the universe in its most challenging traits: the unity, dynamism, rationality, purposiveness, and consciousness in things; it invigorates human morale; it projects and supports morality; it makes the movement of history intelligible; it provides a possible explanation for the mystical experience; it gives hope and direction to life.

Yet this, be it recalled, is not an authoritative or even a recommended envisagement. It is presented only as a specimen to be considered, dissected, learned from, improved upon.

Judaism has never looked sympathetically on the notion that one man can save another's soul. It has no doctrine of vicarious salvation. What is true of man's moral pilgrimage is equally true of his intellectual quest. A man may assist his fellows, but no one can find God or fashion a conception of Him for anyone else. Each man in this respect must redeem himself. He must venture the peril and heartbreak but also the glory and deliverance of finding God in his own way, after his own spirit.

4

This discussion of the common-sense foundations of religious belief would not be complete without reference to one additional reason for faith, relevant only to Jews. I refer to the fact that with faith a Jew is thoroughly at home in his Jewishness, without it always something of a stranger.

The Jew without religious belief, whether he is without it because he has simply neglected to cultivate it or because he is honestly incapable of it, is in a sorry case—as a human being, in the first instance, but more specifically as a Jew. He will read and revere Scripture but disavow its key thesis. He may observe rituals but be out of harmony with their point. He is unfortunate. Yet, given his intellectual constitution and the requirements of integrity, he may have no choice save to accept his disabilities and get along with them as best he can.

But for the Jew capable of belief, Jewishness supplies an additional and final argument on its behalf. The act of faith completed, he is thereafter and forever basically at peace, not only with God but also with Israel and Torah.

PART TWO

III

The Revolt Against Reason:

The Anti-Intellectualism of Henri Bergson

Early in Milton Steinberg's intellectual development he was introduced to the philosophy of Henri Bergson. Henri Bergson—for whom intuition, flux, la durée, the immediacy and presentness of the world was central—was no doubt unsettling to one who had been trained in the twilight of idealism and the early maturity of American pragmatism.

In 1928 Steinberg completed a master's dissertation for Columbia University on "The Relation of Epistemology to Cosmology in the Systems of Bergson and Schopenhauer." It is not a shattering example of philosophic analysis. It does define, however, a preoccupation which runs throughout Steinberg's thought—from its earliest utterance in the dissertation of 1928, the present essay of 1935, to the discussions of anti-intellectualism and the revolt against reason contained in the closing essays of this volume—namely, the modern decline of invincible rationalism and the growing recognition that beneath the surface of the sea of reason there is a vast, dark, inscrutable, and living world.

For Steinberg the relation of reason and divinity was crucial. Anything which breached that connection challenged most profoundly the substance of his own faith, the living link which made possible his conviction that faith held was not philosophy abandoned (see our intro-

duction for further discussion of this point). In all events at the request of THE RECONSTRUCTIONIST *he wrote for it in 1935 (Nov. 1, 1935, Volume I, No. 13) the following review-essay of Bergson's* THE TWO SOURCES OF MORALITY AND RELIGION. *That essay is published here with the permission of* THE RECONSTRUCTIONIST.

EDITOR

One of the most interesting phenomena in the thought life of the modern world is a revolt against reason. This rebellion against the intellect is all the more arresting because it follows so closely upon several centuries during which man deified his ability to think. For from the seventeenth century on, modern man has laid his trust in his mind. He felt that if only he used it adequately he could solve all of life's puzzles. But in the last fifty years a wave of profound disillusionment has swept philosophical and scientific circles. It was discovered in the first place that there were areas of life which were essentially nonrational and which as a result would forever escape capture by logic. Men found to their own dismay that three thousand years of philosophical and scientific thinking had failed to provide them with certainty, that at the end of centuries of hard intellectual work there was no single proposition which was absolutely demonstrable, not even the proposition that two plus two equals four. In addition, they learned recently that, far from being an objective, impersonal force, reason serves often as a device by which men fortify attitudes, desires, and emotions which they maintain on nonrational grounds. Last of all, the intellect has failed to provide men with clear guidance in the business of living. In brief, after thousands of years of thinking, and after three centuries of blind confidence in the powers of thought, the human intellect has been revealed as inapplicable to certain realms of reality, susceptible to perversion for special ends, incompetent to provide certainty, and incapable of giving sure direction to man's activity.

It is inevitable in view of this failure that men seek for other instruments to take the place of rationalism in providing them with an explanation of the world and with direction to their lives. It is this search for a substitute which is revealed in Freud's theory of the subconscious, and in pragmatism which, renouncing reason, endeavors to find a new criterion of truth in the workability of a proposition and a new basis for ethics in the practical results of any line of conduct.

One of the archrebels against the intellect has been the brilliant French-Jewish philosopher, Henri Bergson. In his *Introduction to Metaphysics*, in his *Matter and Memory*, *Time and Free Will*, and *Creative Evolution* alike, he subjects reason to the most scathing criticism which has been leveled against it since the days of the old Greek skeptics. His entire case centers upon the fact that reality is a constantly changing fluidity, whereas the intellect by its very character deals in sharp, concise, and clearly defined concepts. It is impossible, he contends, to catch a flowing reality in stable ideas. Through this critique of reason Bergson has made valuable contributions to modern thought. He has helped to destroy the old psychology which regarded the mind as a series of discrete states of thought. He has solved some of the riddles of philosophy by pointing out that they spring from the artificiality of applying rigid concepts to a reality which is elastic. As a substitute for reason, Bergson advocates intuition. When we look down within us, we discover that our consciousness is a flow of sensation and emotion, of qualitative change. When we consider the physical world without, we find that it too is a restless, unbroken continuum. The material world is the same sort of thing as our consciousness within us. "Physics is simply psychics inverted." In this fashion Bergson arrived at his

114

theory of the *élan vital*. One of the most dazzling passages in modern philosophy is to be found in Bergson's application of this theory of a life force to biology. There he demonstrates that no account of the evolution of life is adequate unless it assumes that behind the universe there moves a driving power, akin to human consciousness, of which reality is only an outer shell.

After twenty-five years of silence Bergson was heard from once again. In *The Two Sources of Morality and Religion* [1] he takes up his argument at the point at which he interrupted it a quarter of a century ago. This time he is concerned not with abstruse philosophical problems but with issues of great practical moment—namely, morality and religion. Once again, he reveals the same anti-intellectualism. Morality, he tells us, rises from two sources. On the one hand, it springs from a sense of obligation which in man is the analogue of instinct in animals. Just as in an ant colony, each individual by instinctive action subordinates his own interests to those of the group, so in man there is an inherent social instinct which moves him to live not for himself but for the community. That which is instinct in the bee is a sense of social pressure in man. In both cases it is Nature's device for preserving the species. Two things should be noted about the morality of instinct. It is in the first place subrational, and in the second place it operates for a limited society only. The bee exhibits patriotism only for its own hive. The instinctive morality is concerned only with the clan, the family, the country—not with humanity.

But there is, Bergson tells us, a second source of morality. This is the morality which is the creation of the moral genius. As musicians invent new musical forms and artists reveal new perceptions of nature, in both cases original

• • •

[1] Henri Bergson, *The Two Sources of Morality and Religion* (New York: Henry Holt and Co., 1935).

creative acts expressive of deep-seated emotion, so certain individuals reveal new perspectives in human relationships. This moral creativity, Bergson insists, is superrational. It is higher than reason as the musical creations of a great musician are above intelligence. But once this vision has been caught by the creative genius, men follow it because of a power of attraction which inheres in it, as men are drawn to great literature, great music, and great painting by an emotional magnetism.

It will be observed that in this account of morality reason plays almost no part. For morality in origin is either subrational or superrational. All that reason can do is study, collate, and compare moralities. It cannot create them. As a matter of fact, a logical ethic might with justification advocate egoism. And even if a morality based upon reason does not urge selfishness there is nothing in man to compel him to accept a reasoned morality. As Bergson puts it, "One can always reason with reason."

What is true of the moral life is equally true of religion. The latter too springs from two sources, the first of which manifests itself in what Bergson denominates as static religion. The life impulse behind the universe drives man to live. It has created intelligence in man to enable him to live more fully. But intelligence can turn against the vital drive. Man, for example, can through his intelligence break loose from the social instinct and decide upon a self-centered life which is destructive of the species. Reason, furthermore, tells man that he must die. This awareness of inevitable doom negates the natural impulse toward life. In addition, man knows that between his desire and its realization there is a vast realm of uncertainty. He would therefore, if he obeyed reason alone, hesitate in setting out to attain what he wishes. Thus does reason inhibit life. But Nature is not content to allow man to destroy himself through his intelligence. It has used this very inhibiting intelligence against itself. By postulating spirits and gods it has allowed the life drive to continue. These spirits are conceived to punish offenses against social morality. They serve thus to suppress the self-centeredness which is born of the intellect. The Gods guarantee immortality and thus lift from the human heart the crushing recognition that death is inevitable. They co-operate with man and thus give him assurance in facing the gap between desire and its attainment. Static religion is then "a defensive reaction of Nature against what might be depressing for the individual, and dissolvent for society, in the exercise of intelligence."

But religion has also another source. There are some human beings who turn back to reality from time to time and catch intuitively the reality of a great life drive behind the universe. These people feel themselves as part and parcel of a storming river which moves through all things. The second source of religion is, then, mysticism, an emotional identification of one's self with the ultimate reality together with the sense of expansion, exultation, certainty, and joy which flow from it. Now, the vital drive behind the world is an active drive. The full and complete mystic, having experienced directly its reality, returns to a life of larger activity.

To those who have followed the development of Bergson's thought, what he says in *The Two Sources* is a natural development of what he said in his earlier works. His theories of morality and religion alike follow naturally from his entire system. And yet there is a profound difference between the earlier works and this most recent one. Brilliant as is the reasoning and gracious as is the style of *The Two Sources of Morality and Religion,* it is not the Bergson of twenty-five years ago. One could not help but think in reading the book of the gestures of an old dancer, in which there are still grace and precision, now grown the least bit lax. So, too, in the Bergson of *The Two Sources,* the argumentation is often flabby and the style, while reminiscent of more youthful vigor, heavier and blurred. Incidentally, I experienced not only a sense of disappointment but on occasion one of sharp irritation. For all Bergson's erudition, he does not know what every Jew ought to know, namely, that the Christianity of Jesus was not an original contribution but an expression of the current Jewish morality and religion of the first century. It is annoying to find a Jew of international importance ignorant of what Gentile scholars have long admitted, and possessed of the exploded notion that Judaism in contrast with Christianity is an inferior religious system. None of these considerations, however, should prevent an act of appreciation of Bergson's newest contribution. His treatment of the sources of morality is immensely significant in the emphasis which it lays upon instinct and inspiration as driving motifs in man's moral living. His treatment of religion calls fresh attention to the fact that it answers vital needs and that the mystical intuition must not be neglected.

But if Bergson throughout makes valuable reading, every one of his works and his last especially reveals the weaknesses of anti-intellectualism. It is more than a little paradoxical for a man to build up a case against reason and to use reason to the full in order to establish that case. And even if we are tolerant enough to overlook this contradictory tactic, that reason is dead, what remains to us? A religion which is entirely mystical is, in the first place, entirely personal, and in the second place, not susceptible to logical examination, for all discussion involves the use of reason. Similarly with morality. If morality be subrational in its sources of instinct, there is nothing which reason can do to change it. And if it be superrational, then it is also beyond intellectual criticism. Both in morality and in religion we are left without criteria of judgment and evaluation. The fantastic aspect of the whole is that, although Bergson himself is obviously a person of good will, his theories play directly into the hands of people whose good will is not so certain. A religion based upon mystical intuition, unchecked by reason, is capable of all sorts of grossnesses and stupidities. And a morality which springs merely from the dream of a creative genius might very well be a destructive morality. Thus, Hitler could very well claim that he has caught a new moral vision of a mankind redeemed through the sense of racial communion. Bergson is not altogether undisturbed by the abuses to which his system lends itself. He merely tells us, however, that in such cases the mysticism is false and the moral vision not truly a vision. But how are we to distinguish between true and false mysticism and between true and false morality without reason as the criterion? It is one of the unfortunate traits of men that, once they have adopted a position, they feel impelled to maintain that position to the exclusion of others. Bergson, having aligned himself in the antirational camp, cannot give his opponents their due.

It is then an intriguing experience—this business of following an anti-intellectualist. One learns a great deal about the inadequacy of human thought, about the meaning of emotion, intuition, and the mystical impulse in man. But the further one travels with an antirationalist, the more one perceives the need for reason. It is a poor staff, crooked and cracked—this intellect on which we must lean. It must be spliced and supported with stays borrowed from the emotional and intuitive. But it is the only staff upon which man can rest his weight with some assurance that it will not break entirely under him at the moment when he needs it most.

IV

The Outlook of Reinhold Niebuhr:

A Description and Appraisal

Steinberg's appraisal of Reinhold Niebuhr, rare when it was written in 1945, is still distinguished. It does not compromise the religious liberalism which he espoused nor does it belabor Niebuhr with those rhetorical strictures of naïve optimism which continue to cascade from the American pulpit.

The present review of Niebuhr's thought, occasioned by the publication in 1945 of his THE CHILDREN OF LIGHT AND THE CHILDREN OF DARKNESS, was but the first of many considerations which Steinberg gave to Niebuhr's thought. Although Steinberg steadfastly refused, as well he might, to accept Niebuhr's modified doctrine of unexpungable human evil, he does evidence from the present essay to its fulfilled exposition in his treatment of evil in "New Currents in Religious Thought" (pp. 214-300) a growing willingness to accept Niebuhr's theological realism. Above all things, Steinberg was fair—his investment in the truth was infinitely more important than his commitment to earlier and more companionable doctrines. The increasing gap between his theology and the theology of Jewish liberalism is signaled less by such observable acts as the manner in which he conducted his pulpit or the liturgy than in such subtle gestures as his genuinely altered view of the extent of human evil and inadequacy. The liberalism *of youth was wounded; the realism of an age that had just barely survived Hitler and might yet not survive communism or nuclear warfare was born.*

"The Outlook of Reinhold Niebuhr" was the beginning of a phase of work—the work that commenced with illness and ended with death, the work of recapitulating a lifetime and judging the deeds of history under the public aspect of evil regnant and the private aspect of death anticipated.

"The Outlook of Reinhold Niebuhr," first published in THE RECONSTRUCTIONIST, *December 14, 1945, Volume XI, Number 15, is reprinted here with its permission.*

EDITOR

Reinhold Niebuhr represents many fine things to a large and steadily increasing number of his contemporaries. He is first of all a Christian theologian of distinction, erudite and profound, one of the best interpreters in modern idiom of the religious outlook generally, of Calvinist Protestantism in particular. Again, he is one of the chief exponents of the thesis that religion belongs in life, indeed that one of its major functions is to serve as a principle both of criticism and of inspiration. In this attitude he is very close to normative Judaism, a fact of which he is well aware, as his own words attest: "I have as a Christian theologian sought to strengthen the Hebraic-prophetic content of the Christian tradition."

In his desire to bring religion to bear on social problems, he is by no means alone. What sets him apart from the crowd is the fact that he is singularly free from the naïveté, intellectual and pragmatic, exhibited by most religionists in economics and politics. If he has all the idealism of "Christian socialists" such as Walter Rauschenbusch, he discloses also a reassuring practicality, a firm grasp on social theory and actuality alike.

Among other things, Doctor Niebuhr is one of the few non-Jews who understand Judaism and the Jewish question. He knows Zionism well and sympathetically. His observations on the Arab-Jewish problem are among the wisest, most penetrating that have emanated from any source. His statement in his introduction to Waldo Frank's *The Jew in Our Day* [1] on the effect of the *galut* [2] on Jewish universalism is, in its perceptiveness and sensitivity, nothing less than brilliant. Jews who are liberals like him for his liberalism. If they are survivalists and Zionists as well, they appreciate him further for his sympathy, strong yet unsentimental, with their aspirations. Religious Jews owe him a special debt. For in focusing the light of the God-faith onto social issues he has aided them in the discharge of their own spiritual commitments.

His largest contribution, however, both to Jews and Christians, both to secular and religious thought, is his reaffirmation of the reality of evil in man and society. This, insofar as one exists, is the central, recurrent motif of his writing and teaching. It is the special contribution of his Calvinism to our generation.

Modern men have with fair consistency been naïvely optimistic as to human nature and society. They have gone ahead on the blithe assumption that neither required much more than a bit of tinkering to be redeemed. As to the character of this tinkering, opinions were divided. In the case of the individual, they ran a full gamut from better housing through improved education to the application of the newer psychiatric techniques. As for society, all that it lacked, most men have imagined, was one or more political reforms, economic reconstructions, or religious revivals to

• • •

[1] Waldo Frank, *The Jew in Our Day* (New York: Duell, Sloan and Pearce, 1944), pp. 3-14.

[2] *Ibid.*, pp. 5-9. *Galut* is the Hebrew word for the "exile" and dispersion of the Jews.—EDITOR.

be well on its way toward becoming the Kingdom of God.

Not that evidences were wanting to shake this light-heartedness. The great religious traditions, including the Jewish, all made much more of the stubborn perversity of man's heart than pleased their modern communicants. Experience, too, demonstrated that each ardently sought-after reform, no matter how beneficial otherwise, left the problem of individual regeneration and social rebirth but little advanced. And recent events have disclosed the depths below depths of bestiality lurking in the human animal. The typical modern man has persisted incorrigibly in his good cheer, in the faith that, despite all evidences to the contrary, men could be saved simply by the discovery of the right formula or device.

This, many of us owe to Reinhold Niebuhr: that he has reminded us of the depth and tenacity of evil in the individual and society.

The central thesis of most of Doctor Niebuhr's writing is this: That, despite all the workings of religion and conscience, man is basically a creature of self-love, that is to say, of pride and selfishness. This self-love is more dangerous, both morally and in its workings, than cruder impulses such as hatred and lust. These latter stand in open, unmistakable contradiction to the ethical principles which most men profess and which consciously, at least, they seek to follow. But egoism is subtle and elusive, insinuating itself into every life interest, perverting purposes, corrupting logic, tainting idealism, and all the time draping itself in respectability, in the robes of dispassionate logic and disinterested righteousness.

To the many uses of religion generally recognized, there is added, in the light of this analysis, one more of supernal importance: Religion offers the sole possibility of deliverance from the tyranny of self-love.

This purpose it serves variously—by pointing out to us the truth concerning our moral natures, by forever subject-

ing our behavior to basic criticism, by posing before us
ideals incompatible with egoism. What is more, only religion can do this job, for only religion posits another transcendent realm of being from which man and history can
be viewed critically. Again, because man partakes of this
other order of reality, he is not trapped in his own naturalistic character. And his history, which by its inherent
nature cannot be self-redemptive, is vindicated on another
plane. Niebuhr's religion, in sum, is not some interesting
adventure in metaphysical speculation, nor some additional
but ultimately superfluous sanction for the good life. It is
a desperate necessity—man's only hope and method of
escape from the evil inherent in himself.

From these key premises flow streams of implications. In
Moral Man and Immoral Society (1936) Niebuhr analyzed
the operations of collective egoism in the nation, the class
—privileged and proletarian, the state and its machinery,
arguing that social conflict is inevitable, that "power must
be challenged by power," that the law at any time represents not theoretical justice but the resolution of colliding
social forces.

Ethics and religion, to be sure, have a part in the social
scene. They set up standards of judgment and values toward which, despite their self-love, men strive. Especially
when one class, party, or nation acquires power and slides
toward its abuse, as it inevitably tends to do, morality,
reason, and religion are mobilized into action by the un-
balance and may operate vigorously for the restoration of
an equilibrium. Spiritual elements, in other words, are not
without influence on the economic order and the state. Yet
society remains an arena of conflicts, and the sooner religious idealists reckon with that fact the better for religion,
moral idealism, and society alike.

In *The Nature and Destiny of Man* (1942) Niebuhr applied his touchstone insight, in the first instance, to doctrines concerning human nature, and then to the concepts

of sin and the sinner. What emerges most conspicuously from this impressive, rich, and immensely learned work is that sin has two faces. One of its countenances is well known: the *undervaluation* in thought and action of the human being who is after all nothing less than the child and embodiment of God. Its other face, limned for us by Niebuhr, is far less familiar: sin as the *overestimation* of man, as the forgetting in mind or deed that he is no better than a creature, as the ascription to him or to his communal institutions of a status more than that of creatureliness and dependence vis-à-vis Deity.

In *The Children of Light and the Children of Darkness* [3] Niebuhr directs his fruitful intuition to "a vindication of democracy and a critique of its traditional defense." Taking his text from the verse (Luke 16:8) which asserts that the children of this world are wiser than the children of light, Niebuhr applies the phrase, "the children of this world" (or of darkness), to those "who know no law beyond their will and interest." The children of light are the idealists, after all their kinds and fashions, who, if they run true to form, are likely to be much less clear-headed, realistic, and tactically cunning than their antagonists. Witness the thinking on democracy by its advocates.

Democracy is on the one hand the by-product of the rise and maturation of bourgeois civilization. As such it is a temporary and contingent device. On the other hand, it is a permanently valuable form of communal organization, rooted in the deepest requirements of man's nature and collective living. It is indeed the only social form that does justice to the twin human necessities, freedom and order, that allows the human being to be, as he must be, both a free spirit and a member of a community.

The children of light, however, for all their passionate

• • •

[3] Reinhold Niebuhr, *The Children of Light and the Children of Darkness* (New York: Charles Scribner's Sons, 1945).

devotion to democracy, fail to understand its true urgency. Therefore they plead for it childishly, apply it naïvely, and in effect contribute to its failure in prestige and action.

They rest their case in its behalf on sentimental notions of the reasonableness, harmlessness, benevolence, and altruism of man, taking it for granted that all which men require is enough light and liberty, and they will find a way, a good way, for themselves. The unhappy truth is that men are capable of refusing to be illumined, of deliberately choosing the evil, that, thanks to self-love, they may calculatingly set their own interests above those of the community, their class above country, their nation above mankind.

This, the children of light are unable or unwilling to concede. Consequently, they often end up disillusioned, or outwitted by shrewder men of ill will, or, for want of realism, prove incompetent in dealing with social problems—developments all tending to the surrender or breakdown of the democratic ideal.

Niebuhr's argument in *The Children of Light* emerges then in this conclusion: Democracy is to be advocated not because men are so rational and good as to make it natural, but because they can be so blind and self-centered as to make it indispensable.

Only through democracy is there any hope for a constructive solution of the deep, terrible antinomies and tensions of human existence: the freedom of the individual which will permit his self-fulfillment versus an ordered community which is both the precondition of that fulfillment and one of its necessary outlets; the preservation of some kind of property right as a natural extension of personality versus such delimitation of that right as is commended by morality, and dictated by the need of preventing property power from becoming tyrannical; that liberty for the religious sect and ethnic minority which will allow it to realize itself and will preserve for mankind the values of variety versus the unity of the community; loyalty to the

nation and national interest versus international organization, a precondition for peace and national survival. For all
these tangled issues, democracy alone offers not solutions—
Niebuhr does not expect any basic human impasse ever to
be finally resolved—but an arena and atmosphere in which
these issues can best and with the least destructiveness be
made viable.

And even as democracy is essential to human welfare,
religion, to repeat a point already made, is essential to
democracy, supplying it with criteria and values from outside man and beyond society, establishing man's transcendence over his natural being, thus assuring his inherent dignity and freedom, providing a vindication of the human
career that is not otherwise forthcoming, since history
neither interprets nor redeems itself.

Here in skeletal form is Niebuhr's plea for democracy
and critique of its traditional defense. A schematism such
as this does not begin to do justice to the richness of his
thinking, to the wisdom to be found in his *obiter dicta* and,
along side paths, to the main lane of his argumentation—
his description, for example, of the sentimentalism and optimistic naïveté concealed in Marxism, his discussion of the
three possible approaches to the problem of religious diversity, more particularly his searching analysis of secularism in that connection; his so-timely presentation of the
problem of international organization, including a vivid
treatment of the fallacies involved in both the utopian and
the cynical approaches to the matter.

Yet *The Children of Light and the Children of Darkness*
and his other works are open to a twofold criticism.

Like all persons molded by a tradition, Niebuhr displays
in his thinking the pattern of that tradition, the tropisms,
as it were, of its reasoning. When he contends that the
individual, try as he will to subject himself to religion,
morality, and reason, can never escape the taint and corruption of self-love; nor can the community, strive as it

may, ever achieve a justice higher than the resolution of contending interests; he is being true to the Calvinist fore-bears of his spirit who held that man was born damned to begin with, and that society was not and could not be the scene of either his or its own salvation. From which the Calvinist drew the rigorously indicated inferences of the need for divine grace and intervention, and of otherworldly salvation.

Niebuhr follows this design boldly to a point. Then his speech, as I catch it, blurs. He obviously entertains in *practice* this-worldly hopes both for the individual and the community, or he would not be so passionately concerned with both. And yet he simply refuses to admit that fact or be cheerful concerning it.

At the same time his *logic* points directly and exclusively to a supermundane denouement. But unlike his ancestors he will not make his assertion of such a position full and vigorous, refusing to go further than to say that man is ulti-mately a citizen of another, nontemporal realm.

But can he have all this both ways? Can he talk inevi-table damnation and act meliorism? Can his logic imply an altogether otherworldly salvation and his final conclusion be something less?

With one other aspect of Niebuhr's outlook I find myself out of harmony. I have long tried to determine in my own mind what it is which makes the tone of Judaism so dif-ferent from the thought-current within the Protestantism he represents. After all both traditions are acutely conscious of the reality of evil. The prophets make much of it, as do the rabbis whose references to the *Yezer Ra,* the evil im-pulse in man, are more numerous than can be quoted. And yet there is a divergence in spirit between the two milieux. Both acknowledge the same actualities, but somehow with diverse responses. There is joyousness, cheer, hope even for this world in Judaism; grimness, pain, and despair of any-thing before death in Calvinist Protestantism.

The difference I have come to believe is one of perspective, of the place to which evil is assigned in the envisagement of the cosmic scheme. In rabbinic Judaism, the central position is held by God and His goodness, against which evil throws a shadow but from the periphery. In Calvinist Protestantism, God and His goodness are, needless to say, also placed in the key position—but it is evil, its roots and flowerings, which get almost as much attention. Observe that it was John Milton, a Christian of this stripe, who, writing a cosmic epic, managed in the end to make not God or the Christ but Lucifer its protagonist and incidentally its most interesting character.

By the same token, Niebuhr's emphasis on the role of evil is no idiosyncrasy, nor is it merely the overstressing of a neglected truth, overstressed to offset the neglect. It is nothing less than a historic pattern of thought and feeling. To one reared in the Jewish tradition, something of morbidity seems to pervade this motif in Protestantism.

Two men, let us suppose, are both afflicted with a chronic and always dangerous disease. One makes that circumstance the focal point of his thought and feeling. He knows all along that he has in himself elements of health, that his life situation is still enjoyable and worth while. His illness, however, looms most prominent in his spiritual landscape and so absorbs his first thought and effort. The other is fully aware of his ailment. He recognizes that he dare not forget it for an instant, or live even most fleetingly in violation of the restraints it imposes, or cease ever to hedge it in. Yet for him the most conspicuous feature of his being is not this, grave as it is, but such basic health as he possesses under his malady. He is, therefore, likely to get along better as patient to his physician, as laborer, as kinsman, as citizen, certainly as a companion to others who, in like case with him, travel the road by his side.

Analogies are always dangerous; no simile should be pressed too far. Yet Niebuhr's outlook does appear to me to partake somewhat of the melancholia of the former; historic Judaism of the cheer of the latter.

All these defects are dwarfed by the brilliance and constructiveness of the intellect of this man, the many and large contributions he is making to our spiritual and social life, and, foremost among these, that he is opening our eyes to actualities which we in our excessive optimism have refused to see, that he has taught us again what our fathers knew and we have refused to credit, a hard, grim truth concerning the place and power of evil in man and society.

V

Kierkegaard and Judaism

In the years before his death—during the wearying years of illness and enforced confinement—Steinberg commenced an intensive reading of contemporary theology and European philosophy. The classics of English and American philosophy—the works of F. H. Bradley, Samuel Alexander, C. S. Peirce, Alfred North Whitehead—were long familiar to him. They had served to strengthen one persistent line of his speculation—the complaisant and caring rationality of God. Upon them he was to fashion his view of the nonabsoluteness of God (cf. "The Theological Issues of the Hour," pp. 155-213, and "New Currents in Religious Thought," pp. 214-300). His awareness of increasing agitation within Protestant theology, already apparent in his early and sustained interest in Reinhold Niebuhr, impelled a fresh consideration of continental thought. In these years, stimulated by close friendship with the distinguished sociologist and intellectual historian, Albert Salomon, and his intense and lively relationship with Will Herberg, Steinberg commenced a careful reading of nineteenth-century German philosophy, with which he had been insufficiently familiar, notably Fichte, Schelling, and Hegel; the decisive spokesmen of a new phenomenology of culture and society, Dilthey, Simmel, Weber, Troeltsch; and the neo-Orthodox Protestant theologians, Emil Brunner and Karl Barth. Above all, in these years, he studied Kierkegaard.

The present essay, "Kierkegaard and Judaism," is distinguished by its manifest respect and admiration, its remarkable and accurate understanding of the theological dilemmas of Reformation doctrine and historic Christianity, and its temperate and judicious assessment of the bearing of Kierkegaardian insight upon Jewish religion.

First published in THE MENORAH JOURNAL, *Spring, 1949, "Kierkegaard and Judaism" is reprinted here with its permission.*

EDITOR

As a thorough Christian—or, as he would have put it, infinitely interested in becoming one—Sören Kierkegaard (1813-1855) addressed himself neither to Jews nor to Judaism. But they have overheard him. In part because they could not help it. Is not Kierkegaard the begetter of Existentialism? Is not the school he fathered all the vogue of late? Are Jews less submissive than others to the tyrannies of fashion?

But Kierkegaard, though made into a fad, was himself a highly original and richly endowed spirit, the author of various fresh critical judgments and insights. But every new truth, every reformulation of an old one, constitutes a challenge to all inhabitants of the universe of discourse on which it bears. In effect then, even if not by intention, Kierkegaard has confronted Jews with a twofold *mai ko mashmo lon*—"What has this to teach us?"

He needs to be considered first of all for his theses of which Judaism has been inadequately aware heretofore. "From all my teachers have I derived understanding"— that is a norm for traditions as well as individuals. Kierkegaard demands appraisal also in still another frame of reference. If Fichte is to be believed, it is from the non-Ego that the Ego becomes conscious of its own nature. Now whatever else Kierkegaard may have been, he was a Christian, marginal and idiosyncratic perhaps, but a Christian none the less. For each of his positions, no matter how eccentric, some authoritative warrant can be found, whether in his immediate Lutheran-Calvinist heritage, or in such a tangential Catholic as Pascal and before him in Duns Scotus and Augustine, or, as is to be expected in a Christian theologian, in Paul, the fountainhead of all Christian doctrine. But if so, if in Kierkegaard we have an *anima totaliter Christiana,* then he constitutes a non-Ego against which the Jewish Ego may whet its self-awareness.

Nor, to this end, is his extremism an impediment. To the contrary, it is an advantage. Just because Kierkegaard represents Christianity at its most intense and distinctive, his evocative effect on the Jewish spirit is all the more pronounced. Approaching him, therefore, Jews are well advised to be on the alert for what they can learn not only about him but about themselves also.

Among the more consequential of Kierkegaard's affirmations are these:

A. That man's plight is desperate, beset as he is by sin and bewilderment, dreading his freedom, shrinking from death, confronting Eternity; forever seeking, never finding, mitigation of his dire lot in the pleasures of the body, the conceptions of the mind.

B. That among human delusions none is more common and baseless than the belief that reason is capable of grasping reality at all, let alone achieving certainty. In this connection Kierkegaard criticizes conceptual thought with such acumen and thoroughness as to win for himself a place in the high tradition of anti-intellectualism stretching from Pyrrho of Elis and Sextus Empiricus to William James and Henri Bergson.

C. That of all conceptualist errors none is more bizarre than the notion of man as a thought-machine who cannot say *sum* ("I am") until he has first asserted *cogito* ("I think"); or the notion of man as a depersonalized, devitalized "something in general" into which philosophy loves to congeal him; whereas, in fact, he is always something particular, dynamic, and passionate, more *sentiens* (emotional) than *sapiens* (intellectual).

D. That the crucial determinations of the human soul are reached in privacy and in decisive instants, not in the public domain and the unfolding of events. This thesis, aimed at Hegel, constitutes the first sortie in modern thought against "historicism," the doctrine that the social and the temporal are somehow involved in salvation.

Such are Kierkegaard's premises, from which flow as consequences:

A. An importunate appeal for subjectivity, for the soul's turning away from the outer world and externalized ideas to its own immediacy.

B. The renunciation of the hope of finality, of attaining to a resting place. To the contrary, man's destiny is to be always "on the way," that dialectical ingress and progress penetrating without end to ever deeper levels of inwardness.

C. And finally—or, more accurately, first of all—a revolutionary re-envisagement, in the light of the foregoing, of the religious life.

The sole principle of religious truth, according to Kierkegaard, is subjectivity. For Christianity is "spirit, spirit is inwardness, inwardness is subjectivity, subjectivity is essentially passion, and in its maximum and infinite, personal, passionate interest in one's eternal happiness." Whence it follows that externality, intellectuality, objectivity—call them what you will—are all obstructive to the religious purpose. Scholarship, Biblical and doctrinal, may be an appealing and sometimes illuminating enterprise; but so far as salvation is concerned—and that is man's only serious business—of no account. So also with formal creeds and rituals; so also with the church as an institution; so even with ethics and all its apparatus of rules and principles.

The religious quest, Kierkegaard insists, is neither so easy, so impersonal, mechanical, or self-limiting. It demands within man a burning with what Pater called "a hard gemlike flame." Even that does not suffice. For God must respond, and who can commit or compel Him? That, too, if granted, is not enough. For salvation and grace are not "things" to be given once and thereafter owned by their recipients. They are not possessions to be held in fee simple: they are ever-receding goals which, once won, must be won again. Hence the most stupid of all complacencies is that of "believers" who suppose that no more is asked of them than the performance of the right commandments or the recitation of the proper confessions. And the most arrogant of offenses is to cease, out of religious pride and self-assurance, from that anguished striving which is the mark of the human soul and its hope of salvation.

Man's freedom therefore is his peril, his misery, and his grandeur. His peril, since all depends on it; his misery, since it consigns him to an infinitely toilsome and ultimately thankless task; his grandeur, for its goal is nothing less than eternal bliss in God.

But there is more to Kierkegaard, much of which is philosophically questionable and some, from the Jewish point of view, nothing short of perilous.

Consider, first, Kierkegaard's radical antirationalism. This, to be sure, is far from total. For Socrates his admiration is as warm as his antagonism to Hegel is deep; and if he has no high regard for the physical sciences, he recognizes them as legitimate fields of human interest, with the intellect as the proper tool for their exploration. But though he pays obeisance to reason and gives abundant evidence of expertness in it, on the climactic issues of living—religion and human salvation—he repudiates reason totally, radically, with zest.

Faith for Kierkegaard is not supplementary to the intellect but its antagonist. This, be it noted, is something different from the usual conflict between faith and reason, whether in religion or philosophy. Here we are not dealing with the *noesis* of Plato or the *theoria* of Aristotle, which, reaching beyond the discursive intellect or *logos,* nevertheless carry it along in their very transcendence of it. Nor are we handling here that more commonplace collision between religious dogma on one side and science on the other.

Kierkegaard makes a different and much more radical point. He argues not merely the conventional thesis that faith and reason can have no traffic with each other, operating as they do in different realms, separated as they are by a "disjuncture" which may be "leaped" but not bridged. His is the revolutionary contention—and it is the core of his doctrine—that faith *of necessity* must "affront" reason, must "spurn" and "scandalize" it. Nor could it be otherwise when faith's climax is the twin declaration that God became man and that His death on the cross, an event in time, is the occasion of eternal salvation.

Can any assertion, Kierkegaard queries again and again, be more paradoxical and absurd? But if the supreme affirmations of faith be absurdities and paradoxes, then manifestly reason is not only insufficient to faith, reason must be faith's natural enemy.

An antirationalist, Kierkegaard turns out something of a nonmoralist also. As in logic, so in ethics, he discloses great forensic virtuosity. Witness the case for marriage and traditional morality in general, which he sets forth in the latter half of *Either-Or.*

But again it is another tack he takes once the issue becomes salvation. As before he sprang from reason to faith, spurning the intellect and trampling it down in his leap, so now he springs above morality. Goodness, he asserts, whatever its other utilities, does not save; it cannot even help to salvation. What is more, when God asks it as He may, or faith requires it as it sometimes does, moral principle must be jettisoned. This is the "teleological suspension of the ethical," propounded by Kierkegaard in his *Fear and Trembling* as the final meaning of Abraham's readiness to sacrifice Isaac at God's behest. This, be it observed, is such a *midrash* on the *Akedah* as no rabbi in two thousand years ventured to put forth.

Closely related to such "secondarizing" of the ethical is that aspect of Kierkegaard's thinking which Buber has analyzed in *The Question to the Single One*—its near solipsism. This is no morally neutral solipsism (the metaphysical view that the self is the only knowable, or the only existent, thing) such as might derive from the epistemological question of how one can know anything. It is rather a projection of self-centeredness, so total a concentration on one's private existence and salvation as to leave no room for concern over anyone else. Indeed, in Kierkegaard's writings "others" simply do not exist as objects of solicitude. There is no community, no society. There is only the soul alone with God.

But if the relation between the individual soul and God be all, then "horizontal" history—the succession of happenings in time—embraces only one true event, the self-revelation of the Eternal. Obviously, however, a history composed of a single and unique episode is not history at all. As for internal or "vertical" history—the soul's confrontation by God—not only is this not history in the usual sense; Kierkegaard, in addition, leaves unresolved whether this is the culmination of a progress in which time is involved or of an instantaneity, a "leap," in which time is not involved. But what manner of history can it be in which the status of time is left questionable? In sum:

nothing, or at most next to nothing, remains of history when Kierkegaard is through.

Consistently, therefore, he strikes the study of history from the roster of earnest concerns. Historical research is not only an irrelevance to the quest after salvation: it can be a hindrance, interposing a "century-long parenthesis" into the urgent business of faith. Indeed, it may prove an active peril, a "most dangerous enemy," eventuating as it does in objective knowledge rather than inwardness and passion.

The main point, however, remains, that history effects nothing toward man's salvation. As Kierkegaard puts it in his *Philosophical Fragments:* "The first and last [generations] are essentially on the same plane. . . . Immediate contemporaneity is merely an occasion. . . ."

From all the foregoing, the anticlericalism and anti-ecclesiasticism of Kierkegaard's last phase, his attacks on institutional Christendom, follow inevitably. That is not an expression of mere unsociability or eccentricity, not even of an ambivalence to the world's esteem which he affected to despise, though all these were factors in the case. Given his points of departure and the direction of his tending, he can arrive at no other terminus. His logic gives him no choice but to reject all churches, regardless of character and denomination. Are they not institutions, externalizations of faith, and so objectivity incarnate? Are they not, further, social entities existing in time, whereas both the social and the temporal are alien to essential religion? So it came to pass that this ardent Christian ended up as Christendom's intransigent critic.

Finally, it should be recorded that when Kierkegaard speaks of the desperateness of man's plight he is indulging in no rhetorical exaggerations. To him the human condition is one of desperation in the most literal denotation of the word. It is, so far as man's own capacities are concerned, simply and starkly hopeless.

For what is it that man can achieve for himself? As all the historic religions have agreed, aesthetic gratifications, whether crude or refined, are unlikely to effect tranquillity in this world, let alone eternal life in the next. And if one seek his salvation in virtue, what man is there on earth who doeth only good and sinneth not, whose righteousness is sufficient to redemption? What can remain then except to transcend pleasure and the good alike, perhaps even— and here Kierkegaard leaves the main road of religious affirmation—to spurn and repudiate them, and go seeking elsewhere?

Only now does the true desperateness of man's plight become apparent. For his very desire and ability to seek belong not to him but to God. As much as the finding is a gift of divine grace, so much is even the setting out to find. Or, to put it in the figure employed by Kierkegaard himself in his *Philosophical Fragments:* Man is not only "destitute of the Truth up to the very moment of his learning it; he cannot even have possessed it in the form of ignorance . . ."; the teacher, that is, God, "gives the learner not only the Truth but also the condition for understanding it. . . ." Which means that facing the alternatives of eternal salvation and damnation, man is all dependence, all impotence; for what he can do for himself is of no avail, and of what avails he can do nothing. Was ever a plight more "dreadful"?

The essence of Kierkegaard, then, at least insofar as he constitutes a non-Ego to Judaism's Ego, consists of the five following antinomies, in each of which the first term is affirmed as against the second:

1. Faith *versus* Reason
2. The Religious *versus* the Ethical
3. The Individual *versus* Society
4. The Moment *versus* History
5. Man's Need *versus* his Powers

It is important that these positions be seen for what they are, not the eccentricities of an individual but the expressions—extreme perhaps, and certainly not exclusive, but none the less authentic—of the Christian *Weltanschauung*. Kierkegaard is not properly understood unless he be taken for the Christian he claimed to be. Nor does our discussion center on anything so unequal as a single person vis-à-vis a historic tradition. What concerns us here is nothing less than the timeless dialectical interchange between the Jewish and Christian faiths.

That it should be necessary to argue now what was asserted earlier in this essay—namely, the Christian character of Kierkegaard—is itself astounding. Few authors have been more explicit about their purposes. He was forever declaring and underscoring his Christian intentions and temper. Of his expositors, however, many have simply refused to take him at his word, some because they have come to him with special interests of their own, others because they were not themselves Christians, or else not Christians of his stripe. Whatever the reason, the role of Protestant doctrine and spirit in Kierkegaard has been consistently underestimated.

The fact is that Kierkegaard was a Christian *ab ovo*. He was raised in a devout Lutheran society, steeped in Christian learning, schooled in Reformation theology, attracted as well as repelled by the prospect of becoming a pastor. The issues of Christian faith and practice burned in him, all the more fiercely for the fierce troubled piety of his guilt-ridden father. Under such influences, under the dynamism of his own genius, Christianity became for Kierkegaard in the end—though not without a terrible struggle— the living heart of his thought, the *pathos* and *telos* of his entire existence.

As for the antinomies above listed, there is no accounting for them in terms of the idiosyncratic or capricious, nor as reactions to Hegel nor as responses to Kant or Schelling or Schleiermacher. They can be explained adequately only as Christian affirmations, restatements in individualistic phrases and insights, of the key assertions of Protestant Christendom in its Lutheran version.

That subordination of reason to faith, that denial of one for the sake of the other, what is it except an exultant obeisance to the mysteries of the Christian faith, the Incarnation foremost among them? On this article the less steadfast believer turns apologist or rationalizer. Not Kierkegaard. Recognizing that any attempt to make sense of it is foredoomed to failure, foreseeing that the sole sure result is to strip away its supernatural power, he elects the bolder course. He sets forth faith not only as beyond, but as radically opposed to, reason. His repudiation of the intellect turns out, then, neither wanton nor philosophically motivated, but rather a doctrinal necessity.

It is also impelled by another, equally weighty consideration. Within Christianity, within all theisms, there have always been two states of mind as to the nature of the divine essence. One holds it to consist in reason and the rational. To this school the Christian Platonists and Thomists belong and, in a drastic metamorphosis, the Hegelian idealists also. In the alternative view, God is Will before He is Reason. What He determines, by the very fact that He determines it, becomes the reasonable and the good. In this line stands Duns Scotus, Calvin, and Luther. This is the foundation stone of all those theologies which teach that salvation is of God's election only.

The logic behind this doctrine is clear. On two grounds salvation cannot be by man's merit. First, all men are sinners and, if the dogma of "total depravity" be granted, none is consequentially better than any other. Shall they then be saved by a righteousness no one of them possesses?

Second, were salvation by merit, God would be *bound* to confer it on those who had earned it, in which case God would not be free—which is a palpable absurdity. This is the classic Augustinian-Lutheran-Calvinist argument. Its effect is to present God as arbitrary in His bestowal of grace. He saves whom He pleases, and for no other reason than that He pleases. But if so God is not only intellectually absurd but morally irrational also.

Little wonder that it comes easy to Kierkegaard, who was reared in such conceptions, that indeed he finds it necessary to make faith the antagonist of reason; for such, in his scheme, it is.

In his nonmoralism, too, Kierkegaard voices an authoritative Christian judgment, one as ancient as the Pauline Epistles.

Having asserted Christ to be the sole medium of salvation, Paul found himself confronted by a dilemma. Obviously, none but the good man should or could be saved. Yet salvation was now a matter not of morality but of faith. But suppose a man had faith but not goodness? The problem was too much for Paul, who ended up by insisting that if the believer were truly a believer he would inevitably be good also. But on the choice between faith and morality, on the issue of what it is on which salvation ultimately depends, Paul was all explicitness. "He who believeth shall be saved; he who disbelieveth shall be condemned."

The "secondarization of the moral" in Kierkegaard, therefore—his "teleological suspension of the ethical," about which such a fuss has been made—that is basically no more than a restatement of a doctrine as old as Paul. Revived by the Reformationists in their rebellion against the "works" of the Catholic Church, it was a conviction imbibed by Kierkegaard with his father's first instruction.

Nor is it otherwise with his near solipsism. In the Pauline-Protestant tradition the crucial tension is always between the individual and God, to which relation other persons and the community are irrelevant. This conception of primitive Christendom, interrupted for centuries by the Catholic Church with its communalizing of the anchorite and its theologizing of society, was revived in an extreme form by Luther. That was indeed, so far as practical consequences went, one of the major differences between the German and Swiss Reformationists: the former yielded up politics and economics to the secular powers and so arrived, by simple subtraction, to a religious life centered on the private soul. Eventually, in the nineteenth century, Lutheranism turned from Luther's precedent toward Calvin's. Some of its communicants evolved a "social gospel." Revealingly enough, to achieve this they had to reach beyond Luther, beyond Paul, beyond even Jesus, to the Hebrew Prophets for sanction and content. But though in the end a rebellion arose against the nonsociality of the Lutheran way, it came after Kierkegaard's time and too late to affect him.

To confirm the already marked individualism of the Reformation religion went its doctrine of the Church. Under the Catholic dispensation the Church was conceived as indispensable to the soul, there being no salvation outside it and the dogmas and sacraments it administered. Religion then, even though it might seek the salvation of the individual, was necessarily social in its expression. With the Reformation, however, that theory was displaced by a congregational conception whereunder redemption became a transaction between each individual man and God. It was Christ directly, immediately, who was the mediator. As for the Church, its proper function was now to serve, before the saving moment, as a guide in its direction; and, after, as an assembly of the Elect in the eyes of men. But since even this limited role could be construed as an invasion by a human institution into the redemptive prerogatives of the Christ, among some Protestant sects the Church was whittled down further until it all but ceased to exist.

Thus, when Kierkegaard ended up an anti-ecclesiast, he

was doing no more than traveling the same road to the same goal at which other tangential Protestant groups had arrived before him.

In the case of his next antinomy—the Moment *versus* History—its traditional Christian derivation, while less obvious than with the others, is nevertheless not difficult to trace. The prevailing Christian tradition has always been strongly historicist. How could it be otherwise with a faith which reaches its apogee in an event regarded as the fulfillment of the ages, and expects an even higher climax in a second event at the end of days? The Augustinian schematization of history as an interplay through the centuries between the City of God and the City of Man—Apocalypse, Millenarianism, Eschatology—these are all expressions of the deep Christian preoccupation with time. But against that there is another, a narrower yet no less authentic stream of Christian thought, which flows not downward through the succession of incidents but circularly about one, which considers as consequential not time and its episodes but a single Moment only, that of the Cross. These were the waters of Kierkegaard's baptism.

As for the texture of man's temperament, as Kierkegaard described it, dread is the warp, powerlessness the woof. A dark fabric to begin with, it is rendered darker still when interwoven with such threads of Christian dogma as Original Sin and *sola gratia*. Under these doctrines man, born in corruption and predestined to damnation, is altogether without the power to save himself. Which is the meaning of the anti-Pelagianism of the Catholic Church, and of the anti-Arminianism of the Protestant. Under the former, Christendom rejected as heresy the suggestion that man can achieve anything toward his salvation outside the Church. Under the latter, he is conceived as standing in even a more parlous pass, first because he is now adjudged a creature of total depravity, without a single merit, and second because not even the Church can aid him. Only God can save; and, since man is deserving of naught, God can save only as an act of pure grace.

This is original Protestantism. Witness the repudiation by the Protestant world of Melanchthon's proposal of Synergism: the thesis that man may co-operate with God in his own deliverance. This is the teaching of the neo-Reformation school in our own time. Witness Barth's insistence that man, the drowning swimmer, is incapable of even a single feeble stroke to keep afloat; that the rescue is to the last effort God's.

Here, then, is the root of Kierkegaard's despair as to man's capacities. It is a despair deriving in part from the precariousness of the human situation, but even more from the inability of the individual to do anything about it—a despair, in a word, which, like the rest of the antinomies, comes to him from the Lutheranism of his rearing.

Now historic Judaism and historic Christianity, being kindred religions, share all sorts of presuppositions. The fact that a thesis is Christian does not exclude it from the possibility of being Jewish. The probabilities, in fact, are quite the reverse. Yet the distinctive points of Kierkegaard's position, those caught in the antinomies, are one and all non-Jewish; indeed, so far as they go, they are the crucial issues at stake between catholic Judaism and universal Christianity. But in varying degrees.

Least clearly definable is the position of Judaism on the first of the five antinomies, that between faith and reason. Of conflicts on the philosophy-*versus*-religion or science-*versus*-religion level Jewish thought has its quota. Such is the purport of the first chapter of Saadya's *Emunoth v'Deoth* and of the entire Maimunist controversy. Like other men professing a revealed religion, Jews have debated whether speculative inquiry is necessary or permissible and, if so, what may be the status of its conclusions vis-à-vis religious verities. But the possibility that faith and reason should be ideally exclusive of each other has little troubled traditionally minded Jewish thinkers.

They neglected to consider that possibility for one simple reason: they had no reason to. Paradox may inhere in all religious affirmation; but where Christianity must glory in it, Judaism need not. Its central position is neither "absurd" nor an "affront" to reason. It is involved in no mysteries like that of the Trinity-Unity, of which one has no choice but to say *credo quia absurdum est* ("I believe because it is absurd"). It sets forth no Gods who are yet mortals. It does not rest on the premise that the death of one man can atone for the sins of other men. All these are notions truly impenetrable to reason. Against them Jewish theology is purely of God, an object of faith to be sure, but by no means of faith against reason; of revelation, miraculous of course, but scarcely a scandal to rationality; of the election of Israel and human redeemability by moral effort, positions complex and difficult enough, and undemonstrable to boot; but in every case, compared to Christian dogma, comprehensibility itself. As is attested by the fact that "natural religion" approaches many of these basic Jewish positions.

Historic Judaism does include some elements totally impenetrable to the intellect—such a tenet, for example, as Resurrection; such a ritual as the *Parah Adumah* (the red heifer, Numbers 19). But even with these, neither virtue nor principle is made of obscurity or mystery. To the contrary, the prevailing effort has always been to rationalize.

Not that such efforts were regarded with universal favor. Some of the ancient rabbis objected to inquiring into the *taamei hamitzvoth*, the purpose of the commandments. The anti-Maimunists sought to ban all philosophical inquiry. But these rabbis, whether ancient or the medieval, were motivated by a kind of antirationalism worlds apart from Kierkegaard's. Their objection to speculation was pragmatic: that with revelation available it is superfluous; or, by its stubborn questioning, disturbing to faith; or, given human limitations, foredoomed to failure. No Jewish thinker is on record as advancing Kierkegaard's contention of the radical incompatibility of religious truth and reason. To the contrary, the common Jewish assumption has always been that the two for God are one, as they would be one for man were his powers of comprehension equal to the theme.

Nor is the Jewish conception of God at all conducive to anti-intellectualism along the lines of the Lutheran-Calvinist.

Kierkegaard, as we have already seen, was predisposed to such a conclusion by, among other things, the notion of a God who is Will rather than Reason. Admittedly, the Jewish tradition shows traces of a similar position on the part of some Jewish thinkers: such a characterization of God as in Exodus 33:19: "I will be gracious to whom I will be gracious, and will show mercy on whom I will show mercy"; such ideas as the *En-Sof* of Kabbalism, whereunder God is pure Being before He unfolds moral or intellectual qualities. Notions of this sort, however, are the exception.

The prime distinction among God's attributes drawn in rabbinic literature is between His justice and His mercy. Medieval Jewish philosophers as a rule demonstrate first the existence of God and then His other attributes, intellectual and moral. That is a matter of forensics almost altogether. The fact is that those thinkers agree one and all, whatever their argumentative procedures, that God is simultaneously and co-essentially existent, moral and free; that, in sum, whatever He is or does or ordains, all makes equal intellectual and moral sense.

From the Jewish viewpoint, God remains beyond man's reason, perhaps beyond all reason. He cannot be counter to it, rationality pertaining to His nature.

Kierkegaard's antirationalism is thus altogether a Christian, more exactly a Lutheran-Calvinist, but not in the

slightest degree a Jewish, necessity. Nor does anything in
Judaism correspond to Kierkegaard's teleological suspension of the ethical.

From the Jewish viewpoint—and this is one of its highest dignities—the ethical is never suspended, not under any
circumstance and not for anyone, not even for God. *Especially not for God!* Are not supreme Reality and supreme
Goodness one and co-essential to the Divine nature? If so,
every act wherein the Good is put aside is more than a
breach of His will; it is in effect a denial of His existence.
Wherefore the rabbis define sin as constituting not merely
rebellion but atheism as well.

What Kierkegaard asserts to be the glory of God is
Jewishly regarded as unmitigated sacrilege. Which indeed
is the true point of the *Akedah,* missed so perversely by
Kierkegaard. While it was a merit in Abraham to be willing to sacrifice his only son to his God, it was God's nature
and merit that He would not accept an immoral tribute.
And it was His purpose, among other things, to establish
that truth.

In sum, the secondary antinomy of Kierkegaard turns
out, like the first, alien to Judaism.

So equally with the third, disjoining the individual from
others and society.

In the Jewish view, as Buber has demonstrated, it is a
false exclusion of which Kierkegaard has here been guilty.
The fulfilled human life requires, in both theory and fact,
the simultaneous affirmation and sanctification of both the
self and the community. "If I be not for myself," asked
Hillel, "who will be for me? But if I be for myself alone,
what am I?" Each man, the tradition insists, must seek the
redemption of his own soul; but at the same time the "per-
fecting of the world under the Kingdom of the Almighty."

In his fourth antinomy, the negation of history, Kierkegaard, as we have observed, is out of harmony with the
dominant Christian tradition itself. As to Judaism, the dis-

crepancy is total. Contemplating a Creation and Revelation in the past and a Resurrection and Kingdom of God in the future, the Jewish tradition is historical throughout. This is not to say that it is "historicist." Judaism does not hold that mere time regenerates men, or history by itself redeems society. Only the decisions of the human spirit are determinative—of the individual to his own salvation, of all men to the achievement of the Kingdom; and neither, of course, ever without God. Yet time and history, like the air men breathe and the space in which they move, are the necessary preconditions for the working out of their destiny.

They are not merely inert, environmental media. They are living, even if not crucial factors, both in the career of the soul (here Kierkegaard might assent) and in that of society (here he would disagree altogether). Indeed, no sharper contrast than on this score can be found between Judaism and Christianity in its Kierkegaardian version. On the latter side is the insistence that "the history of the race" is a merely "quantitative accumulation," that is, a meaningless piling up of more and more of the same thing. On the other hand we have such teachings as Isaiah's "end of days," the rabbinic "future to come" and the "merits of the fathers," and the Kabbalist schema whereunder each soul that lives hastens or retards, by the tempo of its return to its Primal Source, the descent and ascent of the last soul, the Messiah's.

Poles apart on whether the Moment is all, Judaism and Kierkegaard are if possible even further apart on the fifth antinomy—the issue of man's own ability to do anything of consequence toward the alleviation of his plight. The plight is one of anguished intensity, Judaism agrees. But that the human condition is beyond hope Judaism denies, with fourfold warrant.

In the first place Judaism does not, like Kierkegaard, set

up a disjuncture between the aesthetic and ethical, and again between the two of them together and the religious. Nor is this a matter of theoretical import only. Kierkegaard is thereby impelled to regard all pleasures, whether sensual or aesthetic, as at best spiritually indifferent, more likely deleterious; all principled morality as at the most a preparation for something else, rather than as anything in itself; all scientific and speculative thought as a diversion from the religious encounter. Once so much that contributes to the joy and meaning of life has been depreciated or rejected—in any case, ruled out as a field of God's service—little wonder that the human prospect comes to appear inordinately limited and bleak.

Judaism takes a stand of clear opposition to all that. It maintains that God can be encountered, and accordingly salvation can be furthered, in anything man feels and does, so long as it is felt and done "in holiness," that is, in obedience to God's will.

With its pleasures and activities legitimized, its opportunities for service of the Divine multiplied times beyond number, life very naturally takes on another, a brighter guise. If the evil in it is still as grave as in the Kierkegaardian view, its good is larger, more variegated, more readily accessible.

Second, where Kierkegaard can discern but one hope for man, the deliverance of his soul, Judaism espies another also, the regeneration of society. This is no little thing, this goal of the Kingdom. It throws a second light and warmth on all human existence.

Third and fourth, Judaism has greater confidence than has Kierkegaard in God and in man.

This is the Deity which Kierkegaard, after the pattern of Paul and the Reformationists, depicts: a God who first made men imperfect and then demands sinlessness from them—wherefore He took on flesh and died as an atonement for them—who offers them deliverance but on the condition that they believe, a capacity, however, which lies not in their power but in His to give or withhold. The greatest thing of all, Salvation, is altogether by Grace, since no man has the least shred of righteousness to plead for him. Does not this account of God's administration of His world make Him out as questionably just, incontrovertibly unmerciful?

Judaism's appraisal of man's powers is far more generous. They are not unlimited, to be sure; they are often severely circumscribed, as we too well know. But always, the Jewish tradition insists, there is some margin of self-determination. Always a man can do something, no matter how little, with his own soul. And that something may suffice to transform him into a *b'riah hadashah*, a new regenerated creature. If nothing else, a man can do *teshuvah*, he can repent—repent of the evil which heretofore he has loved and affirm the good which up to now he has scorned. By that the whole import of his life may be remade. He may even thereby, and thereby alone, come to merit salvation, according to the rabbinic teaching concerning those who "acquire Eternity in one moment."

How can this be? First because man is a free agent. Everything may be preordained for him, said the sages of old, but not whether he will be righteous. That crucial issue is left to his own decision. It is a determination which not God Himself will coerce. A man's failure to attain perfection is no insuperable obstacle to his vindication. For, being just, God asks but does not exact perfection from one whom He made frail and fallible. "He remembers that we are dust." Not impeccability is required of man, but earnestness of striving toward it. "Not thine to finish the work, but neither art thou free to quit it."

Then is man not in need of God's grace? Of course; all the time and in everything. But that grace is not to be supposed as only exceptional and crucial, as it were, a lightning flash of redemptive mercy breaking unpredictably into and through normality. There is that grace described in the *Siddur* as the "miracles which are daily with us, the wonders and goodnesses which are at all times, evening, morn, and noon." This is the grace manifest in the Torah's guidance and in "the merits of the fathers," the examples and admonitions of the righteous, in the *yezer tov* (good instinct), conscience, and aspiration toward the good, and above all, in the uninterrupted magnetic pull of God. It is a grace always at work, ever available, never failing. All a man need do to have it is to call for it in truth. Even as it is said: "he who setteth out to be purified, from heaven do they help him."

This is the supreme and ultimate reason why Judaism, conscious with Kierkegaard of the human ordeal and peril, does not yield to his despair. It knows that man is stronger, and God is greater in justice and mercy, than he allowed.

Analogies in history are never exact. Yet in many respects Existentialism of the Kierkegaardian stripe is to Judaism in our day what Gnosticism was at the beginning of the Common Era—an alluring but dangerous heresy. There were virtues in that doctrine as in this: inwardness, mystical sensibility, a passion and groping for truths but coldly or imperfectly comprehended by conventional religion, a returning to the primary experiences from which all formal faith stems, and a penetrating feeling for the dilemmas and torments of human existence.

But there were grave failings also. Gnosticism, like Existentialism, abandoned natural reason, the one for esotericism, the other for faith. Like the latter the former also suspended and secondarized and so, in the end, perverted moral values; abandoned the group in its concern for the self; considered only the saving moment but not history, personal salvation but not the Kingdom of God;

and, out of despair, surrendered the world to the demiurge, looking for salvation in flight.

To one doctrine as to the other the proper Jewish response is that of Rabbi Meir when he said, concerning the teachings of his heretic master Elisha ben Abuyah, "As with a pomegranate, one eats the seed and throws the rind away."

PART THREE

VI

The Theological Issues of the Hour

Characteristic of American-Jewish life during the past hundred years has been its consistent, stubborn, and— given the intellectual revolutions of the twentieth century —almost miraculous avoidance of theology. To be sure, in the late nineteenth century the theologians of Reform Judaism set about the task of importing and modifying German Reform theology. Its efforts, notably the work of Kaufmann Kohler and Isaac Mayer Wise, were more of the order of spiritual plastic surgery than of the order of theology. There were justifiable reasons for this neglect of theology—the pressing requirements of social adjustment, the external threat of anti-Semitism, and, in the twentieth century, the deteriorating condition of world Jewry and the rise of Zionism, defined the living situation, in contrast to which theology appeared either frivolous or tragically wasteful.

The situation of Judaism in the forties and fifties has radically altered. Jewry is no longer under threat (although to be sure three million Jews are lost behind the Iron Curtain); Zionism is fulfilled; and American Jews are prosperous and content. With security comes lassitude, and with lassitude boredom. If Judaism is merely to be preserved as a device of survival, as insulation against the ravages of a hostile world, then, the danger past, Judaism may pass.

It is in response to this state of affairs that Jewish the-

ology is redivivus. Survivalist theologies are on the wane; theologies that perform the task of rationalizing Jewish practice and worship as instrumentalities of self-preservation and group identity are under scrutiny. That scrutiny began with the work of Milton Steinberg.

Steinberg was, above all else, a refractor of the influence of his time. He summarizes and focuses both the brilliance and the limitations of his era—its uncompromising rationality and its hopeful and undisillusioned liberalism. Now, a decade later, his summation of the forms of theological speculation in the late thirties and forties may appear yet too unrealistic, too robust, too confident. This was his way and, perhaps, his genius. He succeeded, as no one else had succeeded in the American rabbinate, in translating the concepts of contemporary theology and metaphysics into their Jewish coefficients. He served to bridge the widening gap between Jewish intellectuals outside the synagogue and believing Jews within it. "The Theological Issues of the Hour," an almost personal exposure of Steinberg's own uninterrupted intellectual pilgrimage, is remarkable for its scope, its learning, and its unparalleled (for the rabbinate) familiarity and assimilation of Christian theological literature.

The form which "The Theological Issues of the Hour" takes deserves a final note of explanation. The rubrics, subtopics, methodological cautions and qualifications which mark this essay, derive from the occasion of its preparation. At the instance of the Rabbinical Assembly of America, the membership organization of those rabbis affiliated with Conservative Judaism, Steinberg was asked to deliver a survey lecture on the state of contemporary theology at its annual convention in June, 1949. This lecture, here presented in slightly revised and corrected form, is intended to expose the range and relevance of non-Jewish thought to Judaism.

"The Theological Issues of the Hour" is reprinted with the permission of the Rabbinical Assembly of America.

EDITOR

The winds of theological doctrine now astir, are they random breezes that will soon have blown over or signs of enduring changes in the spiritual weather? Even if they be the former, they merit our attention. May we say of the varieties of the religious life other than of the human, that nothing in it can be alien to us? But if the other alternative hold, that is to say, if these be omens of some new meteorological era, then we would certainly be well-advised to consider them carefully. For in them are discernible the first auguries of the atmosphere of the future, to which we shall, in some fashion or other, have to accommodate ourselves if we and our souls are to survive. What is more, since some at least of the qualities of the new climate are uncongenial to normative Judaism, this paper· constitutes more than a weather report; it is, by implication, something of a storm warning as well.

Procedure

Any attempt at a comprehensive review of the theological innovations of recent years would exceed not only the compass of an essay but, even more hopelessly, my capacities. Instead, therefore, I shall undertake a more modest but also, I believe, a more immediately relevant enterprise. Out of the welter of current religious discourse, so far as I know it, I shall select for presentation and analysis those elements which challenge the positions commonly held among us and which have in them also something of the novel, or, if not that, then at the least of the unwonted.

Thus I shall pass over altogether any elaborations, no matter how original, of positions which are fundamentally conventional: the neo-Kantianisms, for example, or neo-Hegelianisms or epistemological idealisms after their varied species, and, in another direction, the whole horde of scientists who have been busy of late drawing religious deductions from the data of their fields.

Again, I shall make no attempt to deal with neo-Thomism, both because, being as a whole an almost literal translation into modern idiom of a medieval system, it lacks basic originality; but also because it has proved in no way challenging to the Jewish spirit—witness the fact that it has elicited no analogous Maimunism among Jews, and that despite the prestige of Maimonides in Jewish circles, and, in further despite of the old rule: *wie es christelt sich so judelt es sich*.

To this rule, that we shall concern ourselves only with the unfamiliar, there will be but one exception. Mordecai Kaplan's system of thought is no novelty to us. But such is its inherent power, such also the thoroughness of our exposure to it that, as a major influence in our spiritual lives, we cannot consider it too carefully. Without then attempting anything like comprehensive treatment of it, I shall nevertheless not pass it by when reference to it is indicated.

Among the thought currents of the hour we shall concentrate on four:

I. Existentialism, primarily of Kierkegaard but also, though in lesser degree, of others, notably Rosenzweig and Buber.

II and III. Neo-Reformationism, which only a few years ago gave the impression of being a unitary phenomenon but which more recently has split into two divergent schools of thought, namely: the neo-Orthodox or Continental, of which Karl Barth is the founder and chief exponent, and to which Emil Brunner stands half as proponent and half as antagonist; and the American or, to use the nomenclature of Tillich, the neo-Dialectical, which embraces Tillich himself and both Reinhold and H. Richard Niebuhr.

IV. The final universe of discourse which we shall invade lies in a direction antipodal to Existentialism and neo-Reformationism. It is the domain of speculative metaphysics in which are current these days some highly unconventional but also highly stimulating proposals concerning Deity.

Such are the fourfold sources of the materials of our investigation. The fields of interest on which we shall bring them to bear are three:

I. Religious truth and its warranties.
II. The nature of God.
III. Man and society.

●

I • *Religious Truth*

Faith to a degree unprecedented in modern times is being set over against reason, and revelation above self-determining thought.

A. FAITH AGAINST REASON

The boldest and most consequential inclination of the *Zeitgeist* is toward the rejection of the intellect as an instrument for the attaining of truth in general, religious truth in particular, and certainty on any score most particularly of all.

Once men believed in the powers of their own minds with a confidence that penetrated not only philosophy and science but theology as well. Among the Christians, Hegel, Ritschl, and Troeltsch were radically rationalistic; among Jews, Krochmal, Graetz, and Hermann Cohen. As for Kaplan, he is in this respect, as in so many others, *sui generis*. On the one hand, as an instrumentalist, his final criterion of a proposition is not logical tenability but concrete consequence. To that extent he is, like all pragmatists, technically an anticonceptualist. But no one, on the other hand, can be more insistent than he that nothing shall

160

stand exempted from critical analysis, nor is anyone more ready to follow an argument to its end, regardless of whither it may lead—in which respect he is an archrationalist.

As for the rest of us, most of us have been so schooled as to be reluctant to subscribe to any assertion which cannot make some sort of showing before the bar of reason. Wherein we are disclosed as being very much the children of our age.

An age, however, now apparently drawing to a close. In philosophy the beginning of the end began with Hume; it received added impetus at the hands of Lobachevski and his non-Euclidian geometry, of Marx and Freud with their insistence that supposedly objective thought is often actually rationalization; an age, finally, for whose hopes and confidences contemporary pragmatism and intuitionism stand as veritable epitaphs.

As for religion, apart from orthodoxy and mysticism, which have never ceased to constitute a hard core of resistance to the prevailing rationalism, the first significant assertion of an anti-intellectualist position was that of Sören Kierkegaard.

Kierkegaard's opposition to reason in religion derives, as I have sought to show elsewhere,[1] at least in part from specific Christian necessities: from the Church's conception of a God who on one occasion became flesh; from the Protestant notion of a Deity who predestines men, in advance of birth, a few to eternal bliss, the rest to eternal damnation. With a religion affirming such doctrines, logic transparently can have little in common. Little wonder then that Kierkegaard asserts not only that faith transcends reason—a conception which almost all religionists will accept—but that

• • •

[1] "Kierkegaard and Judaism," *The Menorah Journal* (Spring, 1949), pp. 163-80; the present volume, pp. 130-152.

it is its antagonist, an "affront," a "scandal," a "stumbling block" to it.

But the anti-intellectualism of Kierkegaard, while in large share a dictate of Christian creed, represents also a protest of living faith against philosophical abstractions, against such caricatures of religious affirmation as Hegel's God, a complete abstrusity, an absolute Idea which is Mind in general without being an actual mind at all, a God worlds apart from the one Kierkegaard knew from Scripture, from his father's anguished piety, from his own gropings.

The antirationalism of Karl Barth was, to begin with, Kierkegaardian and existentialist in motivation. Later he cut out of his thought "everything that . . . might give the slightest appearance of giving to theology a basis, support, or even a mere justification in the way of Existential philosophy." The anti-intellectualism, however, survived; indeed it took on heightened vigor, but for reasons peculiar to Barth's thought.

God, he insists, is the infinite, the absolute, the subject of all reality. As such He must of necessity be *totaliter aliter*, wholly other from the universe and man, which are the finite, the relative, the created, the object. But if this be truly so, there can be no approach to God through reason.

"Neither my affirmation nor my denial lays claim to being God's truth." [2] "One cannot speak of God simply by speaking of man in a loud voice." [3]

From which it follows relentlessly that there can be no *theologia naturalis*, no knowledge whatsoever concerning the divine nature which derives from the observation of the

•••

[2] Quoted by H. R. Mackintosh, in *Types of Modern Theology* (New York: Charles Scribner's Sons, n.d.), p. 267.

[3] Karl Barth, *The Word of God and the Word of Man*, trans. by Douglas Horton (Boston: The Pilgrim Press, 1928), p. 196.

universe and man. It is this thesis which is the major point at issue between Emil Brunner and Barth in the exchange of essays contained in the volume *Natural Theology*.[4] Brunner holds that though only revelation can afford a knowledge of God adequate to salvation, reason can achieve at least to some intimations of Him. With such temporizing Barth will have no traffic. Revelation apart, he insists, there is no knowledge of God whatsoever. "Every attempt to assert a general revelation," he maintains, "has to be rejected."[5] One theology, and one theology alone, merits to be called a theology, a doctrine of God, and that is the theology which is the *ministerium verbi divini*, the exposition of the word of God as contained in Scripture and even more explicitly in the Incarnation.

From the extremism of this position not only does Brunner dissent but the neo-Dialectical school even more vigorously—which is the first point of departure between it and Protestant neo-Orthodoxy. Thus Tillich is strongly condemnatory of Barth's antirationalist methodology, characterizing it as a state of mind which knows no other device except "to repeat the 'Yes' to its own and the 'No' to every other position."[6] And Niebuhr discerns in Barth's position an attempt "to establish Biblical authority over the mind and conscience of the Christian with as little recourse as possible to any norms of truth or right which may come to us out of the broad sweeps of classical European or modern cultural history."[7]

Yet this very defense of reason on the part of the neo-

• • •

[4] Karl Barth and Emil Brunner, *Natural Theology*, trans. by Peter Fraenkel (London: Geoffrey Bles, 1946).

[5] *Ibid.*, p. 74.

[6] Paul Tillich, *The Protestant Era*, trans. by James Luther Adams (Chicago: The University of Chicago Press, 1948), p. xiii.

[7] Reinhold Niebuhr, "We Are Men and Not God," *The Christian Century* (Oct. 27, 1948), p. 1138.

Dialecticals is itself a condemnation. For though they refuse to follow Barth in his extremism, though they insist
on the utility, the propriety, the necessity of the intellect in
religious pursuits, they do not look to it for the saving
truth. On this score they are at one with their opponent: it
is elsewhere than from thought that deliverance must be
awaited. Only in the revealed word is the *vraie vérité* to be
discovered, and salvation only in the God made manifest
in a God-man.

B. THE NEW REVELATIONISM

Our discussion of Barth and his disciple-opponents has led
directly to a second distinctive doctrine of the hour, the
one which, attending anti-intellectualism, prevents it from
eventuating in a total agnosticism. I have in mind the new
revelationism. This I term "new" because in certain essen-
tials it differs from either form of revelationism known to
the past.

There is, first of all, original, precritical revelationism,
the unswerving acceptance of Scripture as revealing the
nature and the will of God, and this in every idea, word,
and letter. This revelationism, natural and spontaneous during the Middle Ages, survives in our time in one of two
forms. In areas of Jewry and Christendom into which latter-
day thought has not penetrated, it continues in its pristine
spontaneity. Elsewhere, where modernity has made inroads,
it takes the form of fundamentalism, that is to say, a perseverance in faith in the literal validity of the Scriptural
text, but a faith now deliberately and effortfully maintained.

The second revelationism, the modernist or critical, recognizes the relevance of scientific inquiry to the Bible and
accepts its conclusions, all professedly without surrendering
the doctrine of Scriptural inspiration. Not the letter of
Scripture, it holds, nor the text nor the details are divinely
given, but the spirit, the central intuitions, the core asser-

tions. So apparently one investigates the Bible freely and at the same time retains faith in its authority and validity. But only apparently. For among modernists, as those of us who are of this stripe will admit in moments of candor, truth is determined not by the Bible but by reason and experience. Scripture is accepted as binding only insofar as its assertions conform to conclusions derived from other sources, ultimate reliance reposing not in the Bible as God's word but in the powers of human thought.

And now, alongside of these two older forms of revelationism, a third has appeared which in contrast with the other two may fairly be named postcritical. Here one encounters neither orthodoxy's antagonism to criticism nor modernism's capitulation. Unlike the former, postcritical revelationism sets up no resistance against free, scientific exploration into the Bible. To the contrary, it may join in the enterprise. Only it insists that true and interesting as the outcome may be factually, it must be irrelevant to essential religion. Against the modernist, in the other direction, the postcritical position assigns a cognitive role to Scripture. That is to say, it looks to it for the truth necessary to man's salvation, in advance and independent of the disclosure of it by other disciplines, indeed, beyond their reach altogether. In a word, the new revelationism, without withdrawing its hand from Higher Criticism, still holds to the Bible as the supreme, indeed unique, source of religious truth.

The first intimations of this new revelationism appear with Kierkegaard. To him Biblical scholarship is but a "century-long parenthesis" in the quest for salvation, an absorbing pursuit, no doubt, but quite unrelated to man's serious business. Conformably to this viewpoint Kierkegaard does not hesitate to apply the word "myth" to Scriptural episodes, even those of such significance as Abraham's sacrifice of Isaac. But—and this is typical of postcritical revelationism—his use of the term goes hand in hand with an insistence that in this "myth" there is contained a truth which is not only essential to man's deliverance but not otherwise attainable.

So also with Barth, who, schooled though he has been in Higher Criticism, is nevertheless most firm that "the word of God is in the Bible." [8] In contrast to the modernists, he means this so earnestly and thoroughly that he is capable of saying: "We do not seek God elsewhere than in His work, we do not think of Him save with His work, we speak nothing of Him save through His word." [9] Nor is this mere preachment. Barth will assent to no course, whether of thought or action, without Scriptural warrant. "One . . . must always fundamentally think and argue . . . from definite Biblical texts and contexts." [10] And he is quick to accuse even his fellow neo-Reformationists of the "irresponsible attitude . . . to theologize on their own account, that is to say, without asking on what Biblical grounds one puts forward this or that professedly Christian view."

As is to be expected in the light of what has gone before, the neo-Dialecticals who have already refused to follow Barth in his anti-intellectualism refuse to follow him in his total and exclusive reliance on Scripture.

To Reinhold Niebuhr, Barth's position is straight "Biblical literalism." [11] Paul Tillich is as much out of sympathy with this thesis of Barth as with so much else in his thought.[12]

Yet, if these neo-Dialecticals are neither precritical fun-

• • •

[8] *Op. cit.*, p. 43.

[9] Quoted by H. R. Mackintosh, in *Types of Modern Theology*, p. 269.

[10] Karl Barth, "Continental vs. Anglo-Saxon Theology," *The Christian Century* (Feb. 16, 1949), p. 203.

[11] Reinhold Niebuhr, "An Answer to Karl Barth," *The Christian Century* (Feb. 23, 1949). Cf. also Reinhold Niebuhr, *Faith and History* (New York: Charles Scribner's Sons, 1949), p. 166.

[12] Paul Tillich, *op. cit.*, p. xxvii.

damentalists nor Barthians, they are also no modernists.
They do not determine the truth for themselves and then
commend and accept Scripture insofar as it conforms to it.
Their position is that defined by H. Richard Niebuhr in
The Meaning of Revelation. Reason belongs, he contends,
in all things. Nothing is free, he contends further, from
historical relativity, not even Scripture. And yet within
Scripture there is a core truth, a disclosure of God which
is central to human life and beyond time and its permutations. "The revelatory occasion and idea," he says, "have
remained constant." [13] Most pertinently of all, this core disclosure of Scripture is something the intellect cannot have
discovered for itself in advance of the fact of revelation
nor validate after it. Or as Reinhold Niebuhr puts it, the
truth of faith is not "capable of simple correlation with any
system of rational coherence." [14]

Of particular interest to us as Jews is the spilling over
of the new revelationism into Jewish thought. Already an
occasional Jewish thinker is to be found—Jacob Taubes,
for example—who has taken over the Barthian position
almost bodily, with, needless to say, the one immensely
significant difference that where the Christian finds the
supremely unique and sufficient revelation in the Incarnation, Taubes discerns it in the Torah. Contrariwise, antici-
pations of the neo-Dialecticals and especially of H. Richard
Niebuhr are to be found in Buber. In the *I and Thou*
and the *"Zweisprache"* [15] there is implicit a full awareness
of Biblical criticism, and yet the fact of revelation continues as the central actuality, the first and continuing

• • •

[13] H. Richard Niebuhr, *The Meaning of Revelation* (New
York: The Macmillan Company, 1941), p. 111.

[14] Reinhold Niebuhr, *Faith and History,* p. 165.

[15] Martin Buber, *I and Thou* (New York: Charles Scribner's
Sons, 1937); *"Zweisprache"* (1929), translated as "Dialogue,"
Between Man and Man (New York: The Macmillan Company,
1948).

source, of all religious truth. Indeed, as Agus points out,[16] the Buber-Rosenzweig translation of Scripture was designed deliberately to show Scripture forth as a revelatory dialogue. As for Rosenzweig, nowhere does the spirit of the new revelationism find clearer expression than in his suggestion that if divine inspiration is not to be ascribed to the several component texts of the Torah, it cannot be withheld from the Redactor, their editor.[17] Here one sees vividly exhibited the special character of the postcritical position: its readiness to subject the Scriptural text to criticism and a simultaneous perseverance of faith in it as the special and unrivaled source and norm of truth.

The new anti-intellectualism and revelationism, unlike Topsy, have not "just growed." They represent, rather, reactions against prevailing states of religious affairs which have been found unacceptable, indeed intolerable, by men who, whatever else they may be, are indisputably of high intelligence and earnestness. The remedies prescribed may be questionable, the maladies are not.

If there be extremism in the anti-intellectualism of Kierkegaard, there is also a valid protest and a necessary exhortation: the protest, against a rationalism which rarefies the living God of religious faith to an abstract idea, to be apprehended only in remote objectivity and by means of precise, refrigerated concepts; the exhortation, to a God who is infinitely more, rather than less, actual than His believers and who, though He can never be grasped, can be approached, if at all, only in a passion of inwardness and committedness.

In Barth, too, there is something sound and valuable: a repudiation, justifiably indignant, of the *hubris* of the reli-

• • •

[16] Jacob Agus, *Modern Philosophies of Judaism* (New York: Behrman's Book House, 1941), p. 145.

[17] Franz Rosenzweig, *Briefe* (Berlin: Schocken Verlag, 1935), pp. 581-82.

gious rationalists who claim to be carrying God around in their vest pockets, to have Him all tidily packaged, deliverable on request, in neat conceptual containers. Against such arrogance the *totaliter aliter* of Barth is an overdramatic but thoroughly merited slap in one's metaphysical face.

The new revelationism too has its warrant. It is in the first place an outcry against the hypocrisy of modernist religion's pretending that it looks to Scripture for religious truth when actually it does not. It is also in great measure a frank admission of the fact that by logic alone there is no achieving of religious certainty. As Bergson pointed out, one can always reason with reason. A need therefore exists, an inescapable need, for an act of faith. And, since an act of faith must be *in* something, Scripture is as good a locus as any.

There is, then, a case, a provocation if you will, for every phase of the new departure. Yet when all is said and done, our over-all judgment must be that, sound as recent anti-intellectualism may be *qua* protest, it is gravely perilous *qua* program.

In the first place, and as I have already indicated, much of it is a Christian, but not in any wise a Jewish, necessity. Professing no Gods who are yet men, no vicarious atonement of sins, no trinities that are somehow unities, no justification of one man and damnation of another, though both are equally sinners, professing in sum none of the paradoxes of Christianity, we Jews are subject to little of the motivation which impels Christians to the glorification of the unintelligible.

This is not to say that Judaism is a religion of reason after the fashion of Maimonides or Hermann Cohen. To the contrary it has its mysteries and nonrationalities. What is more, it has had its quota of antirationalists, those who have objected to seeking out the "reasons for the *mitz-*

voth,"[18] or engaging in theological speculation. My point is only this, that antirationalism is not essential to it as to the forms of Protestantism we are now considering, and that, in any case, no point of pride or principle has ever been made of spurning the intellect.

Again, there is about the antirationalism we are considering an intellectual disingenuousness. The advocate of the position uses the reason he rejects not only to justify his rejection but also to point toward, if not actually to establish, his proposed alternative to it. Kierkegaard despises conceptualism but he is not above employing it so far as it suits his purpose. And Barth claims to stand on the Word alone; his writing reveals the hollowness of the claim.

Nor could it be otherwise. Reason may be, as its derogators assert, a limited, unsteady, uncreative instrument, but it is one of the few in man's kit; it is the only one by which decision can be made among supposed truths in conflict; it constitutes finally the sole, but literally the sole, pipe line for the communication of ideas. There is then no escaping it by any device, not in any sphere of human interest, not even in religion.

Not even by positing a revelation. The most fundamentalist of revelationists must resort to the intellect, if only to establish the meaning of the text he accepts and to impart it to others. As for the postcritical revelationists, they certainly cannot obviate its use. For how, without it, can they discriminate between Scripture as a whole and that supreme truth which by their lights it contains? How far indeed revelationism fails from being able to dispense with reason is to be seen from the disagreements between Barth

• • •

[18] The Hebrew expression, *"taamei ha-mitzvoth,"* means "the reasons for the divine commandments." Running from the rabbinic literature to the present there is an extensive effort to seek out and define the *raison d'être* of the positive and negative commandments making up traditional Jewish law.—EDITOR.

and Brunner and the even larger differences between them and H. Richard Niebuhr. Here is a trio of postcritical revelationists who, though they agree that the truth is in the Bible, disagree as to its nature in detail and in the large. Which means that even they must end up, willy-nilly and be it ever so reluctantly, in the rationalists' camp, making appeals to reason in the attempt to establish their respective interpretations of Scripture.

But the gravest charges to be leveled against the anti-intellectualists are not disingenuousness and inconsistency, but the fostering of an evil, and this is unnecessary.

To reject reason is to throw off the yoke of speculative responsibility, to give free reign to wishful thinking. Only the critical intellect keeps the religious imagination in check and prevents it from doctrinal license. This anarchy, however, is invited by the anti-intellectualists in their desire to establish religion more securely. Were there no other course than this, were the grounding of faith possible by no other method than the depreciation of reason, this would still be a venture too hazardous to be lightly launched, perhaps to be launched at all. It happens, however—and this is the final offense of anti-intellectualists of the Kierkegaardian and Barthian stripe—that there is another way.

Both Kierkegaard and Barth talk freely about the Dialectical method whereby thought progresses by moving to and fro between opposing poles. But, on this vital instance, the extreme anti-intellectualist is *naeh doresh,* but not *naeh m'kayem.*[19] Forgetting dialectical procedures, he affirms one term absolutely, the thesis of faith, but the other, the antithesis which is reason, he denies with equal resoluteness.

• • •

[19] The talmudic expression, *"naeh doresh, naeh m'kayem,"* means "he who preaches well and acts in conformity with his words."—EDITOR.

Not so does religious thought move responsibly, creatively, securely, but by affirming faith and reason simultaneously: faith to lay first postulates and, when the dialectical process has gone far enough, to evoke final, total, existential commitments; reason to present the possibilities as to first postulates and to exercise a never-ceasing vigilance against reckless, capricious, irresponsible leapings from them. In sum, the proper rule as to the relation between faith and reason is that commended by Koheleth: "It is good that thou shouldst take hold of the one; but from the other withdraw not thy hand." [20]

•

II • *The Nature of God*

A. THE RETURN OF TRANSCENDENTALISM

A rebellion is afoot these days against the immanentist conception of God, the notion of God which envisages Him within the world and man as their ground and life. This is the conception which has dominated religious thought ever since the Renaissance and the scientific revolution, reaching one climax in Spinoza and another in Hegel, numbering among its expositors thinkers as diverse and influential as Schleiermacher and Schelling, Eucken and Bergson, and meeting with sustained opposition only from Orthodoxy which, because of its traditionalism, is irrevocably committed to the older transcendentalism.

In this immanentism Judaism also has been involved. Hasidism partook of it, though for reasons that were social and psychological rather than scientific or philosophical, and in any case peculiar to the Jewish group. In our own

• • •

[20] Eccles. 7:18.

day immanentism is a prime force in American Judaism through Kaplanism,[21] God being conceived as the Power within the world and man that makes for salvation.

Kierkegaard marks the beginning of the reaction against immanentism as of so much else in latter-day religious thought. In him the transcendentalism of the Protestant church, so long automatic and devitalized, came to vigorous self-assertion. A transcendentalist by his Orthodox rearing, a transcendentalist out of disgust with the excesses of Hegel, whose God had been so absorbed into the flow of things that He was only their underlying Idea, he forswore immanentism and all its works. Against it his chief thesis is of the "eternal qualitative difference between God and man"; the "infinite qualitative difference between time and eternity."

In the same spirit Barth proclaims: "God is in heaven, you are on earth." And as for contact between the two, it is not, as the immanentist supposes, a matter of from within outward, but rather, in Barth's oft-quoted metaphor from geometry, an intercepting of the horizontal of time by the perpendicular of eternity.

H. Richard Niebuhr formulates the same distinction when he says: "The favorite predisposition of liberal theology is *within;* that of post-liberal theology, *over against.*"

Between the two alternatives—and this may be significant for more than himself—Buber occupies a middle ground. His God is transcendental, as apart from the world as the Thou from the I which addresses it, and yet not only in relation to it but in some measure determined by the relationship.

One swallow, even a flock of swallows, does not make a

• • •

[21] "Kaplanism," the name by which the philosophy of Mordecai Kaplan is known in Jewish circles. Cf. particularly his *The Meaning of God in Modern Jewish Religion* (New York: Behrman's Book House, 1937), Chapter II, "God as the Power That Makes for Salvation," pp. 40-103.—EDITOR.

spring. But this much seems sure: there is more transcend-entalism in contemporary religious speculation than there has been at any time since the implications of what Galileo read in the heavens and of what the Renaissance humanists discerned in man were drawn for systematic theology.

A considerable measure of immanentism in religion is a consummation devoutly to be wished for. It is of all theol-ogies the easiest to envisage. It gives warmth and dignity to nature and man, where transcendentalism devalues both. It accounts for the good, the true, and the beautiful in the world and the human soul. It brings God near and makes Him accessible.

But on those who set up God-the-immanent in place of God-the-transcendent, to the latter's exclusion, there can be no other appraisal than that their omission compromises the adequacy of what they accept. For they will be alien-ated from the Biblical tradition which is overwhelmingly transcendental. What is more, revelation for them will be little more than man's own discovery of the truth, couched though it is in pietist language. Again, since they conceive God as residing in all things, the individuality of each thing is blurred, tending to be swallowed up in the All, as has occurred not only in Eastern religions but in Spinoza, Hegel, and Schopenhauer. But the individual is both a high concern of historic Judaism and the rock on which any moral life of consequence must be built. They will, furthermore, since they regard all things as manifestations of God, be forced by the logic of their position to view them as good, thus erasing the distinction between good and evil or else at best relativizing it. Finally, since they no longer have a God apart from and above men, things, and events, they will have no stance from which judgment on them can be pronounced.

I have no desire to imitate the rabbi of the familiar tale who informed each litigant in a *din Torah* that he was in the right and then, when his startled *rebbetzin* asked how that could be, assured her that she was right also. Nevertheless both the practical requirements of the religious life and considerations of pure theory unite to compel the simultaneous acceptance of the transcendentalist and immanentist envisagement. As a matter of practice God must be conceived as present within and animating men and affairs or they will be denied both worth and meaning. At the same time, He cannot, for all the reasons already enumerated, be envisaged merely so, but needs to be understood also as standing above and apart.

What man needs is paralleled by the indications of disinterested thought. God must be the transcendent One, the Absolute, or He shall not have served His cognitive purpose of accounting for reality. He must be the Holy and Good, or He shall not discharge his ethical function as Lawgiver and Judge. And yet, the world as we know it is the relative to His absolute, the work of His hands, the arena of His governance, the scene of the fulfillment of His will. He must therefore somehow be in it and implicated with it.

What must be said concerning the new transcendentalism, especially in its extremist versions, as in Barth, is nothing other than what needs to be said concerning radical immanentism, namely, that it has inflated a half-truth to a whole and so perverted even the half.

B. THE NON-ABSOLUTE GOD

The next of the theological novelties to pass in review before us emerges from a universe of discourse radically different from those which have gone before. We set aside for a time Existentialism, neo-Reformationism, whether neo-Orthodox or neo-Dialectical, and Revelationism after its diverse forms. We concern ourselves instead with philosophies, metaphysical and pragmatic, and with a proposal made in certain philosophical quarters of a non-

Absolute God. This is a notion certainly not new in the history of thought. But only now for the first time is it being advocated not by the lunatic fringe of religion, by gnostics and theosophists, but by responsible thinkers making a case that can stand up under critical scrutiny.

Ever since Judaism, in the person of Philo, made contact with Greek metaphysics, the word God has been an unrecognized amphibology. On the one hand it has stood for the God of Scripture, a living Being with whom men enter into crucial relations, who can be pleased or grieved by their conduct, who is the Thou in the I-Thou complex, who discloses Himself in love and ethical demand, whose purposes men can advance, retard, or even defeat, who is therefore affected by and dependent upon them.

Over against this conception has been the other: a God who is an ultimate principle of being, a first and final cause, an unmoved mover of everything else, something timeless and unchanging, whose knowledge of all things must consist in an eternal foresight lest, by His very awareness of their change, He be tainted with their mutability. This is God the Absolute, elevated above all relationships including any of consequence with his worshipers. Such is the God of Philo, Maimonides, Aquinas, Spinoza, Hegel, and Bradley. It is the deity against whom Pascal rebelled when he cried out: "The God of Abraham, Isaac, and Jacob, but not the God of the philosophers!"

Pascal's choice has certainly been that of the masses of men. It has also been, in practical effect, the decision of the sophisticated, indeed of the philosophers themselves. For if they professed a religion and if it ever burst into flame, then, though they might talk the language of Absolutism, it was by a non-Absolute God that the fire was kindled.

And now, in recent decades, a new thing has been created: a non-Absolute conception of God propounded on either rationalist or pragmatic grounds.

An early expression of this doctrine, and one of considerable vogue and influence, is that of William James. James argues his case on this point as on all others from a pragmatist viewpoint, understanding by pragmatism the proposition that "the practical consequence is for us the whole of our conception of the object so far as that conception has positive significance at all." [22]

Consistent with this position, that the meaning of an idea is its affective and effective content, James looks at the actual role of religious doctrine in life and concludes: "Only thorough-going monists or pantheists believe in the Absolute. The God of our popular Christianity is but one member of a pluralistic system; I can hardly conceive of anything more different from the Absolute than the God, say, of Daniel or Isaiah." [23] What is more, "the only God worthy of the name must be finite." [24] And still again, "the line of least resistance, then, both in theology and philosophy, is to accept, along with super-human consciousness, the notion that it is not all-embracing . . . but finite, either in power or in knowledge, or in both at once." [25]

Between the pragmatism of James and that of Professor Kaplan there is one crucial point of agreement and one of dissent. Both are equally indifferent, indeed almost hostile, to metaphysical speculation. But where James, influenced by the theosophy of his father, finds the "affective" and "effective" content of the God idea in the mystical experience, Professor Kaplan, motivated by psychological, ethical, and social purposes, interprets God as "the sum of the animating, organizing forces and relationships which are

• • •

[22] William James, *The Varieties of Religious Experience* (New York: Longmans, Green and Co., 1902), p. 445.

[23] William James, "A Pluralistic Universe," *Essays in Radical Empiricism and a Pluralistic Universe* (New York: Longmans, Green and Co., 1909), p. 111.

[24] *Ibid.*, p. 125.

[25] *Idem.*

forever making a cosmos out of a chaos. . . ." [26] Or again, "the Power that makes for Salvation." [27]

Of this God, as of James's, be it observed that He is *a* force *in* the world rather than *the* force *behind* it. Both God-conceptions are therefore non-Absolutist.

The conclusion of a non-Absolute God is reached also by certain metaphysicians of the neo-Aristotelian school. Neo-Aristotelianism, as the term is here applied, has nothing to do with neo-Thomism, though the latter has Aristotelian origins. It is rather the philosophy of causation first formulated by Aristotle and more recently converted into the philosophy of process by substituting dynamic change for the thing as the basic ingredient of reality. Now, in Aristotle, God is limited in that, though He is the First, Formal, and Final cause of the universe, He is not its material cause, which is independent of Him. So also with the systems of Charles Sanders Peirce and Alfred North Whitehead, which now concern us.

In Peirce's scheme three creative principles account for reality:

1. Tychism, "the doctrine that Absolute chance is a factor in the universe"; [28]

2. Synechism, which is the law of continuity;

3. Agapism, "the law of all laws, the attraction of the world to platonic ideas." [29]

These are the processes at work. As for the ultimates which impel them, they are two: "the nullity . . . the absolute indetermination, the primeval chaos" which was "in the beginning" and survives in the continuing principle of chance; and God who is "the starting point of the universe . . .

---

[26] Mordecai Kaplan, *op. cit.*, p. 76.

[27] Mordecai Kaplan, *The Future of the American Jew* (New York: The Macmillan Company, 1948), p. 201.

[28] James K. Feibleman, *An Introduction to Peirce's Philosophy* (New York: Harper & Bros., 1946), p. 405.

[29] *Ibid.*, p. 408.

. . . the terminus of the universe . . . every state of the universe at a measurable point of time." [30]

The world picture emerging from all this is of an interplay between God and chance, progressing from the original chaos toward a final and total orderliness. "At any time, however, the element of pure chance survives and will remain until the world becomes an absolutely perfect rational and symmetrical system in which mind is at last crystallized in the infinitely distant future." [31]

Observe of Peirce's system that in it God is delimited by another principle, negative perhaps but still independent of Him. He remains the supremely meaningful Being, the meaning-giving Being, but He is no absolute.

Nor is He in Whitehead's design. In this, God is seen under two aspects. He is on the one hand the "principle of concretion," the Being who mediates between the drive behind the universe and the infinite possibilities into which that drive might conceivably incarnate itself. As such, He is, be it noticed, not metaphysically ultimate. Neither the underlying activity nor the forms of possibility derive from Him.

The second aspect of the divine reality, that which Whitehead calls the Consequent Nature of God, results from the "weaving of God's physical feelings upon his primordial concepts," [32] that is to say, it is created in God by the reaction on Himself of the realities He has helped bring into being. This derivative side of God's nature, according to Whitehead, fulfills the function of preserving values. It takes up into itself the best parts of the world and transcends its evil events by embracing them in some higher synthesis of possibility, thus retrieving them for

• • •

[30] *Ibid.*, p. 410.
[31] *Ibid.*, p. 406.
[32] Alfred North Whitehead, *Process and Reality* (New York: The Macmillan Company, 1929), p. 524.

good. "He saves the world as it passes into the immediacy of his own life. It is the judgment of a tenderness which loses nothing that can be saved. It is also the judgment of a wisdom which uses what in the temporal world is mere wreckage." [33]

But—and this the point of relevance to our present purpose—neither as Primordial nor as Consequent is God an absolute. In the former case He is limited by other principles; in the latter, He owes some of His essence and actuality to events. A God created by the world—this is non-Absolutism indeed!

In the same ontological pattern as Peirce and Whitehead, but more after the design of Anselm than of Aristotle, is the metaphysical theology of Charles Hartshorne. [34]

Hartshorne rejects the Absolutism of God not merely because it is inconsistent with historic religion but equally because it is philosophically untenable. Most of the intellectual difficulties associated with the God-idea, the logical contradictions which have always plagued it, he contends, are the result of the intrusion into it of Absolutist excesses and irrelevancies. Once they have been stripped away, once the concept has been disencumbered of embarrassing accretions, it remains, according to Hartshorne, head and shoulders the best of all possible principles of explanation of reality.

But Hartshorne is too astute a logician to leap from a frying pan into the fire. Escaping Absolutism, he avoids also the relativism and finitude of God, according to James. For in that case, he points out, a metaphysical problem has been raised graver than any of a moral or psychological nature which may have been solved. For now we are con-

• • •

[33] *Ibid.*, p. 525.

[34] Charles Hartshorne, *The Divine Relativity* (New Haven: Yale University Press, 1948). Earlier works of Hartshorne related to this problem are: *Beyond Humanism* (1937) and *Man's Vision of God* (1941) (Chicago: Willett Clark & Co.).—EDITOR.

fronted with the question of the ultimate relation between our finite God and whatever it is which limits Him, and the still more formidable riddle of how reality is to be accounted for at all, now that even God has been relativized.

But there is a way out of this impasse, one that restores the God of historic religion and yet retains Him in His function as the ultimate principle of explanation. This is the conception of God which Hartshorne calls a "divine relativity," under which God is an absolute of sorts, yet not, so to speak, an absolute Absolute, but rather an Absolute who is yet relative, entering into living relations with the world and us. So envisaged, God is perfect in some respects but perfectible in others. He is the necessarily existent and yet is subject to change. Indeed according to Hartshorne He responds to all change, knowing and sharing in our thoughts in their flow, our emotions in their mutations, our hopes and fears, our joys and sorrows, and preserving them and so us in Himself.

Thus, without sacrifice of the ontological function of God, indeed with a substantial clarification of it, Hartshorne seeks to restore His "sociality." His role as man's companion and ally, the God, in a word, of living religion.

Subject to three crucial reservations, of which more anon, the proposal of a non-Absolute Deity seems to me to possess considerable merit. Indeed, I should be less than candid if I did not acknowledge the influence on my own thinking, for good I believe, of Peirce and Hartshorne in particular. The former, with his doctrine of Tychism, has offered a helpful hypothesis as to the existence of evil and disorder in a God-directed world. The latter has emancipated me, without any denial, evasion, or obfuscation of the ontological problem, from servitude to the classical metaphysicians and their God who, in His rigid eternal sameness, is no God at all, certainly not the God of whom Scripture makes proclamation, nor whom the human heart requires.

There is then great advance to non-Absolutism, provided always that the three conditions already referred to are met.

First: The God who is set forth as non-Absolute in certain respects must be Absolute in others. Else, the cosmos is left without a ground, the good without a sure criterion, and all things are plunged into a total relativism—a condition which, over and beyond the fact that it is ethically demoralizing, aesthetically distasteful and emotionally depressing, presents also inordinate difficulties, perhaps outright impossibilities, in logic.

Second: Whatever the limitations set on God they must be either *self*-limitations, or else negative in character, such, for example, as the μὴ ὄν of Plato or the Tychism of Peirce. Otherwise a second ultimate principle of reality shall have been established and a metaphysical problem evoked larger and more basic than the theodical problem which has been alleviated.

Third: Recourse to non-Absolutism must not serve as either occasion or excuse for evading metaphysics.

Religion discharges many functions. Among them not the least is the cognitive. That is to say, by his religious beliefs man is helped to comprehend the universe of which he is a part. But when religion neglects this function, when it permits the nature of things to go unillumined, then it is failing in one of the chief purposes for which it was created.

It is on this score that the effort by James must be adjudged a failure.

Refusing on pragmatist principle to venture any definition of the relations among the plural elements in his pluralistic universe, he leaves that universe not only unexplained but even unthinkable.

Here too, in my judgment, is the most serious deficiency in the Kaplanian theology: being a theology without a metaphysic it is really not a theology at all but an account of the psychological and ethical consequence of affirming one.

As with James, Kaplan's refusal to engage in philosophical speculation concerning God, His existence and nature, is deliberate and an issue of principle. Such enterprises constitute "personal" rather than folk religion and are a sign of the disintegration of social life.[35] Again, the God-faith has its roots not in anything intellectual, but in the biological will to live.[36] It is not something reasoned but something willed.[37] Still, again, the mere process of reasoning about God is predestined to futility. "All such argument necessarily moves in a circle." [38] Finally, metaphysical speculation is adjudged irrelevant to any serious human interest. For if the actual meaning of an idea be its affective and effective consequences, then any expedition into it as a *ding an sich* may be interesting as a flight of the imagination; it can have no real significance.

There are many questions which might be asked on these points. Why, for example, is an interest as widespread and persistent as the metaphysical dismissed as merely personal religion of a less worthy sort than folk? Is it not the case that it is most generally something of both? Still again, is it merely theological reflection which is circular and indecisive? Is it not so with all thought about anything at all? What is the proposition in any universe of discourse which can be demonstrated completely? But if so why should theology be derogated while other disciplines, liable to similar deficiencies, are spared?

Passing over all these questions let us return to the point at issue, whether metaphysics is necessary to theology.

This need Kaplan denies. Let us then apply his own

• • •

[35] Mordecai Kaplan, *Judaism as a Civilization* (New York: The Macmillan Company, 1934), p. 337.

[36] Mordecai Kaplan, *The Future of the American Jew,* p. 172; also p. 243 f.

[37] *Ibid.,* p. 182.

[38] *Ibid.,* p. 259.

criterion of practical consequence to the issue and see what eventuates.

Because Kaplan has refused any description of his God as that God is not in His implication but in Himself; because he speaks so generally of the God-idea rather than of God, the *idea* being by his lights what is affective and effective; because, furthermore, he shrinks God to the sum of those aspects of reality which enhance man's life, these being all of God which he regards as mattering to man, because of all this, the following has resulted:

(a) The actuality of God is brought under question. It is asked: Does God really exist or is he only man's notion? Is there anything objective which corresponds to the subjective conception? And who adds up "the sum" in "the sum total of forces that make for salvation"? Is the sum added up "out there" or in the human imagination?

(b) The universe is left unexplained. To say of God that He is a power within the scheme of things leaves the scheme altogether unaccounted for. Which may be well enough for the "tough-minded" to whom, according to James, cosmic issues are of no import, but scarcely for the "tender-minded" whose number, in view of the diffusion and intensity of philosophical speculation throughout history, must be larger than is sometimes supposed.

(c) A need arises for another God beyond and in addition to Kaplan's, who shall account for the world in which they find themselves, concerning which they are insatiably curious.

(d) Something alarmingly close to tribalism in religion is revived. A God possessed of metaphysical standing, a Being who is also a principle of explanation for reality, must be beyond the parochialism of time and space, of nation and creed. He has to be distorted before He can be exploited for particularist purposes. But a God who is all relativist, especially such a God as Kaplan's, who tends to be a function of social life, "an aspect of a particular civilization," [39] is in imminent peril of breaking down into a plurality of deities, each civilization possessing and being informed by its own. Which would bring religious evolution full circle to where it stood just before the prophets arose to proclaim a God who, because He transcended all nations and the world itself, could bind all men and peoples in a unity beyond all division.

It was John Stuart Mill who once said that no argument is refuted until it has been refuted in the best form in which it can be couched. The case for religion without metaphysical theology could not conceivably be presented with greater piety, skill, and integrity than by Mordecai Kaplan. It is a good case as far as it goes, a valuable one. It does not go far enough. God-in-Himself is needed, too, as a principle of explanation in the first instance, but also because otherwise the God-idea itself is emptied of content and potency. This is not to say that all religious people must be metaphysicians; it is to say that, be it by intuition or systematic elaboration, there must be at the core of their belief something ontological, some affirmation, whether naïve or sophisticated, whether guessed or reasoned, concerning the ultimate nature of things.

III · Man and Society

A. THE REDISCOVERY OF SIN

It is questionable whether any cardinal conception of the historic religions has been so devalued in modern times as that of sin.

Here is a doctrine to which in Judaism both the Bible and rabbinic literature bear strong testimony, of which Christianity speaks constantly and with even greater stress. Sin is a matter of universal psychological experience. Its

• • •

[39] *Ibid.*, p. 173.

influence on human affairs, individual and collective, is manifest. Yet under the exegesis of modernist theologians, traditional notions of it have all but evaporated into nothingness.

Not even the Lutheran-Calvinist world has resisted this trend of the times, though the doctrine of man's total depravity was the very heart of both Luther's and Calvin's teachings and was formally elevated to a position of dogmatic eminence in the early creedal formulations of Protestantism, such as the Formula of Concord and the Canons of Dort. Despite all this, the conception of sin was subsequently attenuated until it came to be no more than something negative, the absence of a good, a form of spiritual lag, destined inevitably to be overcome.

As with Christianity, so with Judaism. It is a far cry from the verses, "the imagination of man's heart is evil from his youth" [40] and "the heart is deceitful above all things," [41] and from the rabbinic position which made the *yezer ha-ra* not only a counterpoise to the *yezer ha-tov* [42] but prior to it in the development of man's character—it is a far cry from this to the prevailing attitude of American rabbis, as described by Solomon Zeitlin in his *Disciples of the Wise,* to the effect that sin is no more than "harm to neighbors, friends and business associates; harm to society; support of accepted institutions which are socially harmful."

Rediscovered, the concept of sin is being propounded nowadays with an urgency which is in part an explosive reassertion of original Protestantism, in part an expression of the disillusionment of our generation with its fair hopes concerning the natural redemptability of man, but, most

• • •

[40] Gen. 8:21.
[41] Jer. 17:9.
[42] The Biblical and rabbinic expressions for man's inclination to evil (*yezer ha-ra*) and inclination to good (*yezer ha-tov*).

of all, I believe, an affirmation, the more violent and extreme for having been so long withheld, of an incontrovertible fact of human nature.

True to the doctrines of original sin and total depravity to which he had been reared, reflective of the morbidity of his own temperament which made those doctrines peculiarly congenial to him, Kierkegaard speaks of the "*blessedness* of the thought that we are always in the wrong as against God." And again, "man is not only a sinner because he has sinned, he sins because he is a sinner."

The "continental" neo-Reformationists, Barth and Gogarten, hold to the same position—Barth insisting "the image of God is totally destroyed by sin," [43] Gogarten maintaining that man is "radically and therefore irrevocably evil."

From the extremism of this view not only do the neo-Dialecticals dissent, but Brunner does also. As well as asserting against Barth the validity of some natural, i.e., non-revealed, knowledge of God, he argues, while continuing to use the phrases "original sin" and "total depravity," for a modicum of virtue to be sure not of man's making but flowing from the "preservative grace of God." Such virtue, however inadequate to salvation, is virtue nonetheless.

In Tillich, the normative Protestant doctrine of man is repeated. Listing what in the tradition he accepts, he includes "the infinite distance between God and man . . . the judgment of the Cross over and against all human possibilities." "Man," he asserts further, "in his very existence is estranged from God . . . a distorted humanity is our heritage." [44] Yet though the conventional phrases are there, the *impression* left by Tillich is of a higher estimate of human nature and possibilities than the words imply. Especially is this discernible by implication in Tillich's theses of the "dimension of depth" and the *Kairos*.

• • •

[43] Karl Barth and Emil Brunner, *op. cit.*, p. 74.
[44] Paul Tillich, *op. cit.*, p. xxvii.

What must be imputed to Tillich is clearly stated by Niebuhr. He too holds to the traditional Protestant analysis of human nature. Man, he maintains, is inevitably and inescapably a creature of sinfulness, a sinfulness manifest not only in the grosser and more obvious offenses occasioned by ignorance, lust, and brutality, but also in the higher reaches of his life, his intellectual, social, and even idealistic and religious pursuits. For hither also he comes bearing his self-love, his pride and egoism, whereby everything he is, does, thinks, hopes, and accomplishes is tainted.

"There is," says Niebuhr, "no level of human moral or social achievement in which there is not some corruption of inordinate self-love." [45]

Moral Man and Immoral Society (and for that matter *Faith and History* also) is a "treatise directed against the moralists, both religious and secular, who imagine that the egoism of individuals is being progressively checked by the development of rationality or the growth of a religiously inspired good will." [46]

Nevertheless, and in spite of all this, Niebuhr recognizes, as his associates do not, the actuality of "man's capacity for justice," of which he says that it "makes democracy possible," at the same time that "his inclination to injustice makes democracy necessary." [47]

More explicitly still: "Against pessimistic theories of human nature which affirm the total depravity of man it is important to assert the continued presence in man of the *justitia originalis,* of the law of love, as law and requirement." [48]

• • •

[45] Reinhold Niebuhr, *The Children of Light and the Children of Darkness* (New York: Charles Scribner's Sons, 1945), p. 17.
[46] Reinhold Niebuhr, *Moral Man and Immoral Society,* p. xii.
[47] Reinhold Niebuhr, *The Children of Light and the Children of Darkness,* p. xi.
[48] Reinhold Niebuhr, *The Nature and Destiny of Man* (New York: Charles Scribner's Sons, 1941), I, p. 296.

Which is as far perhaps as one can go and still remain meaningfully with the Reformationist camp.

B. THE DEPRECIATION OF MAN'S MORAL POWERS

Strange as the notion of the total depravity of human nature is to us who have been raised on the Jewish view, a second conception, corelative with and flowing from it, will appear stranger still: the Christian insistence on man's spiritual impotence.

This is the doctrine of *sola gratia*, the thesis that since man in himself lacks all justification, he is totally dependent for salvation on the grace of God. It was on behalf of this position that Augustine combated the teachings of Pelagius to the effect that each man is born in the same condition morally as was Adam's before the Fall; that, being possessed of reason and free will, he may continue sinless; and that grace is conferred not by God's predestination but according to man's merit.

The Augustinian thesis, tempered by the Catholic Church, was revived in full force by the Reformation as its central affirmation. "Man, being totally corrupt," Luther held, "can by nature only resist the Spirit of God, and is converted against and in spite of his perverse will, or must receive a new will before he can accept." [49]

Not an easy doctrine to accept or live with, it was no sooner revived than efforts were launched to temper it once more, most notably by Melanchthon, Luther's associate, with his doctrine of "synergism," the proposal that man makes at least some contribution to his own salvation, and by Arminius. These efforts were suppressed, among the Lutherans through the Formula of Concord of 1577, among the Calvinists at the Synod of Dort in 1618.

The victory was, however, impermanent. Despite what

• • •

[49] Philip Schaff, *Creeds of Christendom* (New York: Harper & Bros., 1931), I, p. 262.

was written in creeds and catechisms, the Augustinian view was no sooner reaffirmed officially than it entered upon a decline. All sorts of forces wore it away. It took an especially vigorous beating at the hands of the demonstration of man's undeniable powers over nature. Its demise was predicted and even reported.

The report, it now turns out, has been exaggerated.

Kierkegaard, describing salvation under the figure of the relation between *God the Teacher* and *Man the disciple,* writes of the latter that he is not only "destitute of the truth up to the very moment of his learning it; he cannot even have possessed it in the form of ignorance." And again, the Teacher "gives the learner not only the Truth but also the condition for understanding. . . ." [50] In other words, man does nothing, but absolutely nothing, toward his own redemption.

In another metaphor,[51] Barth denies that man, the sinking swimmer, contributes so much as a stroke toward his being rescued, the deliverance being entirely and necessarily God's alone.

And Brunner, though he denies Barth's thesis of the obliteration of the divine image, agrees that man "of himself . . . can do nothing toward his own salvation." [52]

On the part of the neo-Dialectical thinkers, *sola gratia* is accorded acceptance in form, but rejection, or something close to it, in effect. Wherein lies still another difference between the right and left wings of neo-Reformationism.

Tillich writes, "No human endeavor and no law of progress can conquer this situation (the estrangement of man from God) but only the paradoxical and reconciling act

• • •

[50] Sören Kierkegaard, *Philosophical Fragments* (Princeton, N. J.: Princeton University Press, 1946), p. 10.
[51] Karl Barth and Emil Brunner, *op. cit.,* p. 79.
[52] *Ibid.,* p. 18.

of the divine self-giving." [53] Nevertheless his doctrine of *Kairoi,* the "times of favor" in which man makes a breakthrough in the direction of God's will, and of the "human boundary situation" when man, in despair over the insufficiency and sinfulness of everything he is and does, yet discovers "the dimension of depth," unsuspected resources of confidence and creativity—these suggest an ascription in fact, even if not in words, of substantial spiritual powers to man.

In Niebuhr finally, while the conviction of the limit of man's powers perseveres, and echoes of the old Protestant terminology of impotence continues to be heard, a keen sense of the decisiveness of man's own will is present also.

As a child of his tradition, Niebuhr writes:

"The order of human existence is too imperiled by chaos, the goodness of man too corrupted by sin, and the possibilities of man too obscured by natural handicaps, to make human order and human possibilities solid bases of the moral imperative." [54]

On the other hand, he speaks repeatedly of man's "transcendent freedom over both the natural and historical process in which he is involved. This freedom accounts for both creative and destructive possibilities in human history."[55]

And in the same spirit, "every new freedom represented a new peril and a new promise." [56]

Niebuhr too alludes to grace, meaning by it in some respects what the fathers of the Reformation and Barth intend. But there is at least one differential character to his use of the term. In addition to the special and unique

• • •

[53] Paul Tillich, *op. cit.,* p. xxviii.

[54] Reinhold Niebuhr, *An Interpretation of Christian Ethics* (New York: Harper & Bros., 1935).

[55] Reinhold Niebuhr, *The Children of Light and the Children of Darkness,* p. 60.

[56] Reinhold Niebuhr, *Faith and History,* p. 7.

grace bestowed by the Cross, which is *sola gratia* in its exact sense, he discerns a second grace, a "common grace" [57] akin to Brunner's "preservative grace," a grace consisting in "family and communal responsibilities, affections, disciplines and pressures" which "serve to draw the self out of itself." In other words, there is that in the normal processes and ideals of living which can mitigate the dominance of self-love. *Sola gratia,* in other words, a special grace available to men only by divine fiat and exclusively relevant to salvation, is compromised, indeed abandoned.

What, then, according to Niebuhr, is the human dilemma? Not that man possesses no freedom whatsoever, as Luther and Calvin taught. Not that the will is by itself totally incapable of the good, as is the contention of neo-Orthodoxy. Man is free and can will the good; being, however, a creature of self-love he is more inclined toward evil, and even when he wills the good, it will tend, owing to his self-love, to come out less good than he purposed, most often indeed not good at all. Or, to permit Niebuhr to speak for himself: "The self finds itself free; but, as Augustine suggested, not free to do good. The self seeks its own despite its freedom to envisage a wider good than its own interest. . . . It is able to make fitful responses to this more inclusive obligation and to feel itself guilty for its failure to make a more consistent response. . . . On the other hand, when it strives for a wider good it surreptitiously introduces its own interests into this more inclusive value." [58]

Having long shared in the exaggerated optimism of our age concerning man's goodness, I for one owe a considerable debt of gratitude to the neo-Reformationists, Reinhold Niebuhr in particular. They have caused me to see

· · ·

[57] *Ibid.,* p. 175.
[58] *Ibid.,* pp. 94-96.

a truth which I had somehow missed in the world about me, though its evidences are everywhere, a truth which I had encountered time and again in the rabbinic tradition but which, being a creature of modernity, I had denatured. They have reminded me of the depth and tenacity of evil in human nature. In this they have supplied me with a frame of reference which hitherto I lacked for the comprehension of the social horrors of the latest decade, and also with a more realistic estimate of the size, strength, and toughness of the Adversary who is not only before and behind, but in us also.

Nevertheless, of the neo-Reformationists, even of Niebuhr, it must be said that they have vitiated their valid insight by exaggerating it. I shall not so much as discuss the neo-Orthodox revival of the Calvinist-Lutheran doctrine of total depravity, a description of man so unrepresentative of him as to constitute a Gothic caricature and to raise questions of the psychic health and benevolence of its authors. Rather I shall apply to neo-Reformationism the sound rule of John Stuart Mill already alluded to, and deal with it in its best and sanest version, that propounded by Niebuhr.

There is a canny realism in Niebuhr over a point in which most of us have too long wallowed in a sentimental naïveté, but it is a realism which by being pushed too far ends up as an unrealism also, though in the opposite direction. For where we, under the seductions of the *Zeitgeist,* have consistently underestimated the evil in man, Niebuhr, under the tropism of his tradition, consistently underestimates the good.

Constantly, insistently, he hammers away at the thesis that men are incapable of heedlessness of self, that all their love is tainted with love of self. Only rarely[59] does he acknowledge with countertruth that phenomenon which the rabbis for example caught in the formula, "acquiring

• • •

[59] *Ibid.,* p. 94 f.; p. 174 f.

eternity in one instant," the bursting forth, often in the unlikeliest persons, of self-sacrificing righteousness or compassion, wherein egoism is burned away, even if only transiently, in the love of another. And when he does take cognizance of this fact—which is, incidentally, far less infrequent than he implies—he does not credit it to human virtue. It is rather "the fruit of some movement of 'grace' which draws the self out of itself despite itself into the love of God and neighbor." [60]

Nor is it true, as Niebuhr insists in a passage already quoted, that responses to "the more inclusive obligation" can be only "fitful." What of the lives beyond number in which, in resistance to all the drag of self-love, onerous obligations are shouldered and faithfully discharged not in one flaming explosion of nobility, but in day-by-day, year-by-year, lifetime dutifulness? As with instants of heedlessness of self, Niebuhr is the victim of a tradition which causes him to see human goodness as smaller in dimensions, less frequent in incidence, more nearly powerless in effect than it is in actuality.

There is, it is my clear impression, considerably less of this underestimation of human goodness in the Niebuhr of *Faith and History* than in the earlier of, let us say, *Moral Man and Immoral Society*. But there is still too much, too much for the actual cases of life, too much for the good of human morale or morality.

All in all, considering this sanest and best representation of the neo-Reformationist position on man's sinfulness, I am left more admiring than ever of the balance of the ancient rabbis on the issue. They never minimized the *yezer ha-ra*. It was to them "the old, stupid king" of Ecclesiastes, compared to whom the *yezer ha-tov* is but a needy, though wise, child.[61] Not guilty of our mistake, they did not commit Niebuhr's either.

• • •

[60] *Ibid.*, p. 175.
[61] Cf. footnote 42; Koheleth Rabbah, IV, 13.

As for the neo-Reformationist doctrine of *sola gratia*, there is a sense in which every religious person accepts it. To believe in God is to believe that it is He who, out of love, makes available whatever good we find about us and in ourselves, including our final salvation. But *sola gratia*, in the special sense in which it has been employed from Augustine to Barth, is unfair to man and to God alike. It is unjust to man because it assumes a total absence of merit on his part. Why, one wonders, is it assumed by neo-Reformationist theologians that to be under God's judgment is the same thing as being totally condemned by it? Unless, as seems to be the case in Kierkegaard, the very fact of finitude is itself a sin.

Sola gratia is even more unfair to God in that it ascribes to him the injustice of exacting perfection from men when it was He, their Maker, who made them imperfect; further it represents Him as morally arbitrary, saving one man but not another, though both are equally without justification; finally, though it prates much of God's mercy, it conceives it as being too little and too late. Divine mercy always, in this scheme, comes onto the scene *after* judgment, and then its appearance is so fitful and so selective as scarcely to be merciful at all.

Once again, normative Judaism, having long anticipated the "preservative" and the "common" grace whereby Brunner and Niebuhr seek to mitigate *sola gratia*, shines the more brightly for contrast with this enveloping gloom. All things are indeed, say the rabbis, by God's grace, but God's grace is available not only in special dispensations addressed to a preselected few but in all its plenitude to all men at all times, through "those miracles which are daily with us, those preselected wonders and benefits which are wrought at all times, evening, morn and noon." All that is required for man to win this grace is that he shall turn to God in his heart. And though all other freedoms be taken from him, of this freedom no man can, and God will not, deprive him.

C. THE RETREAT FROM SOCIALITY AND MELIORISM

That society is a proper sphere of human effort, one in which men may labor in the fair hope of achieving good things, has always been a Jewish affirmation. It is denied both by traditional Protestantism and by the continental wing of neo-Reformationism.

Protestantism, in its original versions, was never particularly concerned with society or sanguine about it. Regarding it as the realm of the devil, Luther washed his hands of the state, confining religion to the salvation of the individual soul. Calvin, with all his concern for the organization of the community, looked upon such activities not as a means to salvation but as a means of affording a demonstration to the world of the election of the Elect. Against this background it is easy to understand the contrast, noted by Tawney in his *Religion and the Rise of Capitalism*, between the continuing attention of the Catholic Church to social problems and the withdrawal of Protestantism from them. Little wonder too that Christian socialism appeared in Protestant circles only tardily and then under sanctions that reached back of Luther, back too of Paul and Jesus, to the prophets of Israel.

Among modern Protestant theologians, this depreciation of society has led, as it did with Luther and Calvin, to two diverse reactions: on the one hand, total disregard of the communal and the social; on the other, alternatively, an engagement with society but in a mood of discouragement.

Kierkegaard is to be numbered among those indifferent to sociality. Not only does the community have no significance for him, but even the self's relation to others means little. Having separated the moral from the religious he arrives at his "teleological suspension of the ethical" wherein the former, that is a man's duty to his fellows, is sacrificed to the latter, his devotion to God.

In the same spirit Barth speaks of "this dreadful, godless, ridiculous opinion that man is the Atlas who is destined to bear the dome of heaven on his shoulders." And again, "the care of the world is not our care." [62]

The alternative Protestant approach, whereunder no abiding spiritual good is expected of society and yet participation in its affairs is required, also finds contemporary manifestation.

It is the thesis of Emil Brunner that "there can never be any of constructing a 'Christian programme of culture' . . . such language betrays an idle and dangerous ideology, forbidden to him who knows the truth about the Creator and about sin. The ethical is not a constitutive but a regulative element in the world. . . . It is not constructive." [63] In other words, such is the nature of society that there can be no hope of molding it after Christian principles. The best that can be achieved is that these principles shall succeed in checking its grosser immoralities.

Formally Tillich holds a similar position. "There exists," he contends, "no direct way from the unconditional to any concrete solution." [64] That is to say, Christianity projects no program for society and is to be identified with none. Its function, as with Brunner, must be critical only, for, if linked with any party or platform, no matter how idealistic, "it loses thereby the unrestricted power to bring both the churches and the parties under judgment." [65] Against this stands Tillich's advocacy of religious socialism and his doctrine of the *Kairos*, both positions predicated on the hope of improving society and leading to involvement not only in it but in partisan movements as well. Wherein the paradox of Protestant social activism finds clear exemplification: on the one side, in practice, a close, hopeful con-

• • •

[62] Quoted by Reinhold Niebuhr in "We Are Men and Not God," *The Christian Century* (Oct. 27, 1948), p. 1138.

[63] Emil Brunner, *The Divine Imperative* (Philadelphia: Westminster, 1943), p. 256.

[64] Paul Tillich, *op. cit.*, p. 256.

[65] *Ibid.*, p. 51.

cern with society; on the other, a theory of despair as to its possibilities.

In Niebuhr the same contradictions find an even more vivid instance. No one can be more scornful than he of meliorist hopes for saving mankind by progressive reform.

"Social conflict," he asserts, "is an inevitability in human history, probably to its very end . . . because of the brutal character of the behavior of all human collectives, and the power of self-interest and collective egoism in all intergroup relations." [66]

So it is according to him and so it must be. For the individual never frees himself from his self-love. Society, an aggregate of individuals, is therefore in effect the interplay of all human sinfulnesses, mitigated by reason which, however, is itself liable to taint; by the ideal of justice which is also corruptible and which, while not impotent, is usually far from decisive; and by religion, itself not immune against perversion and in any case subject to "constitutional limitations . . . as a social influence." [67]

In the end, then, "power must be challenged by power." Which means that come what will, society will always be an arena of conflicting interests. The faith that "the collective life of man can achieve perfect justice" is no more than a "very valuable illusion," [68] as is the expectation that mankind will in time outgrow its selfishness and brutality.[69]

The whole case of Protestantism for social despair is to be found in Niebuhr, couched in contemporary terms and illumined by newer psychological and social insights. The final event, however, is not despair and the passivity which normally flows from it, but, quite paradoxically, vigorous activism and hope. Niebuhr explicitly rejects "the defeatist

• • •

[66] Reinhold Niebuhr, *Moral Man and Immoral Society*, p. xx.
[67] *Ibid.*, p. 63.
[68] *Ibid.*, p. 277.
[69] Reinhold Niebuhr, *Faith and History*, p. 10.

attitude of some versions of the Christian faith, particularly Protestant versions, toward the social existence of mankind." [70] To the contrary, it is his position that "the moral ambiguity in all social structures does not destroy the possibility of an indeterminate improvement in them." [71]

How is the paradox common to Tillich and Niebuhr to be explained? The social pessimism of their theory manifestly comes to them as a heritage from their Lutheran-Calvinist forebears, endowed these days with added weight and momentum because of the tragic spectacle which mankind has made of itself in recent decades. The activism which sits so awkwardly with it would seem to stem from another source—the prophets of Israel, whose influence both thinkers exhibit vividly. Tillich appeals often to the prophetic criticism, launched in the name of the unconditional.[72] But the prophets did more than criticize; they urged courses of positive action. Following them on one score, Tillich goes along on another also, though in doing so he involves himself in something of a contradiction. In Niebuhr the prophetic influence is equally strong and even more explicit. "I have as a Christian theologian," he declares, "sought to strengthen the Hebraic-prophetic content of the Christian tradition." [73]

D. MEANING IN HISTORY

Behind the differences among neo-Reformationists as to sociality and meliorism looms another larger issue, the ultimate one of the meaningfulness of history.

How can it be possible for persons of religious orienta-

• • •

[70] *Ibid.*, p. 199.
[71] *Idem.*
[72] Paul Tillich, *op. cit.*, cf. particularly pp. 32-51, 230, 290.
—EDITOR.
[73] Waldo Frank, *The Jew in Our Day* (New York: Duell, Sloan and Pearce, 1944), Introduction by Reinhold Niebuhr, p. 4.

tion to give negative response to this question? Is not the
world, including the world of human affairs, the work of
God's hand? Can that which God has fashioned be without
significance? What is more, have not the prophets seen a
divine design in such historic episodes as the Exodus from
Egypt, the chastisements which befell Israel and Judah,
the rise of Assyria, "the rod of my anger," the rousing up
of Cyrus from the East? Finally, does not history, in the
scriptural schematism, tend toward an "end of days," a
"future to come," an ultimate "shining forth" of the sovereignty of God, the "correction of the world into the
Kingdom of the Almighty"?

All true enough—so long as society has not been ruled
out as a sphere of divine action and human hope and
concern. But when sociality and meliorism are both denied,
in the fashion just described, when furthermore salvation
is construed as a transaction exclusively between God and
the individual, history, of necessity, loses all point.

Consistently, therefore, historical study in Kierkegaard's
eyes is a total irrelevance, a "century-long parenthesis."
Nor is anything effected by history. "The first and last
(generations) are essentially on the same plane . . . immediate contemporaneity is merely an occasion."

As for Barth's viewpoint, Niebuhr summarizes it as follows: "It is denied that God works in history; the world
of human history is a chaotic and meaningless thing until
it is illumined by the incarnation; since all human actions
fall short of the perfection of God it is denied that human
actions can in any sense be instruments of God; the hope
of a better world in prophetic eschatology is transmuted into
a consistent other-worldliness which simply promises doom
for man in all his works, as far as man is a creature of
nature." [74]

And if it be asked how a Christian can reconcile such a

• • •

[74] Reinhold Niebuhr, "Marx, Barth and Israel's Prophets,"
The Christian Century (Jan. 30, 1935).

position with Biblical religion, which for a Christian includes not only the prophetic "end of days" and Kingdom to come, but also a future second coming, the answer is to be found in the last clause in Niebuhr's description: "The hope of a better world in prophetic eschatology is transmuted into a consistent other-worldliness." Other-worldliness was the solvent with which Kierkegaard, and the earlier Barth, too, purged out of the Christian fabric the threads of historicism seemingly so integral to it. The later Barth, having surrendered other-worldliness, effects the same end with his doctrine of "realized" eschatology. The hope which religion inculcates, he came to hold and holds still, centers not on a life which lies beyond death, nor on some future time to come after history has run its course. It is fulfilled now, in the immediate present, for all selected by divine grace for salvation. Or, as Barth puts it: "Jesus Christ has already robbed sin, death, the devil and hell of their power and has already vindicated divine and human justice in his person." [75]

The divergence between the neo-Orthodox and neo-Dialectical wings of neo-Reformationism, which, in our account, began with a difference over the role of the intellect in religion and widened vastly over the issues of sociality and meliorism, becomes antipodal on this latest issue, the significance of history.

For while both Tillich and Niebuhr are strong anti-historicists, denying that history of and by itself brings redemption to man or that the passage of time will effect "the annulment of history's moral obscurities," both nevertheless are deeply concerned with the theme and see in it vast religious significance.

Thus to Tillich the line of redemption runs horizontally as well as vertically. "History," he says, "is an independent and, finally, the outstanding category of interpreting

•••

[75] Quoted by Reinhold Niebuhr in "We Are Men and Not God," *The Christian Century* (Oct. 27, 1948), p. 1138.

reality . . . true being, or the ultimate good is in a dynamic
process of self-realization within and above temporal existence . . . the religious correlate to the historical interpretation of history is exclusive monotheism: God as the Lord
of time controlling the universal history of mankind, acting in history and through history." [76]

But how does God act in history? Is He bringing it to
an "end of days"? Such a "utopian belief, progressivistic
or revolutionary, in a perfect future" [77] Tillich rejects out
of hand. It is impossible religiously, assuming as it does
a social state which is not under God's judgment; it is
equally unacceptable conceptually, since "an absolute stage
at the end of the dialectical process is a contradiction of the
dialectical principle." [78]

There is then no "far-off divine event" toward which
history progresses. Nonetheless there occurs within it,
though without finality, intermittent episodes of supreme
significance. Any such occasion is a *Kairos*, a time of fulfillment, when finite life, turning toward the infinite, is
open to and accepts its mandates.[79]

The appearance of Jesus is, of course, to Tillich, *Kairos*
in its "unique and universal sense." [80] Nevertheless, he
rejects explicitly "any attempt to absolutize one historical
phenomenon over against all the others." [81] In each *Kairos*
the Kingdom of God is at hand.[82] Recurrently at hand, it
never comes, being ultimately an "impossible possibility."

Niebuhr on history is, as a critic, immensely trenchant
and thoroughgoing, but as a proponent of solutions he is
far less satisfactory.

But first to the criticism. This is directed against histori-

• • •

[76] Paul Tillich, *op. cit.*, pp. 26-27.
[77] *Ibid.*, p. xx.
[78] *Ibid.*, p. 42.
[79] *Ibid.*, p. 43.
[80] *Ibid.*, p. 46.
[81] *Ibid.*, p. 42.
[82] *Ibid.*, p. 47.

202

cism in any of its forms, against the notion that "the historical process is itself redemptive and guarantees both the meaning of life and its fulfillment."[83]

Does this mean that Niebuhr regards history as meaningless after the fashion of Barth? Not at all. "History is creative but not redemptive . . . it enriches life."[84] "There is indeed progress in history in the sense that it presents us with continually larger responsibilities and tasks."[85] What is more, "there is a millennial hope in every vital religion."[86] Finally, given faith and repentance, there is ever present "the possibility of the renewal of life and destruction of evil."[87]

Only "the perils of freedom rise with its promises,"[88] the evil is no sooner achieved than corrupted. Indeed, "the grossest forms of evil enter into history as schemes of redemption."[89]

Then is the score always even? Do the new disabilities cancel out the new gains? It is here that Niebuhr vacillates. The negative Niebuhr describes "the belief that human brutality is a vestigial remnant of man's animal or primitive past" as "one of the dearest illusions of modern culture."[90] Yet he also alludes to the agape of the Kingdom of God as a resource for infinite developments toward a more perfect brotherhood in history.[91]

To the end, Niebuhr remains torn between the meaningfulness and meaninglessness of history. "There is no possi-

• • •

[83] Reinhold Niebuhr, *The Children of Light and the Children of Darkness*, pp. 131-32.

[84] *Idem.*

[85] *Idem.*

[86] Reinhold Niebuhr, *Moral Man and Immoral Society*, p. 60.

[87] Reinhold Niebuhr, *Faith and History*, p. 125.

[88] *Ibid.*, pp. 231-32.

[89] *Ibid.*, p. 214.

[90] *Ibid.*, p. 10.

[91] Reinhold Niebuhr, *The Nature and Destiny of Man*, II, p. 85 *passim.*

bility of a final judgment within history but only at the end of history." [92] The ambiguities and enigmas of man's collective career are resolvable only by God's love. "Human life and human history remain a permanent enigma which only the divine mercy can overcome." [93] "History remains morally ambiguous to the end. The perfect love of Christ is both the ultimate possibility of all historic virtues and a contradiction to them." [94]

Niebuhr is crystal clear on what he means when he refers to the moral enigmas of history, the ambiguities implicit in progress. But, as we shall see, he offers no account, or only the most obscure, of the significance with which he invests his more affirmative concepts: the end of history at which it will be judged; the divine mercy and love which overcomes the enigmas of human existence; the nature of the overcoming; even the role of the Christ which, in this setting, seems not redemptive at all but demonstrative, serving as a supreme instance of suffering innocence and a climactic disclosure of God's love. The upshot is a critique of historicism which remains lucid so long as it remains a critique but which, like Mr. Churchill's cuttlefish, withdraws in the end into an inky obscurity.

In another conceptual framework, Niebuhr reaches the same final opaqueness. Writing of the alternative faiths concerning history, he asserts that the choice is among theories, of which one "(1) envisions an eternity which annuls the whole of history and thereby denies the significance of human life in history; or (2) which falsely reduces the whole dimension of history with its partial and fragmentary meanings to the level of nature; or (3) which assumes that a progressive history ceases at some point to

• • •

[92] Reinhold Niebuhr, *Faith and History,* p. 232.
[93] *Ibid.,* p. 126.
[94] *Ibid.,* p. 135.

be a history in time and culminates in an incredible utopia where unconditioned good is realized amidst the contingencies of history." [95]

So far Niebuhr. But, as we shall soon point out, this catalogue of alternatives is not complete. Missing from it is one other which gives hope and direction to life, which to be sure involves an act of faith but an intelligible one; which therefore, except for those committed to the mystery of the Cross, is the way out of the dilemma.

What shall one make of the neo-Reformationist views of sociality, meliorism, history, from both the Jewish and the universal viewpoints?

The antisociality of Kierkegaard and Barth is, of course, Jewishly regarded, a heresy and, humanly regarded, a betrayal. Man must live both in himself and in his community. Salvation must be both horizontal and vertical.

To deny meliorism, the worth of efforts at communal improvement, is an added affront to both specifically Jewish and universally human interests.

The prophets were concerned not only with the criticism of society but also with its regeneration. The rabbis were no less explicitly concerned, as the very etymology of the word *takanah* suggests.[96] To reject the obligation or possibility of improving man's collective existence is to run counter to a deep Jewish conviction. It is also to dishearten and demoralize the forces of good will within society.

As for the meaning of history, Tillich and Niebuhr are thoroughly justified in their repudiation of historicism, the notion that time automatically brings redemption. Indeed,

• • •

[95] *Ibid.*, p. 137.

[96] *Takanah*, the Hebrew noun for ordinance, particularly remedial or reform ordinance, derives from a root verb meaning to put straight, to mend, to repair, or re-form.—EDITOR.

when one reflects on it, such has never been a Jewish view, though many modern Jews have slipped into the error of taking it to be. In historic Judaism, it is God who redeems, with men as his instruments.

On the other hand, to repudiate an over-all design to history, as do Kierkegaard and Barth, is an impossibility, both Jewishly and as a matter of human sanity and morale. Even to compromise the issue as do Tillich and Niebuhr does not suffice. For men will inevitably ask of Tillich: Is each *Kairos* an event in itself, discrete and unrelated to others, or do all *Kairoi* add up to some sort of total? If the former be the case, then history must be ultimately without design. And if so, what of God?

The same question may be put to Niebuhr who, like Tillich, nowhere speaks forthrightly on whether there is any *cumulativeness* to the good. Thus, in the listing of the alternative interpretations of history, quoted above, he omits the most plausible one, a schematism such as Kaplan envisages whereunder, though mankind never achieves a perfect society, that is, one exempt from God's judgment, the goodnesses wrought by successive generations somehow add up one to another. Only once does Niebuhr approach such a consideration, when in an *arrière pensée* he asks wistfully, "Why should not history be a winnowing process in which truth is separated from falsehood, and the falsehood burned as chaff?" [97] But he contemplates this possibility only to reject it.

And because he rejects it, see what results.

First, the Biblical terminology respecting the future is either emptied of all content or else distorted beyond recognition. What is the sense of talking about an end of days in which history will be judged if there is no end at all, either as *finis* or *telos*? What kind of "Kingdom-come" can

• • •

[97] Reinhold Niebuhr, *Faith and History,* p. 231.

it be which not only never comes but is never a jot nearer at any time than at any other, since each step toward it immediately becomes, by corruption, a step away?

Second, of what avail is a divine love which only judges but never meaningfully redeems?

Finally, given the Niebuhrian schematism, good and evil become impotent in history, or, to put it more accurately, equi-impotent, for neither effects anything abiding. Such a state of affairs can be reconciled with a morally indifferent atheism, but how is it possible in a universe which is governed by a God of goodness?

What then remains, if it be assumed, as Niebuhr and most of us will grant, that a supernatural solution is inadmissible? What, except that one possibility, the most hopeful and rational of all, which Niebuhr—being the scion of Luther and Calvin—cannot admit: the hypothesis of the cumulativeness of the good, i.e., that which conforms to the divine will, and the self-destruction, whether soon or late, of the evil which contravenes it.

Such a construction is, first of all, consistent with a God-motivated world. Under it, furthermore, divine justice and love do avail, for it is they which so order the cosmic economy that the good is treasured up and the evil discarded. Furthermore, sense is restricted to the Biblical terminology. There is an "end" in the sense of *telos*, if not *finis*. It consists in the infinite good toward which mankind strives, without, however, attaining it in its fullness. There is a Kingdom, too—not only a Kingdom latent, but a Kingdom to come. It is that limitless good which we approach, but only as an indeterminate decimal can approximate closer, though it never achieves, final determination.

Into this alternative envisagement no notions of inevitability should be injected. There is no inexorability to the accumulation of the good. Any generation may refuse it, any generation may elect to rebel against God. And yet, always and unfailingly, the goodness of the past is available to any given present on demand, whereas the evil is lost beyond recapture.

The greater survival capacity of good as opposed to evil, its superior retrievability, is the point of the assertion in the Decalogue, that the iniquities of the fathers are visited on the children to the third or fourth generations but their virtues are remembered to the thousandth; of such rabbinic notions as *zechut abot;* and of such Christian conceptions as the efficacy, after death, of the saints and martyrs.

There is then a way out of the impasse of history—rooted in religious tradition, consistent with reason, and, not only consistent with, but an unavoidable implication of, religious faith. It is a hopeful yet realistic way, for, while it denies that history redeems itself or that man will ever achieve perfection, it still envisages him as achieving something of consequence.

How then did Tillich and Niebuhr come to miss it?

Here most conspicuously these eminent and splendid theologians are misled by the tropisms of their theological tradition. Denying man all power to be good or to achieve goodness, they are predisposed against all optimisms, not only "soft" and utopian, but realistic as well.

But the damage wrought on them by the outlook they inherit is by no means limited to the one issue of the meaning of history. It accounts for the deep cleavage in all their thinking, the cleavage between man's total dependence on grace and, on the other side, a doctrine of grace unequal to man's need.

Compare for a moment the architecture of Luther's and Calvin's argument with that of Niebuhr and Tillich.

In the Lutheran-Calvinist case, man and society are totally condemned. They are also accorded the possibility of salvation by grace, which salvation is, however, thoroughly supernaturalistic, entailing the deliverance of the individual soul in a life after death and the regeneration of society in a new world order.

Tillich and Niebuhr have not only retained, they have deepened and extended, the conception of the "lost-ness" of all men and institutions. Being moderns, they are unable to accept or rationalize a supernatural notion of redemption and grace.

The result is a truncated theology, an arrested soteriology, a drama which gets man, the protagonist, as deep into damnation—more deeply indeed than Luther and Calvin ever suggested—but makes no provision for a hero in the wings strong enough to save him at the crucial moment.

Never having dug man into such a pit, Judaism is not at a loss for want of a *deus ex machina* to extricate him.

Conclusion

"There is . . . one plea," writes Will Herberg, "I would venture to make. It is an appeal for a renewal of Jewish theology." [98] "It cannot be that the ancient People of the Book possesses no religious, no theological, no prophetic Word for our time." [99]

A need exists, a great and crying need, for just that analytical exposition of the Jewish religious outlook to which this exhortation summons us. Failing it, Judaism will be poorer and less nourishing than it should and can be. It will, therefore, be less capable of eliciting the loyalty and dedication of better Jewish minds and hearts, which in consequence will depart from it into a religious waste-land, if indeed they do not make their way into those Christian communions which do furnish the required spir-
. . .

[98] Will Herberg, "From Marxism to Judaism," *Commentary* (Jan., 1947), p. 31.
[99] Will Herberg, "Has Judaism Still Power to Speak?" *Commentary* (May, 1949), p. 457.

itual nutriment. In this sense, Mr. Herberg's challenge concerns itself with a factor in Jewish survival as consequential in the long run as those "practical" issues on which American Jewry as a whole, its rabbis included, are wont to expend themselves.

But the quest after the truth has more to commend it than its survivalist value. It is an end in itself, a pursuit requiring no external justification. For Israel to live in the fullest, richest consciousness of God and the good, for the individual Jew to be illumined by it, constitute purposes of which we may properly say what the rabbis said long ago concerning the study of Torah: *le-cach notzarta*.[100] Unless then we bring into being that consummation to which Mr. Herberg invites us, we shall fail in our destiny, and shall go on living, if we live at all, without that which is our ultimate *raison d'être*.

One more consideration remains, compelling us to a renaissance of Jewish theology, the largest of all in some senses. But before I define it, let me first enumerate certain provisos under which alone, I am persuaded, Jewish religious speculation can fulfill either the purposes I have already listed or that yet to come.

The following are, in my opinion, the preconditions for a Jewish theology equal either to the circumstances of modern Jewish living or to its inner necessities.

First: It must be open and receptive to all the winds of doctrine, no matter what the quarter from which they emanate. In this proceeding, no communion or sect may be declared without merit unless first heard. If an idea discloses the least show of verisimilitude, the faintest glimmer of value, it must be examined freely, openly, and without prejudice.

Second: No attempt at theologizing ought be undertaken

• • •

[100] A rabbinic expression meaning, "for this you were created."

except on the basis of a sure, intimate knowledge of Judaism, a knowledge sufficient not only to obviate the *gaffes* and howlers that mar some of recent Jewish religious discussion but also to render impossible what no checking of references can obviate: the unconscious angling or distorting of the normative Jewish outlook under the pressures of fashions of thought from without Judaism or predilections within individual Jews.

Third: Possessing its own character, Judaism is no jellyfish of a faith, complaisant toward any and all religious notions. No new insight or value, no fresh interpretation of an old one is, speaking generally, acceptable among us unless it be compatible with normative Judaism.

Ideas and ideals will arise from time to time, which do not conform to this requirement but which, because they are validated on other scores, cannot be gainsaid. In such instances, one and only one course is open: to acknowledge the new verity or value freely, but as one constituting a new departure.

Beyond all else, there must be no effort at claiming that what is a novelty in fact has all along been present in Judaism, or to "slant" interpretations of the Jewish tradition to give a show of reasonableness to such a claim.

For example, to make of Torah, as does Dr. Jacob Taubes, what the neo-Reformationists make of the Incarnation, that is, the object of faith whereon a man believes and is saved, rather than what Torah is in actuality, a guide to faith and performance; or to propound in a Jewish framework, as he does, the notion of a "realized" eschatology which refers only to the individual in his "vertical" relations to God, whereas authentic Jewish eschatology has always concerned itself also with the end of time and the societal—this is to cram Judaism into a latter-day Procrustean bed.

Likewise, the attempt of Rabbi Emil Fackenheim to define the essence of Judaism, as the "confrontation of finite human existence with the infinite" [101] is a thoroughly well intentioned effort to construe it in the singular light which Kierkegaard has shed. But it is such a characterization of Judaism as renders it unrecognizable. For while there is in Judaism something akin to what Rabbi Fackenheim discerns, it appears inconstantly, indecisively, hardly ever in the form and never in the idiom he employs. Whatever then may or ought to be the role of tension between the Absolute and the individual, it can scarcely be said to be what Rabbi Fackenheim finds it, the key clue to the understanding of Judaism.

Even my very good friend and stimulating companion in study whose lines are my immediate text, Will Herberg, seems to me to approach a similar error. Perhaps the neo-Reformationist conceptions of Original Sin (unbalanced by Original Goodness) and *sola gratia* are sound and ought to be absorbed into Judaism. What is more, there can be no doubt that some rabbinic texts exist which lend some sanction to these conceptions. But such texts are in the minority. In any case, these notions, as Christian theologians employ them, are quite uncongenial to normative Judaism.

Let their introduction then, if they must be introduced, be announced for what it is in fact: a revolution rather than a restoration.

Such are the preconditions for any acceptable speculative Jewish theology. We return now to the purpose which such a theology can serve, beyond its obvious functions, already indicated, as an enhancement of Jewish religious life and a ministry of truth.

Such theological endeavors as Mr. Herberg asks for, and I too urge, have light to offer "to the nations." All Christian religious thought is shot through with the feverish

• • •

[101] Emil Fackenheim, "Can We Believe in Judaism Religiously," *Commentary* (Dec., 1948).

spirituality of Paul. It was he who imposed on it such
vagaries as the corruption of the flesh, Original Sin, justification by faith alone, the incarnation, vicarious atonement and a salvation that is of individuals only and almost
totally "vertical." Because of him these must constitute a
large part of the program and raw materials of any Christian theology.

From concern with such idiosyncratic and artificial notions Judaism has been spared by Paul's departure from it.
It is free then to address itself to the real themes of religion, unadorned and undistorted: God, revelation, and redemption.

Sanity and spiritual realism—these are special endow-
ments of Judaism from which Christianity, at least trad-
tional Christianity, is by inheritance debarred. In Judaism's
case, mystery may attend, but no absurdity mars, the simple lines of its essential faith nor the elemental humane-
ness of its moral aspirations.

Does this mean that Judaism is naïve or superficial, that
it fails to see the depths below depths of riddle in even the
simplest assertion, the mysteries lurking behind every supposed explanation? Does it, as Tillich charges, neglect to
take sin with sufficient seriousness; or is it, as Irving
Kristol [102] has suggested, naïvely trustful of the good intention, ignoring that man's will is never purely good; and
of the good deed, failing to perceive that no matter how
well intended and nobly executed it cannot but eventuate
in some evil along with good; and of justice, overlooking
that no human attempt at it can be anything better than
proximately just?

There have been individuals and periods in Judaism
against which such accusations could properly be leveled.
But normative Judaism, from Genesis, Jeremiah, and Job

•••

[102] Irving Kristol, "How Basic Is 'Basic Judaism,'" *Commentary* (Jan., 1948).

through Hillel and Akiba, to the early masters of Hasidism and Buber, cannot be charged with such culpability.

Here indeed is Judaism's distinctiveness vis-à-vis neo-Reformationism. It has not made a virtue of obfuscation and paradox, the latter of which, as Hartshorne says shrewdly, is often a dignified word for self-contradiction. Recognizing the presence of something unintelligible in all intelligibility, Judaism does not close its eyes to the intelligible where it exists. Aware of the power and tenacity of evil and the likelihood of the good to become the evil or eventuate in it, it still has the realism to acknowledge the good so far as it is that and to affirm it.

That in Judaism which has been called intellectual naïveté is really a maturity that has risen above easy skepticisms, childish delight in riddles for their own sake, self-abasing protestations of an ignorance greater than it has in fact. It has the daring to admit that while man can know little, very little, about God and himself, he can and does know something.

And that in Judaism which has been called comfortable is nothing easier than the injunction to each individual soul, to an entire people, ultimately to all mankind, in defiance of all the evils, the moral ambivalences and obscurities of human nature and the human situation, to become holy and wholehearted with the Lord God.

This then is the final reason which impels me to answer "amen" to Herberg's exhortation. Both in what Judaism is and in what it is not, great opportunities reside for the illumination and inspiration of mankind. We have no right to transgress the Scriptural injunction against withholding good from those to whom it is due.

VII

New Currents in Religious Thought

In January, 1950, scarcely two months before his death, Milton Steinberg delivered a series of four lectures on contemporary theology at the Park Avenue Synagogue. These lectures, drawn from material assembled and incorporated in his earlier lecture to the Rabbinical Assembly convention the previous summer, bear the unmistakable impress of a teacher—a teacher so passionately committed to the problem of teaching that opaque and obscure metaphysical concept and argument are transformed into accessible and relevant immediacies. Were Steinberg to have believed that the subjectivity of Kierkegaard, the neo-Orthodoxy of Barth and Brunner, existentialism, the realism of Niebuhr and the Kairos of Tillich were but extrusions of the theological underground—exciting to the initiated, but essentially arcane and unavailable to the layman—he would not have attempted these public lectures. The intellectual arrogance of which he was sometimes accused is clearly without foundation. Had he more arrogance he might not have undertaken these lectures. They were painful to prepare and excruciating to deliver. The lectures, existing as they did in but stenographic transcript, are marked by labored explanations, patient asides, carefully wrought examples, efforts at concretization, in all an almost desperate search for the right vehicle of communication. As the lectures were preserved they were unsuitable for publication. It was Steinberg's intention to revise them for publication. He died before such could be accomplished. We have undertaken to do the next best thing. The transcript has been used as the basis for completely revising the lectures—in fact, in the effort to recapitulate the style and cadence of their author (which the editor knew well) the lectures were dictated anew, the flow of argument reconstructed, the design and structure rearticulated. As the four essays making up "New Currents in Religious Thought" presently stand they are the work and thought of their original author. For what they suffer in occasional infelicities of style the editor accepts responsibility, trusting only the forbearance of readers who may be assured that had their author lived he would have corrected them.

EDITOR

•

I • *The Revolt Against Reason*

Since the days of the Renaissance and the scientific revolution of the sixteenth century, the distinguishing characteristic of modern man has been his confidence in the intellect; his trust in the powers of reason—scientific reason more particularly, but reason in general; his belief that by sustained and co-operative use of reason he could discover the truth and, in the process, achieve the good life for himself. That confidence has been severely shaken and mitigated of late, and for many thoughtful people it has altogether been destroyed. For those of us who are responsive to this collapse of intellect and rebellion against reason, it is correct to observe that ours is no longer a modern universe, but, in a very real sense, a postmodern universe.

The great faith of modern man is no longer generally accepted and generally shared. In the course of developing his system of inductive logic, Francis Bacon entitled his major work *Novum Organum*. The words *novum organum* can be understood to mean "the new logic," or, according to Aristotle, "the new tool." It was Bacon's conviction that, by the discovery of the free intellect, a new tool had been placed into man's hands; but most profoundly what Bacon meant when he referred to logic as an *organon* was that man had suddenly been endowed with a new organ. For the first time perhaps in the history of man—certainly since the first days of Greek philosophy—the universe was being approached without preconceived ideas. Until the age of Francis Bacon, the universe had been investigated in the spirit of authority and tradition; but with the access of free reason, men were empowered to seek and find the truth for themselves. They had high hope that by this method they could attain the good life—perhaps not in heaven, but more surely here on earth.

Bacon said that "knowledge is power," and Descartes, in speaking of the free intellect, referred to man as "the master and possessor of nature." The free intellect quickly became the new redeemer. In the eighteenth century, Joseph Priestley, one of the representatives of this faith, wrote as follows: "Nature, including both its materials and laws, will be more and more at our command. Men will daily grow more happy. Whatever was the beginning of the world, the end will be glorious and paradisiacal beyond what our imaginations can conceive."

The rationalist and enlightenment vision of the emancipation of man has in great measure been fulfilled. We understand much more about the world about us and about the workings of our own personality than men have ever understood before. We enjoy a high measure of intellectual freedom. We have achieved collectively the exploration and conquest of nature and have won for ourselves and fellow men comfort, luxury, and ease and freedom of time and space beyond the wildest conjectures of Bacon, Descartes, Priestley, and their followers. The faith still remains—the assumed faith—as the articulate faith of great numbers of intellectuals; but it is a faith which has been badly battered. It is readily admitted, however, that while systematic reason and the free intellect have made men more comfortable, they have not succeeded in making men either happier or better; on the contrary, among the powers which they have enlarged are the powers of man's self-destruction. Moreover, in the centuries that have elapsed since man set forth upon the adventure of the free intellect, the initial aspiration has not been fulfilled, the adventure has not led to intellectual certainty. We are sure of nothing after centuries of the free intellect. Where our fathers were sure of their religious beliefs—their superstitions, if you will—we are not even certain of the existence of the external physical world. Philosophy has become uncertain once more regarding the information which our senses give us of the actual world; it is quite common in philosophic and scientific inquiry to question whether the external world does in fact conform to our notions of it.

The sciences, founded as they are upon systems of inductive or deductive logic, achieve certainty only to the extent to which their systems of reasoning are not open to reproach. Characteristic, however, of thinking in the sciences is the fact that both systems of logic, inductive and deductive alike, have been open to serious question in our time. So far as inductive reasoning is concerned, it has never been supposed to yield more than a high measure of probability. The fact that the sun has risen each morning for countless mornings in the past is in itself no reason why it should rise tomorrow. Classic deductive logic, fashioned as it was upon the model of Euclidean geometry, afforded certainty only so long as its geometric character remained uncompromised. We have learned, however, since the days of Lobachevsky that the principles of geometry are no longer as self-evident as we once thought them to be. Certainty, it would appear therefore, is no longer a necessary attribute of philosophy and science.

Philosophy and science are not alone, however, in having called into question the traditional and inherited certainties of the intellect. Karl Marx, as political theorist, demonstrated—or thought he had demonstrated—that all thought is determined by economic interest, and Freud has indicated the irrational and subconscious motivations which lie behind apparently impersonal activity.

There is cause to doubt whether reason has been adequate to the world of experience as science and philosophy sought to understand it. Reason has, it would appear, neither made men happy nor enabled them to achieve the intellectual certainty to which they aspired.

What is an idea, a concept? It is basically an abstract representation of an object. It is like a skeleton figure. When you conceive, for example, the concept "mankind," you project a mental image, an abstract figure representing myriads of individual men. Observe, however, that any discussion about man is at best partial, for it is founded upon a conception that reflects the experience of only a small number of individual men. It is therefore capable of yielding only a partial view of reality. What is more, no abstract idea is capable of communicating the vitality and dynamism which the reality it signifies possesses.

Carlyle once observed that a violin concert was no more than the drawing of horsehair over a wooden sounding box on which is stretched catgut, in such a fashion as to generate impulses pleasing to the ear. Carlyle's description is absolutely true. However, it is not what happens at a concert. It is, however, a substantially accurate description of the analytic intellect when it turns to the dissection of a concrete experience.

In the course of the last generation, Henri Bergson submitted the intellect to another form of interpretation. Conceptions, he argued, are fixed, concrete; they are precise; they are like still pictures; but reality is always in movement. Is it true, however, that an accurate picture of reality results when one seeks to catch it in still images, when it is in the nature of reality that it should be fluid? It might be thought that the intellect has captured reality, but the conquest is of an order of illusion. It is like taking old picture albums and, by flipping them, creating the illusion of a motion picture; there is neither real movement nor fluidity, and the intellect has not seized the movement of reality.

The twentieth century has been a century of multiple revolts—revolts against the intellect, the free mind, the scientific method. There has been the revolt of intuitionism, as exemplified by Bergson, against intellectualist theories of reality. There has been the revolt of pragmatism—the new reliance upon the workable and instrumental. There has been the revolt of authoritarianism—men need a faith by which to live, and if the intellect dissolves all faith, including faith in itself, men often turn to secular and more exacting authorities for direction. There has also been the modern revolt of existentialism.

The history of the intellect in recent centuries has, in great measure, been a history of fulfillment. And yet in the midst of fulfillment, grave deficiencies have become manifest; deficiencies of sufficient magnitude as to cause men to say, "This is all illusion and must be cast aside." What has happened in the course of intellectual history has its parallel course in religion as well.

Both medieval Christianity and Judaism sought and found truth in revelation and authority. The beginning of scientific discovery in the sixteenth century and the awareness of a new method of intellectual inquiry penetrated religion from the very beginning. As soon as it became clear that the intellect could be free, men applied it almost at once to the problems of religion. Reason entered into religion and, with the exception of fundamentalist circles, religion became dominated by the intellect. The climax of this development—the interpenetration of religion by the free intellect—was reached with the achievements of the German philosopher Hegel.

Hegel supplied the point of departure for an organized revolt against the intellect. It was he who carried the achievements of the intellect so far that, although he himself was a complete and committed rationalist, it was he who inevitably invited reaction against his doctrine. The essential Hegelian dogma is that the ideal is the real. "The ideal" meant to Hegel not a preference in the order of values, but a conviction in the order of logic—as the mind functions, when it functions accurately, so reality functions. If it is possible, therefore, to discover the laws of logic, it is possible to discover the laws of the universe. If you have once discovered the laws of logic, whatever is real is necessarily logical and whatever is logical must be real.

The so-called "dialectical logic" of Hegel projects a triangular movement through time. Hegel affirmed that the mind worked in the following fashion: there is a *thesis*—having affirmed a proposition, the dialectic swings to its denial, its *antithesis*. From the thesis and antithesis a *synthesis* results, which becomes the base for a new chain of argument. This, Hegel argued, is the manner in which both the mind and nature work. What logic is for man, God is for the universe. God—or, as Hegel prefers to refer to Him, the Ideal or the Spirit—is, according to Hegel, the dynamism of the process that takes one from thesis to antithesis to synthesis. God, in other words, is the rationality of the world in movement.

Hegel was not content merely to project a metaphysical system. It was necessary for him to bring that system into the closest relation with all the disciplines of the mind—chemistry, botany, biology, and all of the humanistic creations of the spirit, art, literature, and history. One of

Hegel's greatest tracings of the phenomenology of the spirit was in history. It was here, in his monumental *Philosophy of History*, that he showed that every great civilization embodied either a thesis or an antithesis, in order that it might prepare for the synthesis which was to result. Hegel believed finally that the ongoing process of the spirit reached its climax and achieved its ultimate self-understanding through him. It was no longer necessary, he believed, after his death for further speculation to take place. Karl Marx, the disciple of Hegel, both secularized and materialized his thought. Marx removed God—that abstract of reason—from the universe and substituted in His place the dialectical turns of economic determinism. The class struggle becomes the dialectical warfare of society. The secular version of Marx makes it only the more poignant to examine what became of God in Hegel's system. God, according to Hegel, is an abstract system of propositions in motion. Seek to reconcile this notion with the God of the prophets?—the intimate, personal God, who made demands upon men. What has become of human freedom? It works by itself. Freedom, according to Hegel, is the *perpetuum mobile* of history. What, moreover, has become of the individual? He has disappeared completely. If one were unfortunate enough to be a Greek or an Oriental, Hegel's theory of history would consign one to being but an infinitesimal part of a preparatory thesis, antithesis. God becomes an abstraction, His freedom is an illusion, and in its place a great rational process, plunging through history, is released. There can be little doubt in the face of all this that with Hegel the intellect reached the apogee of its domination. It should not be wondered, therefore, that men came to the conclusion that, just as all other forms of truth are discovered and tested by this conceptual apparatus—the free intellect using conceptions according to fixed rules—so religious truth is to be discovered and tested.

The great test for all religious belief is, Is it reasonable? Can it make a showing before the court of logic? A belief which is not reasonable was, for most of the nineteenth century, and is for most of us today, an unacceptable belief; it is perhaps a sign of our continuing modernity that most of us—not having passed into the postmodern age—would continue to test with the intellect any doctrine which presented itself for approval and belief. And yet against all this intellectual domination of life—all forms of rationalism—there began a reaction in the nineteenth century which seems to be gaining momentum in our day. One of the difficulties of interpreting current intellectual developments is that one never knows whether the winds that blow are merely random breezes or whether they represent an enduring change in the climate. It is not possible as yet to be certain whether religious existentialism or neo-Orthodox Barthianism are merely fads in theology, or whether they represent, as did Bacon in the sixteenth century, a major change in the intellectual climate. Clearly, however, there has commenced a great reaction against the kingdom of reason—a reaction which continues to the present hour.

SÖREN KIERKEGAARD

Sören Kierkegaard (1813-1855) was a pre-eminently fascinating human being.

The father of Kierkegaard, a man of great and troubled piety, was haunted all his life by a terrifying consciousness of sin. Among those sins for which he wept—among the sins of which Kierkegaard's father was guilty and of which Kierkegaard was abnormally aware—was the sin of having once cursed God. As a shepherd boy he had defied God and cursed Him. This weighed upon his conscience throughout his life. There were other sins, real and actual, which nourished Kierkegaard's conscience. When his father lost his children, as he did in the prime of life, Kierkegaard became convinced that this was the beginning of the punishment which awaited him in the world to come. It colored his notion of what religion is and must be. Further, Kierkegaard, having grown up in this kind of atmosphere, had a way of regarding his own sins as graver than they seem to have been. This is particularly exemplified in the case of his engagement to Regina Olsen and the arbitrary manner in which he severed it.

We must not make the mistake, however, having conceded that he was a psychological eccentric, of imagining that the basic validity of what Kierkegaard had to say about the human situation is in any way affected by the neurotic accentuation of his character. Kierkegaard remains an immensely gifted, perceptive, and anguished human being, who lived a short, tormented life in which he wrote book after book of enormous spiritual significance. He is a fascinating person, but nothing about him is quite so fascinating as his own spiritual existence. He was a man who, all his life, was acquainted with religious experiences which were passionate, which were intense, which were troubled; who had all his life watched his father trying to make peace with the God whom he had offended, and who himself was always seeking for a God whom he might love; who had an overwhelming sense of the mystery of the presence of God; who had a vivid perception of concrete individual existence, though not of man in the abstract; who was able to write, "I, Sören Kierkegaard, have known sin and have been tormented by it."

It is not unusual that Kierkegaard should have been challenged by the God of Hegel. It is equally no wonder that Kierkegaard, preoccupied as he was with the anguish of his own situation, should argue to himself that if God is all reason, wherefore is the mystery of God? It particularly angered Kierkegaard that Hegel had God all figured out, tied up in a neat package, and carried around in his vest pocket. If the God of Hegel had indeed finished His work, why did the endless questioning, which, from Kierkegaard's point of view, lies at the heart of personal religion, continue to flourish? A religious man, Kierkegaard became aware, had no use for the God of Hegel. Hegel's God was an abstract idea, a force unleashed in history, and brought to consummation in the mind. There was surely a disjunction, Kierkegaard felt, between the God of Hegel and the deep and anguishing God that he nourished within himself. It is no wonder that Kierkegaard should have decided that God has no relation to logic or reason, that reason has nothing to do with God. God is rather, according to Kierkegaard, the object of intense subjective experience and appropriation. Moreover, radicalizing the argument, Kierkegaard insisted that God was a scandal to reason; for when the mind commences to think about religion with reason, it becomes confused and confounded. It is therefore to the glory of religion that it scandalizes the mind.

In consonance with the spirit of Christianity, Kierkegaard sought to define the infinite mystery of Christian experience. How can reason, Kierkegaard felt, seek to penetrate the doctrine of the Incarnation—that an infinite and eternal God should become a timebound human being; or the mystery of the vicarious atonement—that one man, who is really a god, dies on the Cross that the sins of all other men might be ransomed and atoned? How such can occur is indeed a mystery of faith, impenetrable to reason. Clearly, then, for Kierkegaard, there is a mystery within Christian experience that does not yield to the pliant ministrations of reason; moreover, Kierkegaard was aware that if Christianity should submit to the reason of Hegel, Christianity would disappear.

Kierkegaard's objections to Hegel, however, do not stop with his opposition to reason. It was Kierkegaard's insistence that Hegel had lost sight of the concrete man. The concrete man, permitted by the Hegelian system, is one without passions and without anxieties, which is in effect a contradiction of his concreteness, according to Kierke-gaard. The existentialism of Kierkegaard would appear, therefore, to be a revolt against the abstract idea, against any effort to force the reality of concrete existence into the essences that reason projects for the interpretation of the universe. Kierkegaard rebelled against a dependence upon abstract ideas—what we have heretofore been refer-ring to as the constructions of reason and the free intel-lect. He was more concerned that man should plunge into his subjectivity and distill truth from his own inner experi-ence. Each particular man, Kierkegaard insisted, has his own peculiar anxieties and his own concrete fears, his own specific torments and decisions. If a man wishes to know himself truly, Kierkegaard argues, let him put aside abstract ideas. If a man wishes to know the good, Kierkegaard in-sists, let him plunge into himself. Subjectivity and passion become therefore the touchstones of the existential man. The activities of self-scrutiny and self-penetration are the devices of self-encounter and discovery—but through the way of abstract reason there is, according to Kierkegaard, no hope of self-illumination.

The revolt of Kierkegaard against Hegel gave birth to a new form of revolt against reason—the revolt of existential-ism against the abstract and frozen conceptualizations of the mind. It is well known that Kierkegaard has had a potent influence on contemporary thought, but his influ-ence has moved in two directions. There are today religious existentialists—those who would seek to follow and deepen the insight of Kierkegaard—and those who, cued by Kierke-gaard's metaphysical rebellion against reason, are never-theless atheistic existentialists.

MARTIN HEIDEGGER AND JEAN-PAUL SARTRE

Kierkegaard, it should be recalled, sought to plunge man into himself, into those depths of inwardness and subjec-tivity where man might truly confront God. God is for

Kierkegaard pre-eminent and accessible reality. God was that great reality which, not the abstract intellect, but only the passionate inquiry of the heart could apprehend. Martin Heidegger clearly commences where Kierkegaard left off. Where Kierkegaard would argue that the great reality, the being of God, exists, Heidegger commences by arguing that there is no God, and that alone within the world there is to be found the great *Nothing*. If one confronts the universe without presuppositions, Heidegger argues, what is it that one encounters? Basically, one encounters the Nothing. The Nothing keeps breaking into human experience without surcease. And yet, one might ask, how can nothing exist? This is, in fact, the riddle of Heidegger's thought. It should not be imagined, however, that Heidegger's concept of the Nothing is passive. The Nothing is not emptiness, however it may be negation. As Heidegger writes of the Nothing: "The Nothing makes nothing of everything." Ultimately, everything is a nothing. In this no-thingness we exist—with emotions, with fears, with a congeries of feelings. We are real. We are existent. The only thing we do know is our existence. And so Heidegger, denying God, denying all external reality, nevertheless projects a philosophy which insists that there is nothing and yet that we exist. This is a radical form of atheism. It denies God. It denies religious values. Why, however, is man anxious? Because he possesses a terrible secret which he refuses to acknowledge. What is that secret?—That he is going to die. Man is that creature who exists in order to die. It is this horrible reality which no man is prepared to face. Therefore, man constructs systems of philosophy. He deludes himself into believing that there are values in the world which survive him. Immortality?—There is no immortality; man is going to die and death is without compensation. It is when man begins to believe the illusions by which he veils the ultimate reality that he becomes, according to Heidegger, unauthentic.

What does Heidegger wish of man? He wishes man to recognize himself and become authentic again. Jean-Paul Sartre, like Heidegger, is also convinced that there is no God, that there are no immutable forms, that there is no pattern, no order. Sartre insists moreover that the notion that there is an order in the universe (whether such an order is grounded upon an "atheist" metaphysic or not) is essentially a religious belief, because the whole concept of an ordered universe was born in the minds of men who had believed that something orders the universe; whereas, Sartre argues, only chaos is in evidence in the external world.

Like Heidegger, Sartre speculates upon the Nothing. *Being and Nothing* describes a universe into which man is plunged—a universe which we did not make and which we don't particularly like—and yet we find ourselves mysteriously endowed with freedom. Man is completely free because there is no order. Each man, therefore, by his own choice must make his own world. There is no real world, no actual world, except as we make it, and every man, by his own decisions, fashions his world. Each man, as Sartre's *No Exit* suggests, is trapped in a hell of his own devising. We are responsible, therefore we are the unhappy prisoners of our lives. The anxiety of which Kierkegaard spoke, which was an anxiety before God, becomes in Sartre an anxiety of freedom, a fear of freedom. The great blunder, according to Sartre, is for man to take his values and philosophical beliefs too seriously. Sartre objects to what he calls "the spirit of seriousness." When man becomes serious, man becomes unauthentic—he conceals his actual personality from himself and masquerades in the dissimulating garments of objectivity.

In the relations of man with man, Sartre insists that there can only be natural enmity; there cannot be any basic friendship among men. "As soon as somebody looks at me, I am no longer as free as I was a moment before;

I am now an object to him, whereas I am a subject to myself." There can be, therefore, no such thing as an unselfish life. All relations of love are merely attempts to dominate the other or are attempts to allow oneself to be dominated or to manipulate relations to one's own advantage.

The task of philosophy, therefore, is merely to enable man to deepen his grasp of his own subjectivity, to enable him to maintain an authentic grip upon his freedom, and to fashion thereby his universe. Sartre's effort to analyze the inner experiences of man is particularly vividly illustrated by his novel *Nausea*. Sartre analyzes the experience of nausea, the sense of impermanency which we have about ourselves—how we are sometimes overcome by an inexplicable sense of self-disgust. If one analyzes oneself, one can discover, Sartre contends, all the truth that there is to be found. One does not discover God. Whatever truth there is—the only way to find it is by penetrating oneself, not by seeking to formulate abstract theorems about the universe.

It is remarkable that the revolt against reason inaugurated by Kierkegaard should have developed into an articulated atheism on the one hand, and should have at the same time allowed the development of a profound and enriching religious existentialism.

SUMMATION AND CRITIQUE

What are the contributions of the existentialists? What have they added to our lives as human beings and as religious persons? Kierkegaard has made a number of very considerable and very distinct contributions. In the first place, he has taught the philosophers and the theologians a lesson in humility—it is going to be very difficult hereafter to limit God to a Hegelian universe. In the second place, he has supplied a critique of conceptual thought which will have a permanent influence on all of Western philosophy and theology.

Kierkegaard's particular contribution to religion is this: he has reminded us that a God of abstraction is no God at all. He has recalled to both religion and philosophy a recognition of the actual condition of man. One can no longer speak of Man; one can no longer address mankind; there are only particular and individual men, each of whom exists with his own anxieties, fears, and lusts, his own freedoms and his own decisions. Religion, in service to Kierkegaard's understanding of man, must be an affair of passion and not of objective knowledge. It must be a total commitment of the whole personality, risking everything he possesses upon faith.

Flowing from these men, atheist and theist alike, there have been all sorts of new discoveries and insights which philosophy heretofore had obscured through its preoccupation with abstract ideas as the supposedly sufficient instrument of apprehending reality. The existentialists have enabled us to achieve a deeper apprehension of human personality and a more precise conception of the inner geography of the human soul.

It is undeniable that Kierkegaard, and with him Heidegger and Sartre, opened a door into man. Insofar, however, as existentialism represents a total denial of essence, insofar as it represents a total repudiation of philosophic thought and the employment of conceptual thinking, insofar as this is the case, it is not from my point of view an acceptable position for man.

In the first place, it will have been observed, existentialism binds itself into a self-contradiction. It defines a disjunction between the external world and the inner universe of man. If the devices of abstract thought are repudiated, how then is man to investigate reality. To the extent that existentialists must speak in language, existentialists cannot avoid abstraction. To the extent that the existentialists will rely upon intellect as a device of thought and conception, they can ill afford to abandon abstract ideas. They attack the intellect with the intellect. They reject it and then in turn reintroduce the intellect after all. Our objection, therefore, is not that the intuition of existentialism into the barrenness of abstraction is false; it is merely that a partial view makes pretense to being comprehensive and absolute. It is, of course, my conviction that the religious existentialists are of necessity compelled to an antirationalism by virtue of their conviction as Christians. There is, in my view, less necessity for antirationalism in Jewish theology than there is in Christian theology.

The most dangerous aspect of the rebellion of existentialism against the intellect is that, in defying the use of reason, it opens a Pandora's box. One cannot anticipate what will be found when one enters the unexplored cavern of human subjectivity. Whatever else one may say about the intellect, it is the best device availed to man of exploding the bubbles of pretension. If one analyzes a phenomenon conceptually, one can make it disappear into thin smoke or body it forth into substance of truth; but when one repudiates the intellect, as existentialism has in general, one cannot know to what fantastic notions one is exposing human credulity.

Where existentialism seeks to be not an additional avenue to truth, but a rival to reason, my major objection is that it misunderstands and inevitably perverts the entire character of the religious life and the means by which religious truth is to be discovered. From my point of view, religious truth is properly achieved not by reason alone—because reason alone is unavailing. Religious truth, however, is not discovered by faith alone—certainly not in our time. It was possible for our medieval ancestors to close their minds and say, "We believe." Perhaps then, but no more. We are equipped with reason, we know the power of reason, and it is our most potent possession as human beings. Reason cannot be repudiated or denied. It cannot be stifled or put asunder. It will appear *sub rosa,* it will appear surreptitiously whether we wish to admit its presence or not. The real dialectic of the religious life is not a plunge into faith or a descent into inwardness, leaving the intellect behind. The real movement of personality is a continuous alternation between faith and reason.

The dialectic of faith and reason commences with human life. The infant, if we are to believe Sigmund Freud, commences life with a predisposition toward the father's good image. He is predisposed to religion. The child is soon impressed with the inherited cultural notions of the good and the valuable. It is not remarkable, therefore, that the child should project an image of God which he accepts on faith. Yet, as the intellect unfolds, man adopts a more analytical approach, examining his faith and its foundations, and then, having rebuilt it nearer to the intellect, returning to a total existential commitment. The movement from childish image to intellectual scrutiny and the passion of existential faith continues throughout life, alternating and refining, subtilizing and deepening. Faith and reason, faith and reason, faith and reason, in a continual progress. This is the progress of which Kierkegaard spoke. And yet Kierkegaard's concept of progress was inner and inner, deeper and ever deeper, losing sight of the receding external world. The progress which I seek is outward and inward.

The seeking after God as God is therefore ultimately in our time not an activity of faith alone nor of reason alone, but a task for faith and reason in tension.

•

II · *Religious Pragmatism*

There is a sense in which pragmatism contains nothing new. It is as old as man's thought and man's necessity to make conscious decisions. To put it crudely, pragmatism is in essence only this: it is to be guided in thought and in action by considerations of practicality; to make workability the supreme test of an idea or proposition; to ask constantly, as one faces the task of decision: What are the consequences?

Like every other philosophic doctrine, pragmatism has its roots in common experience, in everyday intuitions and in ordinary reactions. But like every other philosophic doctrine, pragmatism represents a disciplining and a refining of these experiences, intuitions, and reactions. There is, however, a great gap between philosophic pragmatism, so-called, and the common-sense practicality which men have always exercised. There is, however, one element which is common to the pragmatism of doctrine and the practicality of common sense: the intellect is set aside.[1]

When the man of common sense sets the intellect aside, he generally does so out of impatience. It is either that he has wearied of theorizing, or else is so hardheaded as to be unconcerned with theory altogether. Common-sense pragmatism characteristically removes the issue from the arbitration of abstract reason to the judgment of human experience. Philosophic pragmatism does the same thing, but for another reason. The philosophic pragmatist isn't impatient and is not usually hardheaded. He moves from the realm of the intellect into the realm of experience largely out of despair with the intellect. Either he is convinced that the intellect is not grappling with reality or else he is convinced that if one persists with the use of the intellect, decision will never be achieved.

In order to make more precise the distinction between

• • •

[1] It is clear that there is some relation between pragmatism and existentialism. Although they are substantially poles apart, they share in common at least one element—they are both adverse reactions to the intellect.

philosophic pragmatism and the practicality of common sense, it is useful for our purposes to turn to the investigation of a specific case. Suppose I were to ask, What is God? I would undoubtedly receive a variety of answers. I might, for example, receive the answer which Hegel gave, namely, that God is Absolute Mind. Or, if I were to open Spinoza's *Ethics*, I would find the page which reads as follows: "God is a Being absolutely infinite, the . . . cause of all things." Or, if I were to turn to the Augsburg Confession of 1630, I would find: "There is one divine essence which is called and is God, eternal without body, indivisible, of infinite power and goodness, the Creator and Preserver of all Things Visible and Invisible Alike. Yet there are three persons of essence and power who are also co-eternal." Whether these definitions would be acceptable is beside the point. Clearly, however, philosophic pragmatism would rise to object. In the first place, it would insist that the words these definitions employ have no meaning. What do such phrases as "absolutely infinite" or "eternal essence" signify? They are merely phrases of abstraction. The heart of the pragmatic critique would not lie, however, in the scrutiny of words, but in the investigation of consequences. The pragmatist would question any definition whose relevance to life and conduct is obscure. Obviously, a definition which seeks to define something of significance and yet which has no significant impact upon behavior and experience is one of emptiness. The pragmatic dissenter does not speak of God's essence but of His consequence. He is less concerned with what God is than with what God does. What does God do? What difference does His reality make to individual human beings? Does He enhance morality, insight, and the impulse to virtue? What difference does He make to society in terms of institutions, ideals, and motivations? In answering these questions, the pragmatic dissenter defines God.

It is characteristic of pragmatism that it should consider

the meaning of anything to be not an object of conceptual analysis but an issue of affects and effects—the consequences of ideas upon the internal life of man, and the consequences of ideas upon the external world. Each idea, the pragmatist insists, is to be measured and defined by its affects and effects. As Charles Peirce, the founder of philosophic pragmatism, suggested: "In order to understand the meaning of an intellectual conception, one should consider what practical consequences might conceivably result, of necessity, from the truth of that conception; and the sum of these consequences will constitute the entire meaning of the intellectual conception."

Pragmatism, in brief, is the doctrine that holds that the meanings of ideas are to be sought, not, as usually supposed, in logical conception or analysis, but in the calculation and summary of the affects and effects of the idea. Classical metaphysics, seeking to resolve the question of God's existence, will resort to numerous devices. It will advance the classic argument that all reality requires cause, that if one traces the chain of causation regressively and infinitely, one must come to the point at which cause has its beginning. That cause would be God. A similar proof might be fashioned from the argument from design. Pointing to the spider web or to the instinctual habits of birds and insects, classical philosophy fashioned a proof for the existence of God. And yet if one were to state the argument from cause or the argument from design to William James, it is likely that he would complain that such arguments never issue in solution or proof. And James would have been right, for it is clear from an examination of Immanuel Kant's treatment of the proofs for the existence of God that either proof or any proof yields the same degree of certainty—and the certainty which all such proofs yield is inadequate to the demands of reason. The pragmatic solution would be fashioned in a different way. Between the alternatives—is there a God or is there not a

God?—the pragmatic question would be, Which hypothesis explains the universe better. James, it will be clear, has gone beyond the conviction of Peirce. Peirce had said that the meaning of an idea is to be *found* in its practical consequences. James has said, however, that the *truth* of an idea is to be *determined* by its practical consequences. Clearly, there is a difference between the assessment of meaning and the acclamation of truth. Moreover, James was convinced that the conviction that something was true had the capacity to make it true. Action, therefore, became the device of validation.

Philosophic pragmatism in America has its origins in the Metaphysical Club, which met at Harvard University from 1872 to 1874. Among participants in this club were Peirce, the mathematician and scientist, and William James, the physician and the scientist in the making. The mood of those thinkers who formed the membership of the Metaphysical Club was one of disgust, particularly disgust with philosophic intellectualism as it had been defined by German idealism and the system-building of Hegel. However, it was not only Hegel that aroused the disgust of Peirce, James, and their associates. They were also in rebellion against the absolute idealist, wherever he made his appearance in philosophy, who believed that the actuality of the world was present before the eternal mind of God. For they felt, quite legitimately, that if this world was ideal before a changing mind, how could the world change and the mind not change, when it itself was aware of a changing universe? The problem which Josiah Royce formulated in his *The World and the Individual* is typical of the absolute idealism against which philosophic pragmatism rebelled. Although the problem that Royce defined was one which metaphysical theology might well consider to this day, it grated against the scientific proclivities of nineteenth-century America. In *The World and the Individual*, Royce raises the question of how it is possible for the eternal, unchanging mind of God to embrace a world eternally in flux without Himself being changed by the flux of which He is aware. Royce offers the suggestion that the world may be before God as a line of poetry. The person reciting the poetry knows the whole line in advance of recitation. The words which have already been recited, the syllables recited and those yet to come—they are all present before him. And yet the line of poetry is in the process of being pronounced. In the same manner, the universe may be comprehended in its entirety by God at any instant, and yet still be in the process of unfolding before the divine mind. Although the problem might have been real to theologians preoccupied with the contrast of change and constancy, the Metaphysical Club at Harvard was nevertheless convinced that such speculations were fruitless and beside the point. American pragmatism had before it the precedent of science. The members of the Metaphysical Club had all been schooled in science and were aware of its methods and procedures. In science, when one deals with two conflicting theories, the debate is not carried on eternally, the principles are not scrutinized and the theorems tested abstractly; rather, the hypothesis which works best in the order of experience to which it is directed is the true hypothesis—the test of truth became the ability of a theory to control and explain reality more perfectly. Clearly, then, the native bent of American practicality and the precedent of a scientific education, turned to the problem of practice and consequence, had a profound influence upon Peirce and James.

WILLIAM JAMES

William James was not only the product of those forces which he encountered at Harvard University; he was also the product of a very remarkable family. His father, Henry James, Senior, was an extraordinary man—a man deeply passionate, profoundly religious, and yet a member of no organized religious sect. William James enjoyed no formal religious training in the household in which the James family grew up. Indicative of the prevailing attitude in the James household is a passage from a letter which Henry James, the novelist, wrote.[2] Referring to the living room in which his father worked as "the inhabited temple" —a temple into which his father entered early every morning and from which he withdrew only late at night, he comments, "we took for granted vague grand things within, but we never paused to peer or penetrate. . . ."[3]

It is true that William James never embraced his father's theology, but he learned from him a good deal else. From his father, William derived a warmth for religion and a profound respect for it. He caught the notion that religion is something subjective, something going on *inside* a human being. Linked to James's apprehension of inner religion was the concept of nondoctrinal religion—religion had little to do with objective principle, but was itself a matter of subjective experience.

To explain James's preoccupation with religion, it is not sufficient that one interpret his family environment. Both Henry James Senior and Junior, as well as William James, went through an emotional crisis. When William James was studying in Germany in his youth, he was on the verge of a breakdown. He suffered great and abiding depressions.

• • •

[2] F. O. Matthiessen, *The James Family* (New York: Knopf, 1947), p. 193.

[3] In the stenographic text of the lecture, "Religious Pragmatism," Rabbi Steinberg commented upon the passage of the letter from Henry James, Jr., as follows: "I suppose the analogy would be that of a typical American Jewish family, in which there still survives an elderly Jew, a rabbinical scholar who by himself maintains the rabbinic spirit of learning, while the rest of the family maintains toward him an uncomprehending, but beneficent, tolerance."—EDITOR.

He had a firsthand experience of doubt and of the sick soul, out of which was born his psychological interest and the genesis of perhaps one of the most extraordinary prodigies of American psychology, *The Varieties of Religious Experience.* During his German dark night of the soul, James experienced the power of will in man as a redemptive influence. He learned how to lift himself out of his depression by an action of volition. He not only succeeded in rebuilding his physical health, but in mending his psychological condition.

The religious philosophy of William James is founded upon an essential pluralism of powers. James regarded God not as the being behind all reality and flux, but as one being among many beings which sustain the universe. God is not the All—He is merely one among many powers. Characteristically, James's conception of God is a response to the prevalent tyranny of monism—the monism, characterized as typically Hegelian, in which one ultimate reality is conceived to be the author and predetermining principle for the unfolding of all reality. I should be personally inclined to agree with James's strictures regarding the temperamental predisposition to monistic and pluralistic theories of the universe. As James divided people into the tough-minded—those who wish facts and only facts—and the tender-minded—those who fret facts—so I am inclined to believe that the pluralist is one who is content with the diversity of fact, while the monist is temperamentally predisposed to the search for the unity lying behind the diversity of fact.

Having examined the constitutive experiences which shaped and molded William James's conception of religion, what emerges? The concept of God is no longer to be raised as a theoretical question. The concept of God is to be validated only by the workability of the idea itself. Is man better or worse off, James might ask, for believing? Does he live with greater resilience and hope and morale by believing rather than by not believing? If he does, then the truth of God is validated by the test of his improved and refined experience. Therefore, let him will to believe in God. Perhaps one of the most dramatic pages in James's work, *The Will to Believe*, occurs at the close where he quotes from FitzJames Stephens where he writes: " 'In all important transactions of life we have to take a leap in the dark. . . . We stand on a mountain pass in the midst of whirling snow and blinding mist, through which we get glimpses now and then of paths which may be deceptive. If we stand still we shall be frozen to death. If we take the wrong road we shall be dashed to pieces. We do not certainly know whether there is any right one. What must we do? Act for the best, hope for the best, and take what comes. . . .' " [4]

In essence, therefore, James comes to much the same conclusion that the existentialist finds necessary—in order to believe, it is necessary that man make a leap. When questioned, therefore, regarding the nature of God, James will respond, "How does God function?" God is essentially something which one experiences within. He functions emotionally, subjectively. The experience of God is essentially a mystical permutation within character. One experiences God not as the Great All, the Omnipresent—one experiences God as one being among many—the first among equals in the universe. God is the great companion.

There can be little question that William James has made a significant contribution to the thinking of modern man. Not only did he successfully challenge the monistic monopoly of metaphysical speculation, but he succeeded as perhaps no American thinker has before or since in so exploring the relation between psychology and experience as to have created a revolution within the American per-

• • •

[4] William James, "The Will to Believe," *Essays on Faith and Morals* (New York: Longmans, Green and Co., 1947), p. 62.

sonality. He has done a valiant job of demonstrating the indecisiveness of reason and the fact that ultimately every decision, not only in religion but in the generality of experience, remains incomplete if it is the object of rational investigation severed from its completion in an act of will. His service to religion may be characterized by the reintroduction of the legitimacy of the emotional; he did much to redignify the value of mysticism among Western men, and the application of the test of efficacy to religious doctrine and religious practice has had a salutary effect.[5]

In spite of the profound contribution of James both as philosopher and as theologian (although perhaps he would deny that he was a theologian), there are a number of inadequacies in his view which ought to be observed. In the first place, the test by experience, however its legitimacy, should not be, in my judgment, the sole test of truth. In the second place, James left the entire issue of value unanswered. Supposing that we do wish to employ the Jamesian test of workability. How are we to judge between different experiences, which is to be regarded as true, when we are afforded no criterion other than the test of experience by which to discriminate the true from the false? If a car is bearing down on me and I wish to survive, obviously the correct tactic is to step out of its path. Pragmatically indicated, this is a wise decision. But suppose that I am bent upon committing suicide.

• • •

[5] In the stenographic transcript of the lecture, Steinberg, commenting upon James's test of workability, observed: "Long ago the Bible said of the commandments of Scripture, 'Thou shalt live by them,' to which the ancient rabbis added, 'You shall live by them and not die by them.' One of the tests of a commandment becomes, therefore, do you live by it or die by it? It is clear, therefore, that the rabbis anticipated at least one dimension of the Jamesian test of truth."—EDITOR.

Quite evidently, the obvious tactic—namely, maintaining my position before the onrushing car—would be infinitely wiser. If the only test of a project is its workability, by what standard, what moral principle, am I to judge the right action from the wrong? James offers us no clear-cut principle of discrimination. This is one weakness of pragmatism which undercuts all its strengths. Pragmatism comes to save man from the indecisiveness of reason by offering a practical solution, but it does not set up the standards by which one can discriminate what is working from what is not. The application of this weakness to the sphere of religion is particularly serious. If one were to follow James alone, it would be impossible to formulate the principles upon which ethical religion is founded. Not only would one scarcely be familiar with the institutional forms in which religious experience is defined, but one would be helpless to judge the foundations of religious practice. For if the only test of truth is workability, the ideal for which religion strives would surely have been convicted of implausibility and error; but it is precisely its characteristic ethical push toward the ideal which sustains religious values in spite of their evident unrealism. There is a sense in which the test of workability in James is less ethically ennobling than the realistic but perhaps impractical pretensions of religion.

JOHN DEWEY

John Dewey, following in the footsteps of William James, is one of the great creative influences of our time. Commencing as he did in rebellion against Hegelian idealism, Dewey was fortunate to encounter early in his career James's *Psychology*. He readily absorbed the Jamesian principle that the purpose of a concept is practical, that the role of conception is not merely analytical, but is devised as an instrument of enabling human beings to live more successfully. Out of this primary apprehension, three representative principles of John Dewey emerge:

The first is the doctrine of *instrumentalism*—the principle that all ideas are instruments for the fulfillment of desires and needs; that there is neither point nor wisdom in the analysis of ideas. If one wishes to evaluate both ideas and ideals, the question which one must put to oneself is, What function do they serve and how can they be purified to serve that function more efficiently? The second of his key doctrines is the doctrine of *empiricism*—the principle that all knowledge derives from experience, and that therefore experience (past experience as well as anticipated experience) is the test of truth. There is no use, Dewey argued, in judging ideals or values with preconceived notions. There are no absolute standards that human beings absolutely require. The science of ethics is founded, therefore, upon an estimation of those courses of conduct which work out more successfully over the long range.

The third of his doctrines is the doctrine of *naturalism*. However much Dewey may protest that he does not have a metaphysics, clearly he has one. Although he wishes to describe and not to define nature, Dewey argues that nature is all things simultaneously—it is purposeful and pointless, organic and yet dead. Actually, however, he has implicitly accepted the principle that there is nothing beyond nature in terms of which nature can be or needs to be interpreted. From such a view of nature, what world picture emerges? Clearly, the world is without rhyme or reason, conceptual pattern or design. It is precisely here that our problem with Dewey's concept of the universe begins. To devise abstract systems of interpretation is unavailing for Dewey. There are no fixed experiences within nature; all experiences are fluid. In addition, experience is always molded by old and tired responses that are unreceptive to the requirements of fresh intelligence and confrontation. Instead of attempting, therefore, to set up a universal timeless ideal, Dewey's advice is to bring one's creative pristine intelligence to bear upon immediate experience. The only requirement of the discriminating intelligence is to examine the present moment in the light of those experiences that lie funded in the past of the race, and to work out their applicability to problems that are at hand.

There follows from Dewey's position a philosophy of religion. This philosophy of religion was articulated in *A Common Faith* (1934). At that time, there was a groan of dismay on the part of many of his disciples, who felt that Dewey's new preoccupation with the problem of religion was almost a betrayal of the principal doctrine of pragmatic naturalism which had characterized his position.

When one reads *A Common Faith*, there is immediately communicated a tremendous sense of urgency. Dewey's religion (if he would not object to our saying that he had one) does not involve a theology; rather, it is an instrument, like everything else, for the enhancement of life. Religion, it would appear, is an irrepressible interest of men, and as such it is a beneficent device if it can be utilized and channeled properly. Although, as Professor Dewey's daughter attests, Dewey received the influences of the natural piety of his wife, he was, like her, an anti-institutionalist, opposed to all forms of supernaturalism. Dewey's approach to the problem of religion is of a piece with his approach to all other problems of human experience. He was concerned that religion should "function beneficently and not destructively." It was characteristic that he held religion to be useful if it served as a device for the enhancement of life. It is this basic principle which underlies *A Common Faith*. In that book, however much he opposed religious doctrine and institutions, he sought to preserve and shore up their contribution to life. He sought to separate the supernatural pretensions of religious institutions and creeds from their socially useful functions. Supernatural ideas serve, he believed, only to divert useful energy in futile directions. There is, he believed, however, a natural religion which is common to all men and which society ought indeed to cultivate. Religion enables man to acquire a sense of belonging within the universe and, more important than that, religion affords a satisfaction which comes to human beings totally dedicated to some moral purpose. "There are," Dewey said, "moments in the lives of all men when you feel yourself completely belonging to something larger, nobler, more permanent than yourself. This experience is the religious experience." Dewey went so far in *A Common Faith* as to be ready to accept the use of the term "God," which, from the point of view of many of his disciples, was an act of supreme treason to his own doctrine. He was able to accept the utility of the word "God" as the means of uniting the ideal and the actual. The union of the ideal and the actual Dewey conceived to be the common element which bound together his own "aggressive atheism" and the traditional supernaturalism of organized religion.[6]

Characteristic of the philosophic enterprise of John Dewey is the debunking of metaphysics. Not only is the metaphysical enterprise, as pursued in the tradition of idealist philosophy, submitted to devastating critique, but the natural proclivity of human personality to speculate concerning the origin and destiny of the universe is itself impugned. There is, however, an irrepressible curiosity in human beings regarding the ultimate character of the universe. This curiosity is one which no merely naturalistic philosophy is capable of adequately expressing or interpreting. Dewey's own effort to avoid the necessity of absolute values was in itself unsuccessful. It is not the first time

• • •

[6] John Dewey, *A Common Faith* (New Haven: Yale University Press, 1934), p. 50 *passim*.

that he has been criticized for using absolute criteria as the device for avoiding the necessity of absolute criteria. He himself has created a set of values by which he tests the success of any instrumental theory. To be sure, those values—democratic values, values of justice, equity and utility—are values which many of us would legitimately assume; but it is somewhat less than frank to imagine that these values do not serve the philosophic argument as criteria for discriminating the right and the wrong, the true and the false. To the extent that these values are operative as discriminating principles, they are, for purposes of argument, absolute—it matters little whether values are treated as instrumental or merely theoretical, for if they serve as absolute principles of discrimination, they are, for all intents and purposes, ultimate values. There is, however, a deeper sense in which Dewey's effort to avoid the appeal to ultimate principles seems hollow to me. Underlying *A Common Faith* is the effort to secure the benefits of religion without the risk, the venture, and the gamble. The religious passion to be at home in the universe is one which may be achieved, however fugitively, only if there is the sense that behind the appearance of things there is a reality which abides. The passion to locate viable meaning in the universe, to establish a bond of community between the individual and the universe, without venturing that act of faith which affirms that there is an immutable although inaccessible reality which defines that meaning, is to wish the prize without the venture. The human consecration to the ideal, the passion to give service to some overarching end greater than the individual, the intuition of beatitude, the willingness to pay the price of martyrdom—all in dedication to an overarching ideal—are not conceivable unless the individual, whether consciously or unconsciously, is proceeding upon an act of faith. The act of faith in this ideal has a significance greater than the expediency of the moment and superior to the requirements of personal predilection; for in essence the pursuit of the ideal is the search for timeless being. As a device of measuring human dedication, it matters little, from the perspective of relative men, whether one speak of God as *ultimate,* as *principle,* as *essence,* or as *ideal;* for it is the measure of human acts which will define the extent and richness of one's belief. Before the divine can be located, however, it is required that the venture and the leap first take place.

There is a sense, therefore, in which Dewey's attitude toward religion may be criticized in the familiar accents of a rabbinic epigram. In the Book of Numbers (25:6-14), two characters appear. One known by the name of Zimri, is guilty of a sordid offense; the other is Phinehas, the grandson of Aaron, who in his zeal for the Lord avenges the offense of Zimri. The rabbis, commenting upon this Biblical incident, describe certain people who do the deeds of Zimri, but who seek the rewards of Phinehas. John Dewey is evidently no Zimri, but there is something in his approach to religion which is characteristic of the rabbinic comment on the deed of Zimri. Dewey somehow wishes all the benefits of religion without having staked his life on the conviction from which those benefits might flow.

MORDECAI KAPLAN

Mordecai Kaplan, one of the few thoroughgoing pragmatists of our generation, is so close to many of us personally and so enduring an institution individually that it is not unusual that many of us have come to take his thought for granted—without having submitted the antecedents of his thought and the tenability of his conclusions to scrutiny.

It is evident that Kaplan has exercised upon the Jewish community two influences deriving from the two stances with which he has confronted us: there is Kaplan the sociologist of the Jewish community and there is Kaplan the theologian. For the moment, I am not concerned with his sociology, but I am very much concerned with his theology.

One of the primary and admitted influences on the thought of Mordecai Kaplan was *The Elementary Forms of the Religious Life* by the distinguished French-Jewish sociologist, Emile Durkheim. Kaplan's first contact with Durkheim was no doubt a traumatic and shaking experience. From his study of religious practice and belief among primitive people, Durkheim indicated that religion was not essentially a personal matter—it was certainly not among primitive people—for the theological issue was never posed to primitive man in terms of the will to believe or the will not to believe: religion was essentially a social matter. It was social in origin. The group creates its religious forms, and defines and perpetuates their homeostatic value. Kaplan also discovered from Durkheim that religion was not, among primitive peoples, a matter of doctrine nor even a matter of ethics. Religion was basically *observance* and the *values* which were attached to the endurance and perpetuation of observance. Only later were myths created, according to Durkheim, to sanction and to give focus and reason to observance already instituted. The function of religion, Kaplan learned from Durkheim, was to preserve the integrity of the group and to protect those *sancta*, those holy devices, by which the group was enabled to survive. It was for Kaplan but a simple transition to link the thought of Durkheim with the thought of Ahad Haam, the Jewish thinker who first defined Judaism as a culture and a civilization, and who subsumed religion as an aspect of a more broad and total culture. Durkheim and Ahad Haam went together very well. From these primary sources, buttressed indubitably by the rich and compelling background of Kaplan's youthful orthodoxy, Kaplan projected certain conclusions: "Religion is almost always social in character. It is non-individual and non-doctrinal." Judaism, it would appear then, bears all the earmarks of "a folk religion." "The Jewish religion is a function of Jewish culture. Theology, abstract ideas concerning God, have a place, but their place is either to enhance the life of the group or, within the life of the individual, to fulfill a pragmatic purpose."

The essential characteristic of Kaplan's theology—reminiscent indeed of the influence of Dewey as well—is well summarized in Kaplan's own definition: "The meaning of an idea," it would appear and even to some extent its truth, "is to be discerned in its affect and effect." It follows, therefore, as a matter of course, that God should be the sum total of those forces which enhance life, which lead to salvation—a conviction of the infinite worth-whileness of life. Kaplan does not decide, nor is it necessary from his own point of view that he decide, whether God is an entity, a being, an aspect of reality, or a useful fiction. All that man can know from experience is that there are things in life which give us courage, evoke love, and inspire joy —which enable us to live with a sense of meaning. These, for all practical purposes, are God. It is a matter, therefore, of personal privilege whether one wishes to speculate concerning the nature of God. It is as well a matter of personal privilege whether one wishes to believe that God has influence or concern for the universe. The search for intellectual imperia is in effect for Kaplan an intellectual game. It is sufficient for him that God be the sum total of those forces which enable us to live and to live better— for in such a conception of the divine nature, man possesses all that is real, necessary, and meaningful.

It is precisely in Kaplan's dispatch of the metaphysical problem that I have always had my most grievous difficulties with his thought. It makes a great deal of difference to me whether God is an entity, a being in himself, an aspect of reality, or a useful fiction. Moreover, upon the answer to this question there hangs the solution of yet another, which is in itself perhaps more profound: when one says that God is the sum total of those forces which make for the enhancement of life, it is material and of moment to ask who is adding up the sum. In other words, it is terribly important to know whether God is anything in Himself or whether He is merely a name by which I have described virtues purely natural in origin and lacking in ultimate status in the universe.[7]

There is yet another reservation which I should wish to suggest concerning Kaplan's theology. Among the purposes of religion is the illumination of the nature of things. Religion is a venture into the dark. One throws a beam of light and hope into the obscurity of the universe, and, in the light of this beam, one reads a particular construction of the scheme of things; having scanned the universe and located its ultimate foundations, one derives hope for the destiny of life and trust in its ultimate meaning and vindication. The function of religion is therefore inescapably creative. It does not merely add up aspects of reality—it makes the venture and the leap to which we have previously referred. Religion must serve a cognitive role. It must inform us concerning the nature of things in a manner which we could not derive from any other science or human discipline. This is the essential task of theology. This is the underlying characteristic of metaphysical inquiry. It is this task and this character which both Mordecai Kaplan and his teacher, John Dewey, avoid.

SUMMATION AND EVALUATION

Pragmatism has indubitably made a very distinct contribution to Western thought. It has recalled us to the

• • •

[7] In the stenographic transcript of this lecture, Steinberg refers in passing to Vaihinger's seminal work, *The Philosophy of As-If*. Although he does not consider Kaplan's theology to be identical with Vaihinger's conception of the useful fiction, he is of the opinion that "it can readily slide into this position."—EDITOR.

necessity of testing the value of ideas, not in abstract or conceptual terms, but in terms of their consequences. We must always bear in mind, however, that the test by consequences, by effects, by workability, is not a sole or sufficient criterion of truth—that actually there should always be, when an idea is submitted to test, three criteria operative at all times. The first criterion is *practicality*. The second must be *plausibility*. If one is choosing between two ideas, one must always choose the idea which covers the facts more efficiently and comprehensively. The test of plausibility is characteristic of the scientific enterprise: When the scientist wishes to choose between two alternative hypotheses, he asks, Which accounts for the facts better? He asks second which works out better; but the scientist also makes use of a third test. The scientist uses the test of *economy*, of simplicity—in essence, an aesthetic test, but a test that has pertinence to the problem of truth: That theory is preferable which depends upon the fewest assumptions. Pragmatism, it would appear, makes reference primarily to the test of practicality to the exclusion of those of plausibility and economy.

In religion there are two choices before us. We must choose between the hypothesis of God and the hypothesis of mechanism, between the hypothesis of spirit and design and the hypothesis of chance. Like every other proposition pretending to absoluteness, neither of these propositions can be demonstrated with finality. One can neither prove nor disprove that God exists. One can neither prove nor disprove that there is only chance in the universe. But given the fact that we confront these choices, how shall we proceed?

It is fitting that we should apply to these hypotheses the tests that we have proposed for the examination of truth.

The test of practicality. This test of pragmatism would seem to favor the theist interpretation of the universe.

If God is at best that which enhances the morale of mankind, it would appear that the energizing of human conduct toward the good is more effectively achieved if it is supposed that there is principle and order behind the universe than if it is supposed that this is but the traditional tale told by an idiot, full of sound and fury, and yet signifying nothing.

The test of congruity and plausibility. Which of our two hypotheses seems to fit the universe better (for neither fits the universe perfectly): a universe which is dynamic and creative, always evoking novelty; a universe which conforms with natural law; a universe which exhibits the purposefulness of animals and the exalted order of consciousness possessed by men? The weight of plausibility would seem to incline as well in favor of the religious hypothesis.

The test of economy. Does the hypothesis of theism or the hypothesis of chance account more successfully for the infinite variety of experience? The spider weaves its web with ingenuity; the snowflakes fall into perfect crystalline pattern; human purposefulness is made manifest in the care and circumspection of both trivial and exalted acts. Which best accounts for the variety and yet order that inhabits the universe—that premise which founds all upon one, or that premise which founds all upon chance? This then is the test of economy, and, as in our previous tests, economy tends toward the theist answer.

The tests of practicality, congruity, and economy all function, however, within the dialectic of reason alone. It will be recalled that we have indicated that this dialectic is insufficient unless reason moves in tension with faith. To speak merely of the hypothesis which is more plausible, which is more aesthetically economical, which is more practically viable, one speaks only within the context of reason. It becomes necessary at this juncture to introduce the existential act of faith. Reason alone will not bring man to that point at which he is able to affirm with clarity and certitude the religious answer. There must be a movement from reason to faith; the act of faith once consummated, the process of reason commences again—downward into the roots of one's existence from which the sap of faith has been drawn, and upward to the elaboration of those consequences which flow from it.[8] On the side of reason, the pragmatic test which James, Dewey, and Kap-

• • •

[8] During the question period which succeeded the close of Steinberg's lecture on religious pragmatism, a member of the audience asked: "How is it possible, once one has moved from reason to faith, to return from faith to that point in reason at which criticism of faith begins?" Rabbi Steinberg responded as follows: "Actually, what happens is that when a man has made an active affirmation, he responds to his active affirmation. He engages in worship, if he has made, in fact, an affirmation of faith. As he engages in worship, his state of faith takes on an additional meaning and intensity. He reads Scripture or other religious literature—however, no longer as literature, but as the expression of his commitment. He begins to live, perhaps, a changed life. He asks, what does this require of me in society? In other words, what happens when he moves into a state of faith is that he commences to live within the ambit of a transformed life. How, then, does he return to reason? Because a human being is always dynamic, living in a dynamic world, even in the midst of pursuing a religious life the religious life challenges him intellectually. The profession of faith does not end the intellectual life; it merely transforms the mode in which the intellectual question is asked anew. A man decides that he is going to believe, and he believes concerning the nature of God. Then he says, shall I conceive God to be transcendent or immanent? In effect, he returns to the life of reason, bearing with him the armature of faith. The point of view of faith supplies criteria in which discrimination commences anew. The life of reason, in effect, is pursued at a different, higher, but equally surcharged and intense level of existence. Reason is not abandoned in the wake of faith; it is merely transformed into the service of new problems and the statement of new concerns."
—EDITOR.

lan would make—the supreme test—is but one of the three that we have proposed. There is need for practicality, but there is need as well for plausibility and economy, and always and beyond all else, there is need, when the rational process has gone as far as it can go at any moment—need, then, for that leap of faith into the heart of things which no man can avoid.

•

III • *Revisions in the Conception of God*

BARTH AND BRUNNER

Karl Barth and Emil Brunner are undoubtedly the two most distinguished contemporary Continental Protestant theologians. Both Barth and Brunner, however distinct and contrasting in their individual theological accents, share in common the revolt against reason with which we have been concerned. Reason, operating independently of the mandates of revelation and disjunct from its source in God, is considered by both to be inadequate to reality— whether it be the inner reality of man's spiritual life, or the external reality of the physical world—reason, shorn of its divinity, is indecisive. The motive consideration which impels them to reject the classic intellectual apparatus as an approach to religious truth is this: that even if, through logical concepts and analysis, one would be able to arrive at the religious conclusion, the conclusion, no matter what its merits in reason, will be inadequate religiously. The religious faith which reason will yield is inevitably limited by the natural and wholly human frame of reference in which it is discharged. It will yield at best the God of the philosophers, and not the God of

Abraham, Isaac, and Jacob. The God of reason is a dialectical God, about whom and with whom one can argue. The God of faith is, however, a God of certainty.

It cannot be denied that the God which reason projects is unavoidably an abstraction. If He be a transcendental God, He will resemble more the God of Bradley than He will resemble the God of the Bible. He will not be a personal God, a God of love and mercy, a God with whom man can enter into relation. What is more, He is likely to be not only an absolute God but an unchanging God, a God for whom sufficiency is a principle of his nature, for whom man can do nothing and who can do nothing for man. Quite obviously, the God of such philosophers is without religious utility. But in spite of all limitations which such philosophic definitions of God might exhibit, clearly such a God is inadequate to the requirements of Christian theology, particularly.

Christianity rises and falls upon the validity of two affirmations. They are that, at a particular moment in history, through a process completely beyond human comprehension, God became flesh in the Incarnation. Such an affirmation cannot be demonstrated logically—it is therefore useless to turn the instrument of philosophy to its investigation. What is more, the second affirmation of Christianity is that that God who became flesh died upon the Cross as an atonement for the sins of mankind—a mankind which is unable to atone for its own sins—and that, by believing in the truth of this redemptive drama, man is saved. To the extent that these affirmations represent the center and heart of Christian belief, reason as a device of discovery and validation is useless. No matter the subtlety of one's concept or the ingenuity of one's argument, reason can never produce the conclusions of Christian doctrine. To this extent, therefore, both Barth and Brunner will argue that metaphysics and rational epistemology are useless as devices of theology. It is characteristic for Brunner to have affirmed point-blank: "It is my purpose to free the Biblical conception of God from the stranglehold of philosophy."

Having rejected the inherited rationalism of European philosophy, where then shall Barth and Brunner turn for confirmation of their doctrine? There is no hope for them in pragmatism—not only does Europe consider pragmatism a distinctively American and therefore slightly vulgar doctrine; it is aware as well that pragmatism, in spite of its cultural onus, leads to debatable conclusions—it is a method of trial and error, a method which, of necessity, even when conclusions are successfully formulated, possesses by its very nature an unavoidable degree of tentativeness. Last but not least, as Brunner himself has commented, not without contempt, a theology which pretends to found itself not upon doctrine but upon life ends in a form of "ethical pragmatism or of mysticism." [9] Clearly, for both Barth and Brunner, essential Christian doctrine is incompatible with pragmatic methods.

If not pragmatism, then surely existentialism? Barth, to be sure, in his early days, was strongly influenced by Kierkegaard and for some time his exposition of philosophy was based upon a form of existentialism. Though Barth later minimized and cast off the influence of existentialism, existentialism has surely had an ever-growing influence upon Emil Brunner and Friedrich Gogarten. Having used existentialism for a time, Barth later came to reject it in its entirety. He said, at one point, "I have cut out of my thinking everything that might give the slightest appearance of giving to theology a basis, support, or even a mere justification in the way of existential philosophy." It may well be asked, Why does Barth reject existentialism so vigorously? What is the risk and

• • •

[9] Emil Brunner, *The Theology of Crisis* (New York: Charles Scribner's Sons, 1929), p. 2.

the danger of existentialism to which Barth reacts so violently? The answer may well lie in a scrutiny of the extent to which subjectivity has ruled existential doctrine and undercut thereby the historic and objective foundations of religious doctrine. Kierkegaard, the first existentialist, commenced as a passionate Christian, seeking in himself the foundations of Christian belief and Christian reality. It is in the repudiation of objective reason and in the reappropriation and deepening of inwardness, passion, and subjectivity that Kierkegaard located the grounds of Christian belief. In a certain sense, therefore, Kierkegaard derived his Christianity from his existentialism. The objective God and the internal God became one and indistinguishable.

Heidegger rejected God and nevertheless made use of the methods of existential analysis. He found in himself, in the end, not God but Nothing. There is a sense, therefore, in which the existential method will yield no more than one possesses to begin with—existentialism makes salvific truth contingent upon resources of depth and understanding which are unavoidably human and, therefore, inescapably limited and unreliable.

Because the existentialist turns within, sundering contact with the formal community and avoiding the contaminating crush of the mass, he remains an isolated individual. Kierkegaard sought to make the isolation of "the single one" into a virtue; if not in oneself, where then, Kierkegaard argued, shall the truth be found? And yet limitation to oneself, although providing an access of vision, builds a wall which cuts off the variety of human contact and the illumination of interpersonal experience. Truth becomes limited to one's own vision and the profundity of one's own inwardness. It is understandable, therefore, that Karl Barth chooses to repudiate the Kierkegaard with whom he began. For Barth is not only a Christian—as was Kierkegaard—he is as well an historical Christian. He is

dreadfully afraid that existentialism will dissolve the community of the Church into isolated and atomic persons
bound to one another by nothing more than subjectivity
and ostensibly released from the objective bonds of Christian faith. Where existentialism would appear to become
a form of exalted self-reliance, Barth believes that man is
not saved by his own self-apprehension but by divine
grace. Finally and last of all—and this is the rock against
which not only existentialism, pragmatism, and rationalism
founder for Barth—the basic doctrines of historic Christianity cannot be established by existential self-invasion.

Then, what remains? For Barth, the answer is transparently clear. What remains is the historic source of all living faith and doctrine. What remains today, as always, is
the Bible. If one wishes certainty before God and the
apprehension of historic Christian faith, the only plunge of
existential risk is not into oneself but into Scripture. Barth,
however, is not naïve enough as to imagine that ours is
anything but a postcritical age. Our ancestors and the
ancestors of Karl Barth found it considerably easier, living
as they did in precritical days when the Bible was universally accepted as the source of all truth, to return at
every moment of question and uncertainty to the Biblical
fount. In our day, however, the Bible is challenged on all
sides. It is not enough that its physics and natural science
are imprecise—no longer is the conflict of science and theology being waged with the same degree of intensity and
fury with which it was waged in the days of Darwin and
Huxley. Nor even is the conflict of Biblical teaching and
evolution particularly aggrieved. To be sure, the Biblical
doctrine of the miraculous giving of Scripture and the
scientific awareness that Scripture was an evolving document reflect an ongoing conflict—but even this conflict
has not destroyed the resources of creative theology. It
would be easy for Barth to say with simplicity and direct-
ness, "back to the Bible"; but we no longer stand where

our ancestors stood; we are no longer precritical or unsophisticated in our approach to Scripture. Those of us who hold a religious position determine its character on the basis of intellect and experience; our religious position is no longer determined with exclusivity by Biblical mandate; we say that the Bible is valid so far as it conforms to the truth at which we arrive from other sources. This is not to deny, for those of us who are modernists, that the Bible is a powerful factor in the molding of religious conclusions; nevertheless, our last court of appeal is not the Scriptures—we look out upon the world and attempt to arrive at conclusions. Having arrived at these conclusions, and noticing their Biblical antecedents, we admire Scripture. And yet our admiration for Scripture takes on something of the hue and form of a condescending compliment.

Karl Barth, to be sure, is not a precritical Christian. Barth does not fall into the trap of either naïve revelationism on the one hand or condescending scientism on the other. Barth is well aware of the trap of condescending scientism—the propensity first to define the truth, and then, having noticed its Biblical confirmation, to admire the brilliance of the Bible. We know no truth, Barth would say, except that which is to be found in Scripture.

The Barthian position is essentially this: Whatever our concessions to the critical analysis of Scripture and the scientific investigation of ancient history, there is a core of truth in Scripture over which time has no dominion. However much we may acknowledge those elements in Scripture which may be relative to time and place and reflect the mores and attitudes of societies long since past, there is a fundamental truth which is independent of time, an essential truth which is independent of all relativity and contingency. Moreover, Barth is exceedingly specific. There is, he argues, a threefold revelation: the revelation of Christianity, the teachings of the Church, and—what Brunner has called the *Tatwort* (the word which is a fact)

—the Incarnation of God in Jesus Christ. In him, say both Brunner and Barth, God is revealed. Only in revelation, they argue, is man enabled to learn anything about God. How, they insist, shall man contemplate and embrace an absolute when his mind and person are so exceedingly limited and finite? God is—and this is indeed a key word for Barth—the *totaliter aliter*. He is, in effect, the "completely other" from everything in the world and everything which we know about the world. If he is "completely other" from everything we know and which the world records, then it is obviously impossible for us to comprehend him through the uses of reason.[10] Barth says, therefore, that only through faith can one apprehend the truth, and only by faith is one's anchor in Christian doctrine secure.

RELEVANCE TO JUDAISM

It may appear at first glance that the affirmation of Karl Barth respecting Scripture is irrelevant to Judaism, but it is not. The fact of the matter is that it has supplied a new foundation and impetus for contemporary Jewish neo-Orthodoxy. The normal and accepted Orthodox position is this: either the assertions of Biblical criticism are denied or an attempt is made to establish the rational plausibility of the supernatural events recorded in Scripture. The anticritical Orthodox tends to fight the scientific critic of Scripture with scientific weapons; he seeks to estab-

• • •

[10] Rabbi Steinberg makes a brief but incomplete allusion to the intense and provocative argument which took place between Brunner and Barth respecting the problem of natural theology. He brings to bear this famous controversy to reinforce his statement of Barth's position that not through the devices of conceptual theology but only through the self-declaring Biblical word of God is there sufficient warrant for Christian doctrine. Cf. Karl Barth and Emil Brunner, *Natural Theology* (London: Geoffrey Bles, 1946).—EDITOR.

lish the plausibility of Biblical event by the same technique with which the critic seeks to undermine it. Barth has defined, however, a new precedent. He is willing to grant that the wording of Scripture, the detail of Scripture, the idiosyncrasies of Scripture, may well be relative. But, he asks, in spite of all relativity, is there in fact a revelation of God contained in Scripture? Clearly, the influence of Barth, whether indirect or direct, is felt in such a position as that expressed by Franz Rosenzweig. Writing to the Orthodox leader, Jacob Rosenheim, Rosenzweig observed: "Where we differ from Orthodoxy is in our reluctance to draw from our belief in the holiness or uniqueness of the Torah, and in its character of revelation, any conclusions as to its literary genesis and the philological values of the text as it has come down to us." [11]

In the spirit of Barth, therefore, Rosenzweig cuts through the relativities imposed upon Scripture by critical science to the heart of revelation which stands unimpeached.

THE REBIRTH OF TRANSCENDENTALISM

The rebirth of transcendentalism is founded upon the conception of God as independent of the world. I have already

• • •

[11] N. N. Glatzer, *Franz Rosenzweig: His Life and Thought* (New York: Schocken Books, 1953), p. 158. It was no doubt impossible for Steinberg to have seen the manuscript of this work which was published several years after his death, but there is little question from his text that he was making reference to a quotation which appears several times in Glatzer's own summary of Rosenzweig's teaching and in the German texts to which Rabbi Steinberg had access. Cf. Franz Rosenzweig, *Briefe* (Berlin: Shocken Verlag, 1935), pp. 581-82. "We too translate the Torah as a single book. For us, too, it is the work of one spirit . . . among ourselves, we call him by the symbol which critical science is accustomed to use to designate its assumed redactor: R. But this symbol R we expand not into Redactor, but into *Rabbenu*. For he is our teacher; his theology is our teaching."—EDITOR.

alluded to the essence of the transcendental position when I described Barth's conception of God as the *totaliter aliter* —the state of being completely different from anything apprehendable in nature.[12]

The God of the reborn transcendentalism is not only different but totally independent of nature—He is the Absolute, the Infinite, the unlimited person; the world is altogether His creation, and man stands at an infinite distance from Him. In the famous exchange between Barth and Brunner respecting the problem of a *theologia naturalis,* one of the points at issue was whether or not the divine image in which man was created is still present in him, however much man may be in bondage to sin. The answer which Barth gives is "No"—there is nothing in man or in human nature which is in the least way divine or in the least degree reminiscent of the image of God; God is infinitely superior and incommensurable with man. It is only possible to speak, therefore, of the divine image being present in man in degree, not in kind.

The transcendentalism which concerns us now is in some form or other the historic line of religious thought until the dawn of modern times. The Bible itself conceived of God as absolutely transcendent and apart from the world. He was the one, almighty and exalted. He surpasses all conceptions and all praises which man can form. Even in Jewish tradition, God is conceived as a being different in kind from His creation and independent of it. And yet, Jewish tradition is not unambiguous. There is unmistakably present in Jewish tradition the conception

• • •

[12] It should be clear that in referring to transcendentalism we do not have in mind the transcendentalism identified with the doctrine of Emerson in the nineteenth century. That transcendentalism was more characteristically identified with the doctrine of the oversoul which is above nature—it assumed the form of a pantheism rather than what we now refer to as a religious transcendentalism.

of an immanent God as well as a transcendent God. This is richly and profoundly in evidence in the 139th Psalm—perhaps the most exalted statement of immanentism in the history of religious literature.

"Oh Lord, Thou hast searched me and known me. Thou knowest my downsitting and mine uprising.

"Thou understandest my thought afar off. Thou measurest my going about and my lying down, And art acquainted with all my ways. . . . Whither shall I go from Thy spirit? Or whither shall I flee from Thy presence? If I ascend up into heaven, Thou art there; if I make my bed in the nether world, behold, Thou art there. If I take the wings of the morning, And dwell in the uttermost parts of the sea; Even there would Thy hand lead me, And Thy right hand would hold me. And if I say: 'Surely the darkness shall envelop me, And the light about me shall be night'; Even the darkness is not too dark for Thee, But the night shineth as the day; the darkness even as the light. . . . How weighty also are Thy thoughts unto me, O God! How great is the sum of them! If I would count them, they are more in number than the sand; Were I to come to the end of them, I would still be with Thee. . . ." (Psalm 139:1-4; 7-12; 17-18.)

It is even observed by the ancient rabbis, reflecting the spirit of Scripture, that when a man dies in pain, somehow God suffers with him; God is in man, so to speak; the indwelling divine presence suffers with suffering mankind. In spite of these unmistakable indications of immanentism, it is the transcendent God that reflects the high tradition of Jewish thought. It cannot be gainsaid, however, that with the Copernican revolution and the dawn of a new astronomy and a new science, it became increasingly difficult to envisage a convincing and viable transcendent God. Immanentism has become the characteristically popular posture of modern man. It is not unusual, therefore, that the modernists to whom we have made previous reference—James, Dewey, and Kaplan—are all immanentists. They conceive of God as a power within the world which makes for human salvation, not as a being independent and apart from the world.

At the present moment it would appear, however, that there is a return to transcendentalism—to the notion of a God apart from the world rather than within it. This return has not been without its salutary influence. In the first place, the criticism which Barth has leveled against immanentist doctrines of God has exposed the hypocrisy with which many moderns have approached Scripture. Actually, it has been the characteristic procedure of modern theology to pursue an independent line of speculation and then impute their conclusions to the Bible. At the very worst, this has been a form of intellectual disingenuousness. Barth has demonstrated the possibility of a post-critical revelationism. He has once again exhibited what runs throughout all of human thought—it is not by reason alone that man arrives at certitude regarding the objects of religious belief, but only with the dialectic of faith and reason can truth be achieved. To be sure, I for one tend to reject Barth's doctrine of revelation. It is perhaps a little smug to say that his doctrine of revelation is more apt for one compelled to define and justify the dogmas of Christian belief than it is to defend and justify the doctrines of Jewish belief. Nevertheless, there would be truth in such smugness. God is not for me, a Jew, a "scandal to the intellect" in the phrase of Kierkegaard, nor do I require a concept of revelation as extreme and uncompromising as the one which Barth requires. Christianity is perforce contrarational. Its contrarationality is as old as the statement of Saint Paul in Corinthians: "Seeing that Jews ask for signs, and Greeks seek after wisdom; but we preach Christ crucified, unto Jews a stumblingblock and unto

Gentiles foolishness"(I Cor. 1:22-23). Christianity is, by its own self-proclamation, disdainful of reason and unsusceptible to its ministrations.

Judaism is not under the same obligation of anti-rationalism. Nor does it believe that certainty is to be achieved only by the route of faith unqualified by reason. Although it acknowledges the inescapable risk of faith; although it testifies to the life wager implicit in the act of faith; although, in the words of Job, "though he shall slay me, I will wait for him," a leap of trust is acknowledged—in spite of all these testimonies, the critical function of reason has not been compromised. By having reposed absolute trust in Scripture at the expense of the intellect, Barth has not succeeded in proving—however much he tried to convince Brunner that he had—that intellect was no longer useful as a means of refining speculative theology. It is one thing to climb Jacob's ladder to heaven and cast down the ladder behind you, and quite another to take the ladder up with you so as to provide a means of returning once again to earth. In the former case, reason is repudiated as a device of scrutiny and refinement; while in the latter, reason is preserved as an instrument of balance and communication. Reason is always required to control the excess of faith. Only with the preservative power of reason is the fine distinction between dogmatism and fanaticism preserved. Barth has, in essence, missed one essential ingredient of historic Biblical faith, the faith which defines most characteristically the Jewish man: that is, that faith ought not to be reposed in Scripture, but only in God. Scripture is simply the means by which God discloses Himself to man. It is not the sufficient disclosure. Faith must always arch over Scripture to the object of faith. The main objection, therefore, which I have to the theology of Karl Barth is that authentic faith is not directed to its proper object. If the act of faith is to be required—and indeed it seems to me that it is required—it

ought to be directed toward the essential core of the religious life, it ought to be in God and in God alone:
for reason may direct us to the palace of the King, even
though it cannot tell us in which chamber He dwells.

IMMANENTISM AND THE NEW TRANSCENDENTALISM

The doctrine of immanentism is, from the human point of
view, the most plausible and easily comprehended conception of God. Immanentism squares well with the natural
and all too finite reach of the human understanding. If
one wishes, for instance, to communicate to a child what
God is, the easiest picture to project is not the picture of
a transcendent being, but of that power or energy which
makes him grow and think—a being which makes him
pursue the beautiful and the good. It is by such tangible
and easily appropriated conceptions that one may best communicate the image of God. The conception of the indwelling glory and pervading presence is one which lends
warmth and dignity to nature and to man. When one
shares such immanentist views, one may see all nature
and creation bound together and linked into a unity sustained through generations; one may interpret physical
injury as somehow a diminution in the totality of God;
one may conceive of death as a deprivation of experience
before God and in some measure a diminishment of
His pleasure. With God in all things, all things share
in God. It is but a small step to negotiate the passage from
likeness and similarity to ontological identification—in
which like becomes same, in which being similar to God
becomes being one with him.

The doctrine of immanentism has indeed been deepened
by the observation of rationality in nature. The stone,
for example, behaves according to rational and predictable
law. There is rationality in the insect, in the beauty of
beasts, and in man. God is in all these things as their

principle of being, their continuity, the law of their nature. And yet, with all the virtues that one can describe in immanentist doctrine, we are in the last analysis compelled to admit that Barth's criticism was right. In the first place, the doctrine of immanentism is alien to the main line of Biblical and religious tradition. In the second place, if God is indeed the power behind and within all things, then God tends to become the all—God is Everything. The danger of a consummated immanentism is that God is no longer either personal or moral—He ceases to be a unique personality and will to the extent to which He is confused with all things, and He ceases to be a moral judge to the extent that all things are considered identical with His nature. To say that God is in the mud puddle and in the flower and in man is to compromise His individuality with a blur. This is the danger to which Oriental mysticism is liable. If indeed all of us are fundamentally God then surely all individuality is an illusion. Immanentism tends to destroy individuality. If God is in all things, and I am but a bubble of God on the river of God, my freedom is useless and my individuality meaningless and ineffectual.

The distinction finally between good and evil disappears. All things are equally God and therefore all things tend to become equally good. To be sure, the main objection to this is transparent: while we experience God as a being within things, we also experience God—and I allude here to Martin Buber's conception of God as the eternal Thou—behind the universe, apart and absolutely other than it. Actually, we encounter God manifest under two aspects—the hidden God and the revealed God, the concealed God and the open and accessible God, the transcendent God and the immanent God.

God is in substance both immanent and transcendent. If he is the infinite source of all things, then he is present in everything and at the same time transcends everything; we are entitled therefore to form two pictures of God—

He who dwells with us, within our fellows, and within all nature, and He who, to be able to participate in all creation, must yet be separate, independent, and transcendent toward it. The intellect may only formulate with success its understanding of the immanent God; beyond its limitations, the movement of faith begins. If God *is*, then He overflows all the conceptual vessels we can fashion to contain Him, and we are compelled to use divers vessels —vessels of varying capacity and intent—for only the seemingly contradictory—the immanent, and the transcendent— will comprehend Him adequately.

NON-ABSOLUTE GOD

We have been dealing heretofore with those thinkers who have conspicuously denied the use of reason in religion. It should be made clear, however, that in spite of all attacks, reason has not abdicated its vaunted throne—not even in theology—and philosophical, rational, theological speculation continues as it always has. The theological Rialto is as crowded as ever—new doctrines emerge, old doctrines disappear into the shadows, traditions are revised, and new traditions are inaugurated. It is not our task here to encompass all that moves with swiftness and brilliance across the intellectual horizon; but there are a number of interesting developments on the religious scene in the course of the past half century which are pertinent to a revision in our traditional conceptions of the nature of God.

The word God, as both Kierkegaard and Barth have pointed out, has really two distinct meanings. These meanings have in themselves inspired two different methods and inquiries directed to His explication. There is, on the one hand, the conception of God which flows out of Biblical Judaism—the living God who is a Thou to the human I, He who enters into relations with man and the world, and who in entering into relation with them becomes thereby a creature open and accessible before them. Whatever the extent of God's transcendence, there is to be sure in God's relation to the world a dimension of relativity (relativity both in the technical and in the moral sense, that is, that God not only effects the world but is effected by it). God needs man as we need Him. Or, as the rabbis often expressed it, God and Israel are partners in the universe, and His fulfillment is in part contingent upon man's dedication.

There is, however, the other God, the God which grows out of the tradition of Greek philosophy. Beyond all else, the Greeks were seeking two things: on the one hand, a principle of being which was sufficient to explain the universe, and at the same time a principle which was sufficiently stable as to remain fixed and unchanging amid the flux of nature. All Greek speculation turned upon the passion to interpret and understand nature, *physis*. Thales, the first philosopher, tried to reduce all things to material components: fire, air, or water. Thales sought to locate principle in discrete aspects of nature. Heraclitus sophisticated the argument of Thales by arguing that, although all things change, there would appear nevertheless to be a logic, a reason, which all things manifest, but which itself does not change. The doctrine of reality formulated by Plato centers about an order of unchanging archetypes, of which the whole physical world is but a transient and sorry imitation. God, from the Greek point of view, was the ultimate, He was the perfect, He was the unchanging, He was the *telos* toward which all moved, He was self-sufficient and adequate to Himself without need of aught else. He was, therefore, an uncompromising Absolute. It is from this tradition of Greek philosophy that the God of Philo, the God of Maimonides, the God of Aquinas, the God of Spinoza, the God of Hegel, and of Bradley derived. The gods of the philosophers were all Absolute gods.

There has been in our day, however, a full-fledged rebellion against the Absolute God. The God of Spinoza, the *deus sive natura,* is a self-caused being, a being which is unchanging and immutable. Such a God, indifferent to the movement of the universe, implicit in all things and yet self-comprehending and without need of anything—such a God can make little difference to the religious man. Moreover, it seems exceedingly difficult to explain a changing world in terms of an Absolute and unmoving God. How can a changing world be the product of an unchanging God? This classic theological question—and it is a question which underlies all theological inquiry—would appear to be responsible for evil as well as good, for deprivation and destruction as well as increase and creation. Finally, and it is upon this doctrine that both Maimonides and Aquinas broke themselves, the Absolute and moral God would appear inconsistent with human freedom. The consequence of these dilemmas has been that in contemporary theology there has been an outpouring of conceptions of God which deny that He is *altogether* Absolute. Both William James and Mordecai Kaplan argue for non-Absolute Gods. To James, God is a being among beings. To Kaplan, God is an aspect of being rather than a being in Himself. The views of both James and Kaplan depend for their significance upon the limitation of God's Absoluteness. Kaplan conceives of God as a power in the world that works for the enhancement of life, and hence for human salvation; he is the guarantee that what ought to be will come to be and can be made to be. It should be emphasized that Kaplan does not regard God as being identical with human intelligence and co-operativeness. Kaplan does discern God in nature—in the beauty, harmony, and creativity of nature. The disclosure of God is not in man alone, but everywhere in the physical world where reason and goodness can be descried. God is not only that which we perceive and apprehend, but He is that which transcends our apprehension. He is not merely a summation of those forces in our lives which help us to live better— He is more than that.

The conception of a non-Absolute God which Kaplan formulated was founded upon the conviction of experience. There are other conceptions of a non-Absolute God which are formed upon the grounds of metaphysics. One may observe that the world does not stagnate, that it always thrusts up new forms, that it constantly issues forth in new powers, new radiance, new beauty, that its variety increases rather than declines, that its coherence and intelligibility is increasingly unfolded to the inquiring intellect. Some theologians and philosophers have come to say, therefore, that God must in some sense "grow" with the world. The unchanging God of the Greeks and the comprehensive God of the Bible becomes the growing God of the "process theologians."

Charles Sanders Peirce, the first American pragmatist, observed: "At any time, the element of pure chance survives and will remain until the world becomes an absolutely perfect, rational and symmetrical system in which mind is at last crystallized in the infinitely distant future." Peirce understood God and chance to be in some metaphysical tension. The rationality of the universe and the dominion of God are somehow related. As the universe is increasingly brought under God's dominion, as the element of chance decreases, the reasonableness of the universe becomes increasingly manifest. Alfred North Whitehead, leaning upon both Plato and Peirce, has defined with philosophic rigor a conception of a growing God. Wherever the observing intellect turns, Whitehead argues, it perceives the presence of process, the presence of growth, development, and the manifest accretion of order and coherence. There is in all things an implicit teleology which does bring forth from the acorn the oak and from the seed the flower and from the womb the child. Out of the infinite range of possibility, there are specific concretions which emerge. What is, then, the principle of concretion? What is the source from which particularity emerges from the spectrum of infinite possibility? This is God. He who contemplates the range of metaphysical possibility according to His *primordial* nature is the same being who brings forth out of the range of possibility the acts and events of concretion. God seeks to make manifest increasing harmony among concrete events. The moral preoccupation of God is therefore the preoccupation with the aesthetic harmony of concrete events. Immortality has, for Whitehead, a metaphysical significance, for God seeks to retain in the presence of memory all events which bring forth increasing harmony. God is therefore never closed. His experience is open toward the realm of possibility and the realm of concreteness; and out of each successfully fashioned and happily matured event, God derives the pleasure and knowledge of increasing perfection.

Clearly, then, the God of Whitehead is not an Absolute God; his is a God in some sense enriched and directly affected by human values and human virtue. In spite of reason and goodness, evil and disorder are evident. Whitehead is able to transmute evil, treating it in a somewhat typically Platonic fashion. God sees "every actuality for what it can be in such a perfected system—its sufferings, its sorrows, its failures, its triumphs, its immediacies of joy —woven by rightness of feeling into the harmony of the universal feeling. . . . The revolts of destructive evil, purely self-regarding, are dismissed into their triviality of merely individual facts; and yet the good they did achieve in individual joy, in individual sorrow, in the introduction of needed contrast, is yet saved by its relation to the completed whole." [13] However real evil may be for man, how-

• • •

[13] Alfred North Whitehead, *Process and Reality* (New York: The Macmillan Company, 1929), p. 525.

ever obdurate the presence of destructiveness and disorder in the universe, it is the *consequent* nature of God that evil is transformed into a metaphysical coefficient of contrast and enrichment. In God's conspectus, evil is but a moment and the totality is unmarred. This is one view of evil which, however agreeable to God, leaves man's predicament essentially unaltered. It is rather difficult for the individual passing through crisis and despair to rationalize his torment by the recognition that it is serving some constructive purpose in the ultimate and metaphysically unapproachable domain of ideal possibility.

Edgar Sheffield Brightman offered a somewhat different contemporary solution to the problem of evil. Believing as he did that God was the principle of meaning and reason in reality, Brightman nevertheless acknowledged the presence of what he called surds. A surd, technically speaking, is an irrational number. It is a number which neither makes sense within itself nor makes sense in terms of any other numbers. In the same fashion, says Brightman, as there are surds, in mathematics, so in God's creation there are elements of nonrationality. If one observes, for example, a field strewn with pebbles, it is possible to explain reasonably how every single pebble got there. There is a regular history of pebbles, a history of cause and effect, a consequential outgrowth of glacial deposits, the expansion under cold and the contraction under heat, and so on. To the same degree, however, as there is a rationality which may be discerned to explain the pebbles in the field, there is also an irrationality. Why should the pebbles be distributed as they are, why should large pebbles be set amid smaller pebbles, why the enormous variety of color, shapes, sizes, and textures? There is amid every structure of order and coherence observable elements of irrationality and disorder. As in mathematics there are surds, so in life there are surds of nonrationality. These surds, unyielding as they are to any theist explanation, constitute an implicit limitation upon the unerring, perfect, and absolute dominion of God.

Another conception of the non-Absolute God has been proposed by Charles Hartshorne, who holds that God is both an absolute and a relative being—absolute as the ground of reality, but relative in His power in relation to men and creation.

There are, to be sure, a considerable variety of doctrines which may be proposed for grounding the reality of God with increasing and satisfactory philosophic cogency. My own position, however, is this. Having come to religion from philosophy, I now feel, if it does not sound unduly arrogant, that I have religiously outgrown philosophy. The kind of God with which one ends in Spinoza, Hegel, or even Whitehead may be suggestive and illuminating for the religious man, but in itself of no particular religious use.[14]

The philosopher's God is of limited use: if He is Absolute and unchanging being, He is inadequate to the manifest change and flux which make reality so problematic for us; on the other hand, if He is a being among beings, if He is but superior in degree and quality to all else, He is religiously unavailing. It is my own conviction, and alas it is not one which the scope of this discussion permits me to develop adequately, that God is Absolute in the sense of being a creator to whom we stand as creatures while being at the same time a self-limiting power. To the extent of the reality of our freedom, God is limited in His power. The metaphysical and moral quality of freedom involves not only that God is somehow conditional to our action, but that God is somehow structured by it. If man is to

• • •

[14] I warmly commend a very brilliant little book on Whitehead's conception of God by Stephen Lee Ely, *The Religious Availability of Whitehead's God* (Madison, Wis.: The University of Wisconsin Press, 1942).

have real freedom, God's control cannot be complete. To be sure, we must acknowledge that our experience is incommensurable with God's; and yet, on the other hand, if we cannot analogize from our own experience to that of God's, we have no grounds for basing a rational theology. I am unwilling as yet to surrender the possibility of a rational theology.

In *The Mind of the Maker*, Dorothy Sayers takes the classic creeds of Christianity and proceeds to investigate their meaning in terms of the creative process through which the novelist passes in the formation of the novel's characters and plot. Among the many marvelous points that she makes, Miss Sayers observes that every novelist forms character from scratch; but, once it has been created, it begins to possess a personality of its own which the novelist is no longer able to thwart or contradict. The world in effect, once created, is endowed with a character and a purpose which draws strength from its own motivation and reason. It is no longer completely submissive to the rule and sway of God. We are God's handiwork as well as free agents; although there is still the command of God to choose the good and to reject the evil, as His created characters we come to act out our own destiny.

I am inclined as well, in the spirit of Peirce and Brightman, to accept the limitation on God's power which is implied in the concept of the surd and of chance. God is indubitably the power of rationality, of design, of order, of meaningfulness, of creativity; yet traditional conceptions of God, whatever their success in dealing with the general structure of reality, are somehow inadequate to deal with the problem of evil. I had occasion to visit recently someone who was stricken with a wasting paralysis. There is no principle which can make intelligible the selection of that particular individual among the range of individuals—

his paralysis is quite as irrational as the paralysis of any other creature. To be sure, there is a line of causes, a succession of plausible events which can interpret to this particular individual the event of his suffering and the intelligibility of his affliction. On the other hand, both he and I are certain that there is a power within and external to himself who is fighting for his life and his return to health. The concept of surds, of the irrational, of the fortuitous, of the chance events that crop out of the normal stream of life, seems true to reality, acceptable to the afflicted, and consonant with the essential goodness of God. The concept of irrational evil prevents us from ascribing to God that which probably should not be ascribed to Him. God is exempted, not from the struggle, but from the responsibility for the elements of chance within his universe. Both He and His creation are then faced with a common task and a common battle. They may share together in opposing the same unreason and bringing greater light and order into the universe. It must be admitted, however, that if we deny to God responsibility for *all*, we must at the same time admit that His power is limited and His perfection is not complete. There are elements, therefore, of the non-Absolute conception of God which I personally require to account to myself for the reality of evil.[15]

• • •

[15] Interpreting parenthetically Brightman's principle of the surd, Rabbi Steinberg drew the following distinction: "Not all evil needs to be reduced to surds, and not all irrationality needs to be reduced to evil. For example, if, knowing the better way, I elect to pursue the worse, that is not a matter of a surd, that is a matter of my having made an immoral choice. If there is going to be real freedom and responsibility, men must be free to make both good and bad choices. The presence of the surd defines a metaphysical dimension—it may enter into the formation of a moral decision, but in itself it is not sufficient to explain away or compromise the responsibility of man to choose the good."—EDITOR.

276

SUMMARY

Existentialism has been found wanting, not for its reaffirmation of faith, but for its precipitous and unwarranted dispatch of reason. The religious life, we have affirmed, is not a matter of exclusive faith or omnipotent reason, but a tension and polarity between them. Pragmatism was found wanting because its understanding of reason was deficient. Whereas reason requires as well both plausibility and economy, pragmatism made too exclusive use of the demand of practicality. Our present exploration of a variety of doctrines—the new transcendentalism, the new immanentism, the non-Absolute conceptions of God—express my own private doctrine of the "escalator clause." Once faith in God has been determined—as I am convinced it must be—once the existential commitment has been made, then diverse possibilities are open. God so far transcends us that it would seem presumptuous and arrogant to claim any unique, abiding, permanent, and unalterable conception of God. A variety of conceptions becomes possible consequential to faith, and each conception, to the extent that it is directed to the true God, must in measure possess an aspect of truth. As there have always been diverse theological doctrines within Judaism, there may be presently diversities of conception concerning God. There will be times when one's capacity for faith and comprehension will be diminished, when one may withdraw trust in certain areas, maintaining however a threshold below which one may not descend; there will be other times when one's capacity and need for faith is greater and one's sensibilities are more keenly attuned; at such moments, the affirmation will be more intense and its comprehensiveness will be greater. Given the existential act, the escalator rises and falls, the scope extends and narrows, the affirmations multiply or contract. There is always, then, an allowance within the religious life for the free play of speculation, imagination, and affirmation above and beyond a threshold of minimal commitment. Both faith and theology open windows of possibility. The depths are charted and the minimal requirements are known: faith and reason define a dialectic below which man must never fall, but above the existential act and the openness of reason, there is indefinite room for the freedom of the individual against tradition, the play of the imagination, the reach of the mystic, the call of the prophet, and the anticipation of a consummated vision which has been vouchsafed as yet to no man.

•

IV · *The Re-evaluation of Man*

The postmodern man, he who no longer accepts the characteristic creed of modernity, has rejected the inherited faith of the eighteenth and nineteenth centuries in the intellect and in its capacity to win through to the truth. There are, however, more articles to the creed of modern man than merely his confidence in reason, and these as well are being scrutinized and repudiated by those who consider themselves no longer modern, but postmodern.

It is not our intention in what follows to create a caricature of the modern man; however, selecting at random, there are certain articles of faith which modern man has held sacrosanct, which at the present moment are being opened to the "blasphemies" of criticism.

1. Modern man has a sense of the irrelevance of the concept of sin, whereas throughout the ages characteristic of Western sensibility there has been an acute, and at times agonizing, preoccupation with sin. It is typical of modern man that this notion no longer seems applicable to himself; that, if he be a typical and characteristic son

of modernity, he has almost no conception of sin whatsoever.

2. Typical as well of modern man is that, when he confronts evil in both individuals and society, he is serenely
confident that it is remediable. He is convinced that there
is nothing in society or within human nature so objection-
able and ineradicable as to be unyielding to the medicaments of reason and social correction. To be sure, the
medicaments vary and the techniques of solution have been
diverse and often contradictory. There have been those
who argued, such as the Marxists, that were society to be
noncompetitive and classless, the purely superficial evils
that attend upon our economic disorder would evaporate.
There are those, more naïve and perhaps therefore more
benign, who place their trust for the correction of society
in education, in science, and, more particularly, in the
correctives of psychology and psychoanalysis. And then of
course there are those who insist upon fashioning confec-
tions blended out of all the solutions available. Inescapably, however, we must acknowledge that characteristic of modern man is his almost irrational and stubborn
insistence that evil can be removed and the individual
and society perfected.

3. Yet another characteristic of man which indeed follows from his conception of evil and its eradication is a
form of radical individualism which insists upon the sub-
lime virtue of self-sufficiency and self-reliance. Believing
in salvation, modern man nevertheless believes that he is
its own agent and author. Salvation is to be wrought by
man's own efforts. He believes in his own absolute and
invincible moral autonomy. If he discerns within himself
that which is unacceptable, he is also convinced that he
has but to rouse his own initiative and address himself to
the task, apply the proper methods, and eventually he will
right his own wrongs—similarly with the evils which exist
within society, the source of salvation is within.

4. Finally, modern man has a strong sense of the reality of progress. Progress as a concept is of relatively recent coinage. Neither the ancients nor medieval man had any such conception; but modern man not only believes that progress is actual, that the future can be improved and the ills of the past obliterated, but there has been, in modern thought—expressed both in popular and philosophic form—almost a dogma concerning the inevitability of progress. The line which stretches from Condorcet to John Dewey and Mordecai Kaplan is one which, at least as it refers to the doctrine of progress, is unbroken. The typical man (if such there be), notwithstanding the fact that he may be philosopher or believer on other grounds, has tended in our century to conceive the whole of the human enterprise as an ascending plane, a mounting spiral, in which, through trial and error, man rises higher, erecting ever more stately chambers for his soul.

The characteristic attributes of modern man—his atrophied sense of sin, his concept of remediability, the working of his own salvation, the reality of progress—have in our day been submitted to searing examination and critique. Every one of the doctrines we have described has, in some fashion or another, whether in whole or in part, been modified or at the extreme repudiated. The concept of sin has been returned to primacy, the capacity of man to initiate his own salvation has been held up to ridicule, and the reality of progress has been shown to be a tissue of willful delusion.

SIN

One of the strongest currents in the flow of contemporary religious thought is the rediscovery of the reality of sin and the sinfulness of human nature. I say "rediscovery" because, to be sure, sin and sinfulness are conceptions as old as man—conceptions which have always occupied (and

I am compelled to emphasize this, because in our modernity we have forgotten it) sensitive human beings and enjoyed a central position in Jewish and Christian thought. Consider for a moment how large the conception of sin bulks in the Hebrew Bible. Even in the opening passages of the Book of Genesis, Cain is warned against sin, which "coucheth at thy door" (Gen. 4:7). Moreover, shortly thereafter we find: "The imagination of man's heart is evil from his youth" (Gen. 8:21). And, to pick but a glaring instance from among many, when Moses, summarizing his teaching to the house of Israel, addressing his chosen and stiff-necked flock, says: "Lest there be among you a root that beareth gall and wormwood" (Deut. 29:17)—this I take to mean a Biblical allusion to the principle of perversity which, though the good way is laid out before man at the instance of God, and although it be understood by him, yet there is within man an obstinacy which will cause him to sacrifice God and His way in order to elect the way of evil and death.

The prophets themselves were no less realistic about the nature of man than was the Pentateuch. Jeremiah, among many other things, says, "The heart is deceitful above all things, and it is desperately weak" (Jer. 17:9). And yet in spite of the complex of utterance which emphasizes the Biblical sense of human sin and sinfulness, the Bible is articulate as well in its awareness of the wonder and dignity of man, its recognition of his inscrutable moral preciousness: "Thou hast made him but little lower than the angels" (Ps. 8:6). The Biblical awareness of human sin and the Biblical recognition of human grandeur are not in themselves contradictory. The rabbinic literature testifies to the fact that the good is often fashioned out of evil, that the *yezer ha-ra* is often the instrumentality whereby good is to be wrought. When the rabbis, however, do discuss the *yezer ha-tov* in contrast with the *yezer ha-ra*, however much they acknowledge the dignity and glory of human personality, they tend to ascribe greater power and depth to the evil than to the good. Thus, for example, they point out that the *yezer ha-ra* is in a child before the child is born, else why would the foetus kick against the womb? And one of the most perceptive (however much it may be farfetched) and revealing of rabbinic passages on this theme is a homily on a verse from Ecclesiastes (Eccles. 4:13-14): "Better is a poor and wise child than an old and foolish king . . . for out of prison he came forth to be king; although in his kingdom he was born poor." Within the text of Ecclesiastes this passage is obscure, the exegesis of the rabbis makes it both translucent and rich with meaning. " 'Better is a poor and wise child'—this is the *yezer ha-tov*, the inclination to good. Why is it called *child?* Because the inclination to good only attaches itself to a man when he has reached the age of maturity. And why is it called *poor?* Because all do not obey its instruction. And why is it called *wise?* Because it teaches human beings the right way. And to the phrase 'than an old and foolish king'—this is the *yezer ha-ra*, the inclination to evil. Why does the Preacher call it *king?* Because all men obey the inclination to evil. Why does he call it *old?* Because the inclination to evil attaches itself to man from youth until old age. Why does he call it *foolish?* Because it teaches man the way of evil." Continuing their exegesis, the rabbis then ask, How does one interpret the phrase "for out of prison he came forth to be king"? The rabbis answer, "The evil inclination is so described because it entangles human beings as if among thorns." [16]

The rabbis end their interpretation by saying that never-

• • •

[16] At this point the rabbis are interpreting from the Hebrew word for prison (*ha-zurim*) which is like the Hebrew word for thorns—it is a traditional mode of rabbinic exegesis to seek parallels and interrelations among words, even though their literal meanings may be disparate, in order to effect their interpretation of the parable. (Midrash Rabbah on Eccles. 4:13). —EDITOR.

theless, through obedience to the Torah, the young child may go forth to receive the sovereignty of virtue, though he came into life under the sovereignty of evil.

The rabbinic view of evil stands, however, in radical contrast with the view projected by Paul the Apostle. It was Paul who contributed to Western religious thought the notion that man does not become a sinner when he has sinned for the first time, but that man is born a sinner—not merely with a predisposition to sin, but that he is actually guilty of a sin committed by his first ancestor. By reason of this primeval sin, every man is inescapably tainted. Man is therefore, as Kierkegaard later formulated the doctrine, not a sinner because he has sinned, but rather he sins because first he is a sinner, and his essential sinfulness arises from the primordial rebellion of Adam against God. In Augustine, the doctrine of Paul is given additional depth, and in Luther and Calvin an insistence upon the total depravity of human nature becomes strident. In the view of that tradition which runs from Paul through the Protestant Reformation, man is adjudged incapable of good—every act of virtue is tainted by the evil which is born within him, and it is only through grace and through an unmerited gift that man is transformed in such fashion as to be capable of redemption in spite of ineradicable sinfulness.

The doctrines of original evil, utter depravity, and ineradicable taint have in recent generations enjoyed no particular following in Western religion other than in the camps of fundamentalist Christianity. The religious base upon which these doctrines were founded had disintegrated. People no longer accepted the normative instruction of church and synagogue regarding the character of human nature and the potentiality of human nature for good and evil. Most "enlightened" Westerners were inclined rather to rely upon their own capacity to achieve virtue and avoid vice. Those conceptions of sin formulated historically by the Church—the notion of sin as a breach of law and a blasphemy against the divine person—enjoyed no significant reputation. Added to the modern disenchantment with theological speculation regarding the character of human nature has been the deteriorative influence of comparative religion and anthropology. The moral codes formulated and perpetuated by historic Western religions were observed to vary from land to land and from time to time; more and folkway interblended in such fashion as to shade and texture with ambiguity the pretensions to absoluteness which Western moral codes assumed as a matter of course. There has been unquestionably a rebellion against the tyranny of hard and fast conceptions of sin and the inescapable confusion of sin with offenses against the inherited moral code. The failure of theologies to draw a distinction between fundamental idolatries and self-arrogations and slight and socially conditioned transgressions against inherited codes, such as smoking and drinking, led inevitably to an attitude of contempt and disrespect for the moral professions of the churches. Though the code was historically accepted, it was always viewed with suspicion, and when the opportunity presented itself for junking these codes entirely, modern man responded with alacrity.

It is possible, however, that modern man threw out the baby with the bath. The entire apparatus was judged wanting, and its conceptual foundations were jettisoned as well. The code was found to be hypocritical and the conception of evil was repudiated. Indeed, Aldous Huxley has confirmed the cavalier response of modern man. He observed that in his youth his desire to carouse and make merry was always inhibited by the presence of a Christian conscience. His conscience had an insistent way of tapping him upon the shoulder to say, "no, no." It became necessary, therefore, if he was to enjoy life as he conceived it, to modify conscience and repudiate its Christian foundation in the doctrine of sin. To be sure, this is a subconscious rationalization of behavior otherwise desired, but it is indicative of the characteristic stance of modern man: to identify all too closely the concrete moral code with the philosophic and theological foundations of which it is merely a temporally conditioned and exchangeable example.

Lying, to be sure, at the base of the modern repudiation of sin and sinfulness has been the inescapable self-admiration of man. So many of the disabilities of man have been overcome, so many of the old inhibitions have been discarded without damage, that man has developed a high estimate of his powers, his capacities and benevolence, his presumed reasonableness and virtue. The tendency of modern man has been to regard the doctrine of sin as but a device of retarding the spiritual development of mankind. The assumptions which underly the naïve optimism of a generation now past are founded upon an essential idolatry—the assumption that man can by his own efforts, unaided by God, bring himself to perfection. As long as this assumption remained unchallenged, the concept of sin was useless and beside the point.

It might be said—with some risk of historical overestimation—that Sören Kierkegaard rediscovered sin. His rediscovery of sin was but a corollary of his investigation of many areas of human nature which modern man had glossed over too easily. His superb analytic work, *The Concept of Dread*, illustrates only too clearly how Kierkegaard was enabled by an investigation of obscure areas of personality to project an image of man, for which the reality of evil and the meaning of sin were both indispensable as means of understanding the total man.

Kierkegaard's rediscovery of a principle of perversity in man, "a root that beareth gall and wormwood," might well have remained an idiosyncratic insight of an idiosyncratic thinker. Time has, however, played into Kierkegaard's hands in this regard. After more than a century of blithe and naïve confidence concerning human nature, after more than a century of assuming that everything wrong in man was due to the fact that he was inadequately educated, or politically shackled, or economically retarded, we have come in our generation to discover that the depths of evil in man were yet untapped and uncontrolled. The recent decades of totalitarian fascism and communism have made it clear that there is no crime of which the most sophisticated, literate, self-determining civilization is not capable. In fact, among the great villains of our time have been those who did not lack for education or want for food or thirst for opportunity. The advantages of modern civilization alone are not sufficient to blunt or put asunder him who hates mankind and himself, the good and the beautiful. The Biblical view of man and the tragic impasse of modern civilization have together served to form the basis on which "crisis theology" is being erected.

Man, according to Karl Barth, is forever under the judgment of God. We are always inadequate to the moral law, and before the will of God, each man, without exception, is a sinner. Man not only stands before divine judgment, but, according to Barth (and this is indeed in the main line of Christian tradition), he stands condemned under divine judgment. There is no man who is not victimized by his own self-glorification. There is no man who has loved his neighbor as much as he has loved himself. There is no man whose deeds are adequate to his professions. In the scrutiny of God, each man is condemned. Relying upon Luther and Calvin even more profoundly than upon Kierkegaard, Barth argues that the image of God has indeed been expunged from human nature by man's sinfulness. This is not only to say that man's reason is no longer capable of comprehending God and man's will no longer satisfactory to fulfill God's. Barth is rather saying that man is totally depraved, that there is nothing which he is capable of doing in goodness.

The theology of crisis according to Karl Barth and Emil Brunner has undergone significant modification in its American transplantation. So-called "neo-Dialectical" theologians (a barbarous phrase by which the thought of Paul Tillich and Reinhold Niebuhr has been characterized) are, it seems to me, more astute than either Barth or Brunner. They make a better case because they have tempered the extremity to which Barth and Brunner lend themselves. They do not say that man is totally depraved or divested of all virtue; as a matter of fact, they insist upon the natural virtue of man, the natural justice to which Niebuhr has made particular reference; they concentrate heavily however, perhaps in reaction to the prevailing climate of modern times, on man's sinfulness.

There has not been, in modern times, a more astute analysis of the depths and perversities of human nature than one can find in the writings of Reinhold Niebuhr. What Arthur Koestler discloses in *Darkness at Noon* to be the character of Rubashov, Reinhold Niebuhr, from a Christian point of view, has dissected. The prevailing conception of Niebuhr is that man is a creature marked by pride and self-love. This is his besetting sin; though man has been appointed by destiny to be a servant of God, he has become in fact a rebel against God. Loving himself—vain, prideful, self-satisfied—what happens to man? Not only does he indulge the vices and lusts of which all of us are conscious, but even his idealism—and it is this which is the crux of Niebuhr's argument—becomes perverted. The quest for truth, the search for justice, the pursuit of virtue and beauty, are indubitably meritorious endeavors. Where is a man closer to God than in the pursuit of ultimate ends? And yet, when man sets out to search for the truth, or justice, or virtue, or beauty, his own self-love becomes so profoundly involved that each end—truth, justice, virtue—is perjured and distorted. The self and the end become confused, and the pursuit of truth is compromised by the defense of the ego. The ostensible love of truth becomes a ready instrument for the aggrandizement of self and the expanding kingdom of sin. There is no such thing, says Niebuhr, as an *objective* quest for truth. There is always the love of self operating as the subtle instrument of perversion. And so it goes in the pursuit of religion or the pursuit of politics or the pursuit of economic well-being—ideals become modes of self-aggrandizement and the virtues of power yield to the corruptions of power. Niebuhr has not been content to expose the self-love which lies at the root of individual pursuits, but he has turned as well to an investigation of the corruption of ideals within society. Justice is at best an abstract principle which may serve successfully to regulate the vision of society and social relations, but as well yields to corruption when it enters the arena of pressures. Concrete justice is always vastly different from abstract justice. This, because society is a congerie of pressures. Religious idealism has all along been transparently a failure because it was incapable of realizing that virtue—instead of merely being preached—had as well to be organized. Not only injustice is a consequence of the pressure group, but so is justice.

Niebuhr's own recognition that self-love is ineradicable, that it cannot be educated out of a person, has served him well, for it has provided the basis for a more realistic appraisal of what is and is not possible to human nature. His extraordinarily acute political sensibility has been well exposed in his book, *The Children of Light and the Children of Darkness.* The children of light are the idealists —they may have been more virtuous, but they were immensely more naïve than the children of darkness. The children of darkness have always had the wrong cause but the better strategy.

"One of the great blunders," Niebuhr argues, "of the children of light has been to misread the nature of democracy." The general theory of democracy rests upon the somewhat sentimental conception of social contract formulated by both Rousseau and John Locke. The viability of the doctrine of social contract depends upon the illusion of the natural goodness of man. If society had not corrupted man, so the illusion goes, men might very well have lived quite nicely with one another without government. The great villain in this sentimental tableau is society. Society, it was thought, corrupts and distorts the essential good will of man. It was believed that if the natural order of human relationships could be restored, so might the virtue of man be restored. It is upon some such naïve optimism, Niebuhr argues, that democratic theory from the seventeenth to the nineteenth centuries is founded. Such a version of human nature and history is not, according to Niebuhr, accurate to the facts. Actually, democracy is necessary not because human beings are so good that it is natural and inevitable, but because human beings tend so easily to be corrupted.[17]

Democracy becomes, therefore, not the consequence of our natural development, but the only device by which we can prevent self-destruction.

Niebuhr's critique of democracy and its political institutions has been a negative one. His efforts to recall us from an ideal, but naïve, estimation of human nature to a realistic appraisal of its capacities and limitations would not have been possible were it not for his interpretation

• • •

[17] Reinhold Niebuhr, *The Children of Light and the Children of Darkness* (New York: Charles Scribner's Sons, 1945), xi. "Man's capacity for justice makes democracy possible; but man's inclination to injustice makes democracy necessary."—EDITOR.

of human sinfulness. Sin is neither obsolete nor unreal. It is, both as fact and conception, as potent as ever. It is, moreover, a reality whose presence we need to reappropriate the more ardently because we have forgotten it.

SALVATION

If indeed man is entrapped by the snares of sin, how shall he extricate himself?

In raising this question, we expose one of the most profound and abiding perplexities of historic religious thought. By whose initiative does man overcome his prevailing self-love? How is its hold over human personality to be broken? The problem of initiative, as stated in the terms of the new theology, is in fact the classic problem of autonomy versus grace.

Judaism, the tradition out of which we speak, has always held that man needs both autonomy and grace together. Realistic as it is to the depth of evil in man and to the adverse circumstances which surround him, Judaism has never supposed that a human being might redeem himself by his own efforts alone; nevertheless, the general Jewish view has been that, in addition to grace, man requires freedom and self-initiation as well. The world, according to the rabbis, is so constituted that if man makes the first move, heaven will come to help him. Man is free—his freedom may remain a mystery (indeed, one of the profoundest of mysteries), but according to Judaism, he must be free, otherwise there can be no real meaning to the moral life. The reality of remorse and the power of repentance both depend upon the presence of freedom. Each man can, by a single act in a single moment, retrieve the errors of a whole life. It is for this reason that the extreme situations of life—the presence of danger or the brushing wings of death—are associated in the liturgy with self-scrutiny and penitence.

The emphatic direction of Jewish tradition would seem to be that salvation may be wrought by human initiative in disjunction, indeed even without, divine grace. There are numberless examples in the rabbinic literature which would suggest that man can be the agent of his own salvation. The rabbis often speak of him who by a single act acquired eternal life in one instant. By one exemplary act of mercy, while serving as the executioner of Rabbi Hanina ben Teradion, a Roman executioner was enabled, say the rabbis, to acquire eternity. The recognition of the precedence of human initiative to divine grace is deep-seated in Judaism. Divine grace may well be indispensable, but it does not come first.

In the Christian tradition, the whole conception is reversed. It is distinctive of the Christian tradition that it denies that autonomy in salvation is primary, that man can initiate his own salvation; indeed, the extremity to which Christianity moves is that man is incapable of doing anything whatsoever toward his own salvation. Salvation is by grace alone. Having once confused imperfection under the law with incapacity before the law, Paul the Apostle was persuaded that only by external and vicarious atonement could he be redeemed from his sins. Salvation came by the grace of the Cross, and the only merit that might be brought in self-justification was faith in the redeeming power of the Cross. Paul was, however, troubled by one consideration: Who gives man faith? By the time of Augustine, this question was also resolved: Salvation was by faith in the Cross, but faith was the gift of God. If one possessed, therefore, the power to believe properly, that power was a divine gift. The latter theology of the Catholic Church saw fit to modify the extremity of the Augustinian view. It held that although salvation was by faith as understood by the Church, it was also by works—deeds of charity and the power of the sacraments. As Jesus Christ was understood to have had the power to forgive sins by virtue of his own sacrifice, so the Church, being the vicar of Christ, was empowered as well to forgive sins. The Mass, being the central act of Catholic Christian worship, brings together in mysterious union grace and human initiative. Being in essence a re-enactment of the sacrifice of Christ, the faithful are enabled by participation in it to relive the sacrifice at Calvary. In reaction against the Catholic Church, Luther and Calvin alike repudiated works altogether: There is no salvation by works, only by faith. Believing as they did that human nature was totally depraved, it became inconceivable to them that man should be possessed of that kind of faith which might have the purity and perfection needed to work salvation. They returned, therefore, to the position of Augustine: Faith is possible in a depraved human nature only if that nature is regenerated by the grace of God. Obviously, with a corrupt spirit, man cannot make himself pure—only God is capable of such purification. So, with Luther and Calvin, man is damned unless God takes the initiative to redeem him.

These doctrines were no sooner stated than the desire to revise them asserted itself. To be on the one hand uncertain as to whether one is saved and on the other hand to be disqualified from being able to do anything about it oneself had the consequence of consigning man to a dreadful passivity. Philipp Melanchthon (1497-1560), a contemporary of Luther, went so far as to suggest a revision of the doctrine of total depravity. Melanchthon's more generous appraisal of human nature was more than confirmed and extended by the position adopted by Arminius (1560-1609), the celebrated Dutch Reformed theologian. Arminius, in his attacks upon the Calvinist doctrine of predestination, left himself open to accusations of Pelagianism and disloyalty to the confessions of his church; however, this did not prevent him from affirming in contradistinction to both Lutheran and Calvinist tradition that divine sovereignty was quite compatible with a real free will in man. Unfortunately, the humanistic modifications of Me-

lanchthon and the reaffirmation of genuine freedom by
Arminius ceased to be influential in the theological coun-
cils of the church by the eighteenth century. Lutheran
churches, before and to this day, would, if faithful to the
orthodoxy of their tradition, hold with the doctrine of total
depravity. By the late nineteenth and early twentieth
centuries, however, the persuasion of modern man had
moved outside of the church and left the doctrine of total
depravity within.

The revival of both continental and American preoccupation with the problem of human evil can—like other revivals—be traced to Kierkegaard. With cold, philosophic,
dispassionate frankness, Kierkegaard makes a fascinating
point. If the Cross is to save man at all, it must save man
completely—if it does not save completely, it is not a
miracle. For salvation to be miraculous, for the doctrine
of *sola gratia* to be reinstated, there must be on God's part
an absolute, comprehensive, and complete act. Therefore,
says Kierkegaard, God is like a teacher who not only
teaches us the truth but endows us with the capacity to
understand the truth which he has given to us; we have the
capacity neither to seek the truth nor, being endowed with
that capacity by God, to find the truth without him. Everything is done by the teacher of truth; the pupil does nothing at all. Karl Barth has expanded the Kierkegaardian
metaphor of God the teacher. Man, according to Karl
Barth, "is a swimmer who is sinking"—when God rescues
him, man does not even contribute a single stroke. The
rescue is entirely the work of God. Emil Brunner, who
generally tends to moderate Barth's position, speaks of a
preservative grace.[18] The love of God is, according to

• • •

[18] Karl Barth, to be sure, does imply a partially nonsupernat-
uralist conception of grace. It is his doctrine of so-called "realized eschatology." Barth says that the true Christian is already
redeemed within time and history; that he enjoys a serenity,
peace, and confidence which nobody else possesses—a conviction of being at one with God.—EDITOR.

him, always present and available to everybody. Brunner denies, therefore, that God's image is expunged from man. There is a kind of common grace open to all; but, and here Brunner is in the high Reformation tradition, this common grace is insufficient to save mankind, because there is too much evil in it.

Tillich and Niebuhr present us with an interesting paradox. By virtue of the astute psychological and sociological analysis which Tillich and Niebuhr have grafted onto the conception of sin and salvation, their conception of sin is deeper and more comprehensive than is that of their predecessors. They have worked harder to articulate the devices and strategies of sin and self-love. Although they do not accept the doctrine of total depravity, their conception of sin is more richly textured and embracing, notwithstanding the absence of abstract and systematic statement. The danger which their theology runs, however, is that although they possess a deeper conception of sin, they have, it is my conviction, a much less adequate conception of salvation.

Were one to pass before Luther and Calvin and ask, "Behold! We are totally depraved; what must we do?" they might well have answered, "You must fold your hands, trust, hope, and pray that Divine Providence, which was asserted before the world came into being, has predestined that you will be among the saved; that God will bestow His grace upon you and that receiving it you will be able to accept His truth and be redeemed." And if so favored, it might be asked, in what does redemption consist? The Reformers might have responded, "If you are among the elect, you will enjoy immortality; and if you are among the damned, you will burn forever." The answers of Luther and Calvin were apodictic and utterly clear; the answers of Tillich and Niebuhr to the problem of grace and salvation are shot through with ambiguity. Luther could always speak out supernatural injunctions and declarations; but Tillich and Niebuhr are not availed of the ease of supernatural solutions. Somehow Tillich and Niebuhr—and Niebuhr more emphatically—have succeeded with their doctrine of sin in pushing man into a considerably deeper ditch than ever before; however, the machinery of salvation by which to extricate him has broken down entirely.

In sum, it would appear that the continental and American neo-Orthodox theologians have succeeded in deepening our understanding of sin, but have not succeeded in making the meaning of grace more vivid. The predicament of man is brilliantly described, but its resolution is left hazy and imprecise.

There can be little question but that Barth and Brunner, Tillich and Niebuhr, have made a substantial and profound contribution to modern thought. I know, indeed, that they have made a substantial contribution to my own thought. I was raised a typical modern. I held typically naïve and innocent conceptions of the depth and tenacity of evil in man and in society. I think that I have learned from these thinkers—particularly from Reinhold Niebuhr—a salutary lesson in the strength of the Adversary against whom we are wrestling, both within ourselves, in other men, and in the world outside. My utopianism is toned, and a realism is born. Although I cannot share with neo-Reformationist theologies their insistence upon the total condemnation of man under the judgment of God, it is crucial to be aware that all things do stand condemned, that all things fall short of the moral requirement of God and His law. There should be no final faith placed in any human being, any institution, any concept, any value. Beyond every institution and human being and principle and value there is the judgment of God. The task of realism in theology is to anticipate both the inadequacy in man, in society, and in ourselves, and to struggle against it; and to guard against the danger of making any partial truth, whether it be the truth of science or philosophy or institutional religion, into a god. We must always be watchful, I have learned, against idolatry. No church, no institution, no system of values should be regarded as being beyond the judgment of God. All things should be viewed as compromised before his scrutiny. If we remember this, we will be less likely to succumb to idolatry— the assumptions of finality when there is no finality, the Absolutistic delusions by which mankind has been so widely and so consistently seduced.

On the other hand, having acknowledged my indebtedness to neo-Orthodox Protestant theology, I must affirm my conviction that it is subject to a desperate imbalance. The pit of sin has been dug so deep, and supernatural grace has been rendered so questionable a concept, as to leave man's predicament seemingly irresoluble. Returning from the deliberations of neo-Orthodoxy to a reading of rabbinic literature, one becomes aware again of the balance, the astuteness, the penetration, and the enduring hopefulness of the rabbis. They recognize full well the depth and intensity of evil in man. Though denying that man is totally depraved, the rabbis are not without realism when they recognize and extend the insight of the Book of Genesis: "If thou doest not well, sin coucheth at the door; and unto thee is its desire, *but thou mayest rule over it*" (Gen. 4:7). Evil there is and sin is intense, but man has the power to rule over it. There is need for grace, but the ultimate initiative is man's. "Open unto me," the rabbis say, "in the name of God but the breadth of a hair, and I will open unto you so that chariots may ride in."

HISTORY

One of the primary acts of faith, indeed one of the dogmas of contemporary man, is the belief in design and progress in history. The notion of design in history has, to be sure, its antecedents in Judaism. All individuals and nations were seen by Isaiah to have their appointed role and destiny within the economy of God's Kingdom. At the heart, though, of the Jewish view is the conception that the redemption of society is both horizontal through time and vertical through grace and salvation. The rabbis believed that society could be improved, that its conditions could be ameliorated, that the environment of man could be bettered—for this reason, they consistently legislated for the improvement of society. They believed as well, however, that history has an end, that it is moving toward an ultimate purpose and fulfillment; that fulfillment was to be the Kingdom of God—when society shall have been purged of its evil and a domain of freedom, justice, and peace will have been inaugurated. The Kingdom of God, according to the rabbis, must be the work of God. Men are the necessary allies of God. The Kingdom of God is not imposed upon man, and man cannot inaugurate it by himself. Both God and man are necessary to the beginning of the Kingdom.

The Christian tradition is indescribably more pessimistic than the Jewish. The world of the apostles was a dying world, and all men waited until the wickedness of the created order passed away and a new order and a new creation was brought into being. The savior was born, the savior died, and the savior will come again. What passes in between is but an interlude of inadequacy and incompletion. Christianity conceives of man as that creature which must endure history rather than make use of it.

The conception of history held by modern man stands in contrast both to Judaism and to Christianity. At heart, modern man believes in a *secular meliorism*. The world is somehow getting better. It will continue to get better because man is making it better. Salvation is of this world, and salvation is social (the individual having become, in modern times, but a function of society).

The neo-Orthodox revival, as on other issues, has had

something profound to say. In an effort to radically disengage the concept of salvation from secular perversions, Karl Barth has argued that religion has, in fact, nothing to do with society, that religion deals only with the salvation of the individual. Brunner, on the other hand, admitting some relation between Christianity and society, insists that religion is not integral to society, but is rather its external and interested critic. "Society has no Christian phase of culture," Brunner has said, "because every actuality is tainted with sin." Christianity cannot therefore, in their view, put forth a program for society, because in the process it fears it will be corrupted and compromised.

Tillich and Niebuhr, true to their predicament, are both active social reformers and antimeliorists. Man's sinfulness endures, human nature cannot improve, and the world as a consequence cannot get better. They share on the one hand the traditional Protestant assumption of the irretrievable sinfulness of man, and on the other they affirm with unparalleled vigor the prophetic tradition which reaches out to them from the Bible. Niebuhr has, for example, convincingly demonstrated that time by itself cannot redeem mankind, that patience and the passing of years will result in inevitable progress. And yet to the question whether or not history has design or meaning, Niebuhr is not clear. Tillich's thought on this question is no particular improvement. Although making much of his doctrine of *Kairos* [19] (what he calls the unfulfilled moment, the moment of time approaching us as fate and decision),[20] it is unclear whether each *Kairos* is a unique and ahistorical break into time, or whether each *Kairos* becomes itself a moment within his-

• • •

[19] Judging from Rabbi Steinberg's reference, it may be assumed that he refers to Tillich's discussion of *Kairos* in *The Interpretation of History* (New York: Charles Scribner's Sons, 1936), and *The Protestant Era* (Chicago: The University of Chicago Press, 1948).—EDITOR.

[20] *The Interpretation of History,* p. 129.

tory and by the addition and accumulation of *Kairoi*, the wisdom and understanding of man are extended. If the former, each *Kairos* is an irreplaceable event; if the latter, it is equally irreplaceable, but enters the stream of history and the collective experience of mankind. Niebuhr leaves equally unresolved the question as to whether there is any cumulativeness to man's achievement of the good. Although he holds that human history cannot redeem man, he admits that it does enlarge the scope of human freedom and choice. The ambiguity remains and the disjunction between history and the ends of the Kingdom of God is as vast as ever.

I must confess that while I am able to follow Tillich and Niebuhr part of the journey, I cannot follow them all the way. As they have exaggerated the evil in human nature, they have in my view exaggerated the evil in history. Their uncompromising denial of meliorism strikes me as being in contradiction to Jewish tradition; it is both morally debilitating and in my view unrealistic. If indeed evil and good are equally impotent to gain the final triumph, if the content of history is but the endless record of struggles without resolution, then we would appear to be no better off *in the world* for having faith in God. To borrow a phrase from the gaming table, in a world vitalized by God, the world must be *tilted*. To the extent that God enters the world, the world must be tilted toward His ends, toward the good. There can be no certainty that the good will be achieved, but there must be a predisposition in its direction. It should be made clear that I do not hold with a doctrine of inevitable progress, with any trust in the finality of human decision, with any conviction that however much we stand upon the shoulders of our ancestors we stand higher than they. Within the economy of Providence, I would hold however that there is more abundantly available to us the goods of the past than the evils of the past. Every generation stands at Sinai, every generation hesitates between the two paths, and the merits of the Fathers do not automatically redeem any generation or individual; neither do the sins of the Fathers damn any generation or individual; yet the virtues of the Fathers are present, are available, are always more available than the sins of the past. There is truth, therefore, in the rabbinic doctrine of *ha-zechut avot* ("the merits of the fathers") —as the precedent of Socratic discretion is with us in our acts of judgment, so the moral discrimination of the patriarchs, the prophets, and the rabbis is with us in our moments of moral decision. Socrates cannot redeem us nor can the rabbis redeem us—but both are available to illuminate our actions.

Each generation stands at Eden and each generation stands at Sinai. Each has the accumulated reserves of the past at its disposal if it chooses to draw upon them; nevertheless each generation, because it has greater spiritual resources available to it, is potentially capable of approximating ever more closely to the Kingdom of God. The Kingdom of God will never be attained in a society ruled by self-love and idolatry. There will never be a time in which society will not be harrowed by conflict, but we may conceive and work and pray for a society in which human beings have so expanded their sensitivity to the moral quality of thoughts and acts as to have succeeded in expanding the foundations upon which the true Kingdom of God shall one day be built.

SUMMATION AND REPRISE

The new currents in religious thought which we have examined are neither necessarily new nor necessarily confluent. They just happen to be the currents which are flowing at present. The fact that they flow in itself does not compel them to flow in harmony; yet we have sought throughout these essays to locate the common undertow which drags and pulls these currents into unity.

I. *The revolt against reason* was explored with a view

toward indicating that neither faith nor reason are sufficient as devices of apprehension by themselves, but that both are required in an unending and eternal dialectic.

II. *Religious pragmatism* was explored with a view to ascertaining the mechanics whereby a reason, grounded in nature, seeks to approach faith; and an examination of the criteria by which the operation of religious pragmatism is to be judged.

III. *Revisions in the conception of God* as they have emerged in our time were investigated. Faith is not a state of being at rest, although to be sure it enjoys moments of serenity and peace. Faith is not a peace of mind. Faith, on the contrary, should be a constant striving. As soon as faith is attained, one moves from the position of faith in which one's whole existence has been risked, downward into one's assumptions and outward into the exploration of all its implications.

IV. And lastly, in the discussion of *the re-evaluation of man,* the crisis theology of our time, it is proper that a concluding word be spoken about the spirit in which the entire religious enterprise is undertaken.

Religion is more than theology. Although religion is theology, to be sure, it also comprehends the entire array of culture. The enterprise of faith is, however, not an enterprise of reason alone or of faith alone. True to the heart of Jewish religious belief, above both faith and reason, hope reigns supreme. The spirit which must invest the religious enterprise is the spirit of hope. The prophet Zechariah, in an exquisite phrase, said of those believing in the world that they were "prisoners of hope" (Zech. 9:12). We are indeed all of us imprisoned by hope. But, and we should not forget this, hope may be of two kinds: hope may be delusive, narrowing, unrealistic; and hope may also release and redeem us.

Name Index

Adler, Cyrus, 33
Agus, Jacob, 167
Ahad Haam, 247
Akedah, 136, 147
Aleichem, Sholom, 18
Alexander, Samuel, 130
Ansche Chesed, Congregation, 29
Anselm, 179
Aquinas, Thomas, 175, 268, 269
Arminius (Arminianism), 143, 188, 291, 292
Aristotle (Aristotelianism), 101, 135, 177, 179, 216
As a Driven Leaf, 22, 48-53, 56
Asch, Sholem, 52
Augsburg Confession, 233
Augustine (Augustinianism), 101, 141, 143, 188f, 194, 282, 291

Bacon, Francis, 65, 215f, 222
Barrie, J. M., 24
Barth, Karl, 57, 130, 144, 158, 161f, 163, 165f, 168f, 170f, 172, 174, 186, 189, 194, 195f, 199f, 202, 204f, 214, 222, 253-259, 261, 263f, 266, 267, 285f, 292, 292n, 294, 297
Basic Judaism, 56-57
Believing Jew, A, 47n

Ben Abuyah, Elisha, 22, 48-50, 52, 152
Bergson, Henri, 27, 59, 74, 111-118, 132, 168, 171, 218f
Bernstein, Alex, 36
Beth El Zedeck, Congregation (Indianapolis), 42f
Bin-Gorion, 18
Boehme, Jacob, 101
Bradley, F. H., 57, 130, 175, 254, 268
Brightman, Edgar Sheffield, 272f, 274, 275n
Brunner, Emil, 57, 130, 158, 162, 170, 186, 189, 190f, 194, 196f, 214, 253-259, 261, 264, 286f, 292f, 294, 297
Buber, Martin, 58, 136, 158, 166, 167, 172, 266
Buddhism, 82
Butler University, 43, 44

Cahan, Abraham, 20
Calvin, John (Calvinism), 121, 127f, 140, 141f, 185, 188, 191, 195, 206, 207, 282, 285, 291, 293
Canons of Dort, 185, 188
Carlyle, Thomas, 218